SOWING CRISIS

SOWING CRISIS

The Cold War and American Dominance
in the Middle East

RASHID KHALIDI

Beacon Press
Boston

BEACON PRESS
25 Beacon Street
Boston, Massachusetts 02108-2892
www.beacon.org

Beacon Press books
are published under the auspices of
the Unitarian Universalist Association of Congregations.

12 11 10 09   8 7 6 5 4 3 2 1

This book is printed on acid-free paper that meets the uncoated paper
ANSI/NISO specifications for permanence as revised in 1992.

Composition by Wilsted & Taylor Publishing Services

LIBRARY OF CONGRESS CATALOGING-IN-PUBLICATION DATA
Khalidi, Rashid.
Sowing crisis : the Cold War and American dominance
in the Middle East / Rashid Khalidi.
p. cm.
Includes bibliographical references and index.
ISBN-13: 978-0-8070-0310-7 (hardcover : alk. paper)
1. United States—Foreign relations—Middle East.
2. Middle East—Foreign relations—United States. 3. Cold War.
4. United States—Foreign relations—1945–1989. I. Title.
DS63.2.U5K495 2009
327.7305609'045—dc22   2008037146

THIS BOOK IS DEDICATED TO MY
NEWBORN GRANDSON, TARIQ:

MAY HE GROW UP TO SEE A MORE PEACEFUL,
MORE JUST, AND MORE EQUITABLE MIDDLE EAST
THAN THE ONE I HAVE DESCRIBED HEREIN.

CONTENTS

The Middle East (c. 1985)

PREFACE

The Cold War and how it played out in the Middle East have fascinated me for many years. I began researching Soviet policy in the region in the mid-1970s, and soon afterward began teaching about Soviet and American Middle East policy at the American University of Beirut. Things looked quite different from the vantage point of Beirut than they appeared from either Moscow or Washington, or than they did in most of the scholarship on the Cold War. Being on the receiving end of the superpowers' policies and actions imparted to the latter an immediacy and vividness that they may not have otherwise had. At the same time, the realities of the regional situation looked quite different from a local perspective than they may have to superpower policymakers thousands of miles, and often a mental world, away. That was the germ of this book, the disjuncture between superpower and Middle Eastern perspectives, between the "metropolitan" and the "peripheral," and it is also in some ways its justification. In the pages that follow, I examine the superpowers' four-and-a-half-decade-long contest over and in the Middle East, not just in terms of their perspectives and the documents they generated, but of how they affected the region. This book does not purport to be a comprehensive, primary-source-based history of the Cold War in the Middle East, although I was fortunate in being able to rely on valuable archival material unearthed from the old Soviet archives by the Cold War History Project, and from the American archives by the National Security Archive. Based on this and other documentation, the work of other scholars, and earlier research of my own,[1] this book is an extended essay that encompasses my reflections on the Cold War rivalry in the region as much as possible from a perspective different from that of Washington and Moscow, while always —indeed, perhaps inevitably—trying to take their viewpoints into account.

Although I have been thinking about and researching aspects of this topic for over three decades, when I first began working on this project in earnest a little more than three years ago, it looked as if this period and the attitudes it engendered were a relic of the past. I had hoped that the old passions had cooled enough that I would be able to go beyond the defensive, partisan rhetoric that the Cold War produced on both sides, and that had found its way into much of the previous scholarship on the topic. As I worked on the book I did, however, see both the contemporary relevance of a study of the Cold War in the Middle East and parallels with the current situation. For example, the American-Iranian confrontation in the post–Cold War era resembled nothing so much as a regional version of the Cold War, with an exaggerated emphasis on terrorism taking the place of "international communism" as a bogey, and a "global war on terror" targeting an "axis of evil" standing in for a cold war against an "evil empire."

As I reflect on this topic today, in the waning months of 2008, that parallel may still be valid. Of course, much will depend on how the incoming American president decides to deal with Iran, and how Iran responds, and on whether the war on terror continues to be the centerpiece of the next administration's foreign and security policies, as it was of the Bush administration's. But the relevance of this book today is even greater and more immediate given the sudden upsurge of American-Russian tensions in the wake of the conflict in Georgia, and in light of the broader issue of NATO expansion into the former East bloc, and the stationing of American weapons systems immediately adjacent to the borders of Russia. Listening to voices in Washington and in Moscow after the standoff in Georgia, or to that of Vice President Dick Cheney, speaking immediately after a visit to Tbilisi in September 2008 about Russian actions as an "affront to civilized standards,"[2] it almost sounded as if the Cold War had never ended.

Although it appears from some of the current rhetoric that there are those who would like nothing more than to see the Cold War revived, the ideological thrust on both sides is certainly different today than it was at the height of the twentieth-century superpower confrontation. American critics of Russia speak of the extension of democracy rather than of capitalism and free markets, while Russians defending their country's actions speak in terms of protection of its great-power prerogatives and its security, not of the triumph of communism. So while some elements of American and Russian policy justifications have remained the same, others have clearly changed.

If the Cold War taught us anything, however, it was (or should have been) to look beneath these sorts of statements for other, deeper motivations. One underlying objective in the Middle East for both superpowers during the Cold War, as chapter 2 of this book shows, was access to oil. Another was achieving strategic advantage in this vital region. It is worth asking, as I do in the pages that follow, whether these and other similar motivations may not have been more important throughout the Cold War than they were credited with being at the time, while ideology was perhaps less important than most on both sides of the iron curtain then believed or claimed to believe. The fact that ideology does not explain everything is shown by the persistence of deep differences between Russia and the West over the expansion eastward of NATO to countries like the Baltic republics, the Ukraine, and Georgia. That these issues have arisen long after communism collapsed in eastern Europe, and Russia became a capitalist country awash with millionaires and billionaires, would seem at least in part to validate this line of argument.

And if access to energy resources and strategic positioning played a larger role than is sometimes realized in the Cold War, the American-Russian standoff over Georgia certainly appears to fit the same pattern. Georgia is the *only* route to the West for central Asia's rich oil and gas deposits which does not pass through Russia. It is a former part of the Soviet Union, and before that, of imperial Russia, and it is part of the sensitive southern belt around the Soviet Union that abuts on the Middle East and that was perceived in Moscow as crucial to Soviet security from World War II onward, as we shall see in the pages that follow. Moreover, just as the Middle East and adjacent regions have always been a crucial arena for the functioning of the international system before and during the Cold War, as I show in chapter 3, so has the Georgian crisis raised system-wide questions. Writing in *Le Monde* about Russia's recent "demonstration of force," columnist Daniel Vernet stated: "This is a matter of asserting [Russia's] place in the definition of a new world order. The post–Cold War period when the West, and in particular the United States, could try to remodel the international system in [its] image, at best hoping that Russia would accept this, and at worst without paying attention to its interests, is past."[3]

If this book has any impact, I hope that it will be in alerting its readers to some of the damage and the dangers imposed on small countries and vulnerable peoples in the Middle East (as in other regions) by the ill-advised grand designs of great powers situated far away and generally—but not always—insulated from the consequences of their own actions. The Cold War had a potent overriding logic of its own for both sides, which generally took precedence over all other considerations, whether solicitude for the interests of countries and peoples directly affected by the conflict, or even acknowledgment of the realities on the ground where these contradicted fixed ideological imperatives. This Cold War logic often led the superpowers to ride roughshod over these realities, which nevertheless frequently had a way of asserting themselves, whether for the United States in Lebanon in 1983 or for the Soviet Union in Afghanistan in the 1980s. A similar logic seems to have driven the sole superpower in the wake of the Cold War, with similar consequences, as the United States has discovered to its dismay in Iraq and Afghanistan. We may have seen the same logic at work as the Bush administration wittingly or unwittingly encouraged the volatile Georgian president to provoke Russia, which apparently was waiting to take advantage of just such a provocation. As some Georgians are ruefully beginning to realize, the cost for Georgia may prove to be great,[4] which I show in these pages was also the case for small Middle Eastern clients of the superpowers throughout the Cold War, and of the United States since then.

This brings me to another theme discussed herein, which is that in the Middle East in the post–Cold War era, and especially over the past eight years, the United States often appeared to be operating in many respects as if the Cold War had never ended. This was true even before the recent recrudescence of American-Russian tensions in and around the Middle East, as starting in the 1990s the United States built more bases and poured more troops and equipment into the region than at any time since World War II. It is too early to say whether this dynamic will continue now that a new wariness has entered American-Russian relations. But the United States seemed to move almost seamlessly in the Middle East from mobilization against the Soviet Union to a high military profile that eventually found its justification in George W. Bush's global war on terror. It may be that the same dynamic will obtain in light of the new American-Russian tensions over Georgia, and that the Middle East will continue to be a major focus of American strategic attention, albeit now directed at Russia. It is worth noting that in his speech, cited above, Vice President Cheney made a point of stressing that "in the Middle East, Russian arms-dealing has endangered the prospects for peace and freedom in that region," referring in particular to arms sales to Syria and Iran, and to the former channeling some of these weapons "to terrorist fighters in Lebanon and Iraq."[5]

I would venture, on the basis of the experiences of the Cold War and of the post–Cold War era thus far, that whatever happens in American-Russian relations and regarding the war on terror, the Middle East will indeed continue to be a crucially important arena. The history I survey in this book will help to explain why this is so, and will give us all yet another opportunity to determine whether men and women learn anything from history. The signs for the post–Cold War era so far are not entirely encouraging.

SEPTEMBER 2008

INTRODUCTION: RETHINKING THE COLD WAR IN THE MIDDLE EAST

The period that is always most difficult of access is the one that is just within living memory. Not yet written down, its primary sources often still inaccessible, it is at the disposal of fallible memory and prejudice. No generation is ever fair to its parents.

—ROSEMARY HILL[1]

For nearly half a century, the Cold War rivalry between the United States and the Soviet Union created a glacial divide that loomed over international relations. Its icy tentacles extended across the globe, with often devastating effects. The Cold War provoked a high degree of polarization, as states and political parties aligned themselves with the two superpowers in virtually every region of the world, exacerbating and aggravating pre-existing local conflicts or producing new ones, and envenoming the political atmosphere in numerous countries. Once it became a full-blown ideological and great-power confrontation in the wake of World War II, the East-West division dominated deliberations at the newly established United Nations and became the main focal point of international affairs. Its chill was felt in the domestic politics not only of the United States and the Soviet Union but of countries the world over.

The Cold War did not begin immediately after World War II, although precisely when it did start is a subject of some dispute. Former British prime minister Winston Churchill's famous observation, in a speech at Westminster College in Fulton, Missouri, on March 5, 1946, that "from Stettin in the Baltic to Trieste in the Adriatic, an iron curtain has descended across the Continent," is often seen as a decisive indication that the Cold War was already under way by that point, less than a year after the war's end.[2] Historians, however, cite various key events from 1945 until 1947 as marking the end of the World War II alliance between the Western powers and the Soviet Union and the beginning of a cold war between them. It is clear, for example, that Churchill and some of President Harry S. Truman's advisors were much more hostile toward the Soviets than were others, or than President Franklin D. Roosevelt apparently had been. It is also clear that over time, political circumstances changed, as did the views of decision makers on the Anglo-American side. Although Soviet decision-making was more opaque, it appears as if similar differences regarding American intentions may have existed in the minds of Joseph Stalin and the small circle of advisors around him.[3] Once the Cold War had started in earnest, however, it rapidly came to constitute the central axis of world affairs, and any such differences of opinion as may have existed on either side lost most of their importance.

We now know that this rivalry had been presaged by deep wartime suspicions and devious maneuvering among the Allies at the height of the colossal joint effort against Nazi Germany during World War II. In the case of those wary old adversaries Churchill and Stalin, antagonism to each other's system was of very long standing.[4] Beyond the crucial questions of the postwar future of Germany, Central Europe, and the Balkans, the concerns of the Soviets and the Western powers extended into the Middle East and the adjacent regions south of the USSR, whence Britain had launched its repeated interventions to crush the Bolshevik regime during the four-year Russian Civil War after the 1917 revolution. It is unlikely that either Churchill or

Stalin, both of whom were central figures in this earliest phase of the East-West rivalry, ever fully forgot the impact of that deadly struggle. In some measure, these intense early experiences can be said to have shaped each one's view of the other side.[5] Indeed, Churchill's entire career shows that he was always profoundly anticommunist, while Stalin's long-standing obsession with Britain as an imperialist power, notably in the Middle East, at times seemed to override his strong concerns about the growing role there of the United States in the early phases of the Cold War. Meanwhile, to complete this triangular picture, American policymakers, less experienced in international affairs than their British counterparts, often tended to be influenced by the latter's deep concerns about the spread of communism in the Middle East (which they often conflated with nationalism and anticolonialism). At the same time, the United States was for many years frequently at odds with Britain in different parts of the region, until their simmering differences in approach exploded during the 1956 Suez War, when the United States openly opposed Britain and its French and Israeli allies. This sub rosa rivalry between the two Western powers is an underappreciated aspect of the early years of the post–World War II era.

The Cold War and the fears it engendered haunted several generations.[6] It had this impact not only in the United States and the Soviet Union, and in Europe, which at the end of World War II lay battered by combat and virtually prostrate between the victorious armies of the two nascent superpowers. It also had a powerful effect in East and Southeast Asia, notably in Korea and Vietnam, where less than five years after the end of World War II the Cold War soon developed into ferocious hot wars. These were the only such wars directly involving the United States and its allies on the one hand and communist satellites and allies of the Soviet Union on the other. There were also less overt proxy confrontations between the superpowers in Central America and the Caribbean, Africa, South Asia, and the Middle East, all of which were important arenas of superpower rivalry for decades. The first such non-European confrontations between the USSR and the United States and its allies (even before the wars in East and Southeast Asia) transpired in the Middle East. They were to have a special importance, as we shall see.

The Cold War has now been over for nearly two decades. For students of college age today, it is beyond their experience and their memory. If they know anything at all about it, this period is at best a matter of dim, distant history to them. And yet if time seems to fly for those of us who grew up during the Cold War and do remember it, changes in the way people see history progress very slowly. This may be especially true of recent history, about which many of those who have lived through the events in question may have deeply felt views, views that they are reluctant to modify. Thus, a serious rethinking of this crucial and well-defined period of modern world history, free of the Cold War shibboleths and the intense partisanship that distorted so much earlier scholarship, only began slowly. A reluctance to readdress the period has especially afflicted the "winning side," where certain aspects of the orthodox, long-accepted interpretation of the conflict have yet to be challenged.[7] Indeed, the continuing identification of many older Cold War historians with the received truths on "their side" of the now vanished iron curtain has been a hindrance to the writing of balanced, objective history of the Cold War.[8]

Although much good historical work has been done in recent years, particularly on the origins of the Cold War, there is still significant room for further reconsideration of the broad story of this rivalry's origins, development, and course, and of its effects, especially as considerable new archival documentation on the Soviet side and from other sources has become available since the collapse of the Soviet Union.[9] A new look at the Cold War is particularly timely now that even after the demise of communism and the rise of capitalism in Russia, and the end of the ideological struggle that supposedly undergirded the Cold War, Western relations with Russia in East and central Europe, in the Caucasus, and in the Middle East are once again characterized by considerable friction. This is a perfect example of how one's vantage point in time makes possible a completely different view of history. After the West's warm embrace of the first two post-Soviet rulers of Russia, Mikhail Gorbachev and Boris Yeltsin, and after the triumphalist proclamations of the "End of History,"[10] who could have foreseen the emergence of grave differences only a decade later between the United States and Europe, on the one hand, and Russia, on the other, over Iran, energy supplies, the expansion of NATO to countries like Georgia and Ukraine, and missile defenses? All of this should perhaps make us rethink at least some of the conventional views of the causes and motivations of the Cold War. Perhaps ideology was not quite as important as some on both sides made it out to be, and perhaps traditional great-power conflicts of interest over strategic issues and resources, the likes of which continually plagued Russian-Western relations before the Bolshevik Revolution, deserve more attention.

Beyond the need for further rethinking of Cold War history in general, relatively little new research has been done about the central role of this great international rivalry in a number of regional conflicts.[11] This follows on a period, from the late 1950s through the early 1990s, when much scholarship in a variety of fields, much of it policy driven and some of it of uneven quality, was devoted to exploring the impact of the Cold War on these regions. The inquiry into regional impacts of the superpower rivalry was a branch of an entire field, Sovietology, which grew up in the shadow of the Cold War and has now virtually disappeared. There has been a similar drop in recent decades in the number of such works in various Cold War–related fields. Ironically, this has come just as some distance in time has developed between us and the most dramatic events of the Cold War, and when new archival and other primary sources have been made available, at least in theory making the writing of the history of this period easier. The relative paucity of new scholarly work on this vital era is as true of the Middle East as it is of most of the regions that were deeply marked by the impact of the Cold War rivalry from the 1940s until the 1990s.[12]

These regions, whether Africa, Latin America, South and East Asia, or the Middle East, have been marked further since then by what might be called the ghosts of the Cold War. The most striking example is the blowback of United States' involvement in the Afghan war against the Soviet occupation of that country, but there are many others.[13] Understanding these powerful and lingering aftereffects of the Cold War requires going back in time and reassessing that conflict, especially its less-studied final phases. I will seek to explore further on in this book the lingering impact of these Cold War ghosts in the Middle East long after the Soviet Union itself had disappeared and the Cold War was forgotten.

It is important to revisit this period, in the Middle East in particular, for several other reasons. Immediately subsequent to the rapid disappearance of its Soviet rival, in 1990–91, the United States engaged in an extraordinarily confident assertion of its suddenly unrivaled power in the Middle East via its leadership of a grand coalition against Iraq's invasion of Kuwait in the Gulf War of 1991, and in convening the 1991 Arab-Israeli peace conference in Madrid, which led to the 1993 Oslo Accords, signed on the White House lawn. Both were unprecedented initiatives in various ways. Although nominally a collective effort, the 1991 Gulf War was the first American land war in Asia since Vietnam. Meanwhile, Madrid witnessed the first multilateral peace conference in history bringing together all the parties to the conflict, Arab and Israeli, and all relevant international actors. Moreover, it constituted the first and only serious and sustained American (or international) effort in over half a century at a comprehensive resolution of the Palestine conflict.

In light of these apparently radical departures in American policy immediately after the collapse of the Soviet Union, it would be useful to revise our understanding of the Cold War as simply a prolegomenon to the current era of unfettered American dominance over the region. Such a revision would help us answer a number of questions: Was the United States previously as constrained by the presence of its Soviet rival as sometimes seemed to be the case, and as these two novel departures immediately after the demise of the USSR seemed to indicate? Alternatively, was America in fact more dominant in the Middle East throughout the Cold War era than may have appeared at the time?

These are important questions, since for the United States the Cold War was at least the ostensible reason for an enormously expanded American post–World War II global presence. Similarly, the perceived Soviet threat was the pretext for the establishment of U.S. military bases spanning the globe, and for the development of a vastly enhanced American international intelligence, economic, and diplomatic profile compared with the relatively modest world role of the United States before December 7, 1941.[14] Before that date, the United States was a Western Hemisphere and Pacific power with a major fleet and great economic might, but with limited military and air capacities and narrowly defined international interests. It thereafter became the dominant world power, the sole possessor of atomic weapons, with fleets and air forces that dwarfed those of all other powers, and an unrivaled global economic, diplomatic, and intelligence presence. The post–World War II expansion of American power around the globe contrasted strikingly with the isolationist aftermath of World War I and the rapid decline of American involvement in European and Middle Eastern issues in 1919–20. The post-1945 expansion was in large measure predicated, at least as it was presented to the American public, on the newfound "need" to confront the Soviet Union (although it is striking to note that certain important aspects of this expansion, especially in the military sphere, well antedated the Cold War).[15] What drove this expanded vision of the role of the United States in the world in the waning years of Roosevelt's presidency was a sense that the global presence of American power was necessary to prevent yet another world war, and that America's previous refusal to play such a global role was a major reason for the disasters of 1914 and 1939. Such a view might not have convinced an American public skeptical of shouldering expansive international burdens, whence the utility of the easy-to-understand "Soviet menace" to Truman and those around him in justifying the efforts involved.

In many regions, this expansion of America's global reach meant that the wartime arrival of U.S. troops—in the case of the Middle East this occurred in North Africa and Iran in 1942—was not followed after the end of the war by their disappearance back over the horizon, as had happened in Europe immediately after World War I. These initial wartime deployments of American forces, and the later establishment and postwar maintenance of major U.S. air bases at Dhahran in Saudi Arabia, at Wheelus Field near Tripoli in Libya, in Morocco, and in Turkey marked the beginning of a continuous U.S. military presence in different locales in this region, a presence that is ongoing to this day. It was the beginning as well of what has become a well-established role for the United States as a major Middle Eastern power. Indeed, I would argue strongly that these early war-time and postwar moves constituted the beginning of an American role as *the* major Middle Eastern power, a reality that was masked for a time by the power and proximity to the region of the USSR.

Although overshadowed at times by other Cold War arenas, the Middle East was not just a secondary region where the United States and the USSR contended. Already during World War II, the crucial strategic importance of the Middle East had been amply demonstrated in terms of its central geographic location on the southern flank of Europe and astride vital sea and air lanes, and the vast energy reserves it was known to contain. The region's importance in terms of strategy and oil was further established during the Cold War, perhaps to a greater extent than some observers realize, as later chapters of this book will show. And since the Cold War ended, the significance of the Middle East to the United States has only seemed to increase with every passing year. Evidence for this assertion can be found in a series of major recent American initiatives in the region, including those already mentioned such as the defeat of Iraq in the 1991 Gulf War and the 1991–93 Madrid-Oslo Middle East peace process. Further evidence is the Iraq sanctions regime from 1991 until 2003, which involved constant bombing and overflights of Iraq, followed by the invasion of that country in 2003 and its subsequent occupation, which in 2009 will enter its seventh year, the largest, longest-lasting, and most costly such American overseas military effort since Vietnam.

Some of these post–Cold War American actions were unilateral in essence, even if they may have been superficially multilateral in form, while others emerged more genuinely from collective decision-making in the United Nations and elsewhere. Since the end of the Cold War, perhaps only American involvement in the Balkans and the North Korean nuclear crisis have been actions of the same level of gravity. In any case, these initiatives in the Middle East have been among the most dramatic taken by the United States in the world arena in the wake of the collapse of European communism and the end of the Cold War. They indicate a particular and continuing importance to American policymakers of the vast stretch of North Africa and West Asia running from the Atlantic Ocean to central Asia, even after the end of the Cold War.

Given all of these facts, a reexamination of the Cold War in the Middle East has the potential to clarify several important issues. The first is with respect to achieving a historical understanding of the unprecedented current American involvement in this extensive region. How did the United States get into the situation in which it finds itself today, with a huge military, political, and economic presence in this unstable part of the world, where it is currently fighting two potentially open-ended wars, in Afghanistan and Iraq? Beyond this, the United States appeared at times as if it were on the verge of a third Middle Eastern hot war, with Iran, even as the two powers engaged in a fierce covert rivalry throughout the region that often looked very much like a cold war. Does this extended forward American military posture indeed have its roots in decades of deepening involvement in the region linked to the rivalry with the Soviet Union? Alternatively, is this involvement entirely new in nature and entirely different from that during the Cold War, and was the main reason for it really the changed world situation after 9/11, and the "global war on terror," as the Bush administration argued?

The second issue is the broader and more general one of the nature of the transformation of the United States from being essentially a power whose ambitions were limited to the Western Hemisphere and the Pacific region before World War II, to being one of two superpowers, to its current position as the

sole global hegemon. Is explaining the growth of American involvement in the Middle East crucial to our understanding of
the United States' new post–Cold War global role? What was
the importance of the region's energy resources, and those of
adjacent Transcaucasia and central Asia, in the ambitions of
the team that surrounded George W. Bush to extend American
global hegemony through the rest of the twenty-first century?
This ambition was clearly indicated by the manifesto issued
by the Project for a New American Century (PNAC), to which
many of the key members of the Bush administration adhered
before they came into office in January 2001.[16]

A final issue that might be clarified by an examination of the
Cold War with respect to the Middle East is the extent to which
today's massive American involvement in the region is an aberration, no more than the most egregious of the many foreign
policy missteps and excesses of the Bush administration. If the
current situation is indeed the result of one administration's actions, the pendulum is likely to swing back and we will eventually see this aggressive new course reversed by George W. Bush's
successors. By contrast, is this assertive new high-profile American posture in the Middle East no more than a logical—albeit
more extreme and violent—continuation and development of
what came before in the way of U.S. policy there, going back to
the Cold War? If so, the approach inaugurated under George W.
Bush may mark the beginning of a new pattern of direct, unilateral American military interventions in this unstable region
that is likely to continue into the future, and is also likely to ex-
acerbate further its instability.

THE SAUDI CONNECTION

In considering the issues just raised, and the questions that arise
from them, it is useful to start with a little-appreciated episode

near the end of World War II, to which I will have occasion to return.[17] This was the meeting between President Franklin D. Roosevelt and the Saudi king 'Abd al-'Aziz ibn Sa'ud (known variously as 'Abd al-'Aziz and Ibn Sa'ud) in Egypt on February 14, 1945. Roosevelt, infirm and only two months from death, was on his way home from the Yalta conference. Why did the weary president of what had just become the most powerful country on earth spend the better part of a day meeting with this apparently minor Middle Eastern potentate? The answer is that this encounter was arranged because of Saudi Arabia's importance in the eyes of those in the State Department, the military, and the Office of Strategic Services (OSS)—the wartime predecessor of the Central Intelligence Agency, established by Maj. Gen. Bill Donovan—who were already planning for the postwar era. The organizer of the 1945 meeting, Col. William Eddy, the head of the American Legation at Jedda, was an Arabic-speaking son of missionaries who had grown up in Cairo. He was a key figure in the OSS, and his account of the meeting, which he arranged and at which he served as the translator, provides much valuable detail.[18] We know that by this point the vast extent of Saudi oil reserves was familiar to American strategic planners and oil executives.[19] Saudi oil had just begun flowing to support the Allied war effort, an effort that was simultaneously strangling both German and Japanese oil supplies, measurably shortening the war.[20] Finally, in 1945 the United States was already planning to acquire a major air base at Dhahran, which it continued using until 1962, and used again for a decade starting with the 1991 Gulf War, nearly thirty years later.

The United States and Britain had by this stage launched major invasions of Sicily, Italy, and southern France from bases in the Middle East, and were supplying massive quantities of Lend-Lease equipment to the Soviet Union across Iran, which was occupied by British, Soviet, and American troops. Saudi

Arabia was only one link in this vast wartime chain, which stretched right around the globe, but the kingdom had one crucial characteristic, besides its strategic position and its possession of vast reservoirs of oil and gas beneath its soil: it was one of only two fully independent states in this crucial Middle Eastern region that had never been occupied by the troops of European colonial powers, and it had no foreign bases on its soil. Moreover, Ibn Sa'ud had twelve years earlier signed an exclusive agreement for the exploration and exploitation of its oil reserves with an American consortium of companies that became the Arabian American Oil Company (ARAMCO).[21] This consortium had thereby managed to secure the first major exclusive American oil concession in the Middle East, an area that had heretofore been virtually an exclusive British preserve.

President Roosevelt was thus meeting with the absolute ruler of a nation with something unique to offer the United States: an alliance with a Middle Eastern power that was not already part of another great power's sphere of influence. Such an alliance gave American access to oil and bases in the kingdom even more meaning. Moreover, importantly for the coming postwar era, Saudi Arabia's ruler was staunchly anticommunist, and he did not have to worry about a large body of nationalist public opinion, as did governments in other major Middle Eastern countries like Egypt, Iraq, Syria, and Iran, where large urban populations, organized into political parties, enjoying slowly growing literacy and attached to a culture of newspapers and books, were deeply anticolonial and suspicious of foreign bases and foreign concessions.

Nevertheless, because of his concern about his standing both in the Arab world and with public opinion in his kingdom, however rudimentary the latter may have been, the Saudi king felt unable to go along with the request of his American interlocutor that all the Jewish survivors of the Nazi Holocaust be settled in Palestine. He stressed that happy though he was to co-operate with the United States in a variety of spheres, he would have to insist on the importance of one issue, that of Palestine, about which he asked: "What injury have Arabs done to the Jews of Europe?"[22] In response to this expression of the king's position, in April 1945, just before Roosevelt died, the president sent a letter to Ibn Sa'ud confirming what he told him in response to the concerns over Palestine that the king had expressed during their meeting: that the United States would consult with both Arabs and Jews before acting in Palestine, where it would never act against the interests of the Arabs.[23]

Roosevelt's successor, Harry S. Truman, was to deny initially that the United States had ever made such commitments.[24] Although he was later provided with Roosevelt's April 1945 letter by the State Department, in the Palestine policy Truman crafted over the next few years he proceeded to violate blatantly both of his predecessor's commitments—to consult with both Arabs and Jews before taking action in Palestine, and to do nothing there that would harm the Arabs. Four American diplomats based in the Middle East who had been brought back to Washington in October 1946 to brief Truman were left cooling their heels for over a month because, the president finally told them, his advisors "felt that it would be impolitic to see his Ministers to Arab countries, no matter how briefly, prior to the November Congressional elections." It was to this group that Truman uttered the infamous words: "I'm sorry, gentlemen, but I have to answer to hundreds of thousands who are anxious for the success of Zionism; I do not have hundreds of thousands of Arabs among my constituents."[25] Not surprisingly in light of these views, starting with Truman's presidency, the issue of Palestine became a continuing irritant to the Saudi monarchy in its dealings with Washington, and indeed in those of virtually every single Arab regime, democratic or autocratic, ever since. It remains so down to the present day. It has, however, been an irritant that most Saudi and other Arab leaders came to accept as the price of doing business with the indispensable power of the United States. This fact has not been entirely lost on the Palestinians or on those many others in the region concerned about Palestine.

By giving an oil concession to an American consortium in 1933, the Saudi monarch had already managed to assert his independence of Great Britain's heretofore exclusive and pervasive influence over his kingdom, influence that the king had long resented bitterly.[26] Whether far-sighted, fortunate, or both, between 1933 and his meeting with Roosevelt, Ibn Sa'ud managed to link his realm and his dynasty firmly to the growing power of the United States, doing so well before many world statesmen had realized the future superpower's full potential. In the end, this crucial connection was to prove more important to him and to the five of his sons who have succeeded him as kings since 1953 than were their concerns about Palestine, notwithstanding any contrary opinions, which since have often been strongly expressed by Saudi and Arab critics.

Perceived by Washington to be valuable to postwar planning in terms of both its economic and strategic value, Saudi Arabia soon turned out to have the world's largest proven oil reserves, which is still the case today. Oil produced by ARAMCO was crucial to the postwar recovery of Europe, to keeping oil prices extremely low for several decades after World War II, and to increasing the profits of the big American oil companies that dominated the world oil market.[27] Saudi Arabia had importance in other realms, however, linked to the fact that it was one of the first countries in the Middle East where the United States was free to establish bases without having to take permission from, or incur the jealousy of, the traditional powers that dominated the region, Britain and France.[28] The Dhahran air base (originally called an "airfield," in deference to Saudi sensitivity about having foreign bases on their soil), on which construction began in late 1945 and which was utilized by the United States Air Force until 1962, was especially useful to American global airlift capabilities, and for rescue, reconnaissance, and combat aircraft, as a link in the chain of bases strategically located along the Soviet southern frontiers. This was particularly the case in the early years of the Cold War, when American strategic bombers like the B-29 had more limited ranges than would more advanced craft later on.[29]

Feeling itself under pressure from Arab nationalist sentiment and the anticolonial propaganda of the Egyptian regime, which increased in intensity in the late 1950s, the Saudi government requested termination of the basing arrangement in 1961, and the U.S. Air Force ceased to base units there the subsequent year, although Americans (ex-military personnel contracted by the Vinnell Corporation) continued to run the airfield for the Saudi government thereafter. The U.S. Air Force in any case had ceased to need the base in the early 1960s when the development of longer-range weapons systems made it possible to give up a variety of American bases, including Dhahran and later Wheelus Field in Libya, as well as others, for Jupiter intermediate-range ballistic missiles (IRBMs) in Turkey and Britain.[30] I will return to these Cold War strategic issues in chapter 4.

It was not until after the advent of a completely different post–Cold War American strategy, one involving a large-scale, long-term, multicountry American military presence in the Middle East, that, starting in 1991, U.S. forces were once again based at Dhahran, as well as in Kuwait, Bahrain, Oman, Qatar, and elsewhere in the region. It is noteworthy that this new strategy came after the demise of the USSR removed any existential nuclear danger to the United States itself. However, these newly arrived American forces in the Middle East were not directed against "international communism" and its proxies, as was the case from the mid-1940s through the early 1970s, but rather against local Middle Eastern actors. The American presence in the region was clearly intended for entirely different purposes than those for which U.S. bases there were first envisioned. I will examine in a later chapter the little-remarked-upon shift from a Cold War emphasis on the formidable power of the Soviet Union—an emphasis that over time came to require fewer bases in the Middle East, and indeed by the 1970s relied largely on an "over the horizon" posture (whereby the United States depended almost entirely on naval and air forces based outside the region, together with some pre-positioned equipment, for the projection of American power)—to the current American post–Cold War strategy. This has produced the largest U.S. military concentration in the region since World War II, albeit one directed against foes whose nature is not always entirely clear.

THE ARAB COLD WAR

As the Cold War penetrated the Middle East, and as the United States gradually replaced Britain and France as the dominant Western power in the region—not without a little friction, as we shall see—the American-Saudi connection continued to be important. It was cemented in 1957 by the adherence of the new Saudi monarch, King Sa'ud, to the Eisenhower Doctrine.[31] This follow-up to the Truman Doctrine—which ten years earlier had marked the first formal American recognition that the Cold War had extended to the Middle East—was enunciated by President Dwight D. Eisenhower before a joint session of Congress in January 1957. In it, Eisenhower proclaimed American support for any Middle Eastern government targeted by "overt armed aggression from any nation controlled by International Communism."[32] King Saʻud's public adhesion to the American camp in the Middle East through his acceptance of this doctrine after a visit to Washington, D.C., was a major coup for the United States. American policy thereby separated Saudi Arabia from Egypt, its erstwhile ally in inter-Arab politics and a vocal advocate of nonalignment, even as the Egyptian regime of Gamal Abdel Nasser gradually moved closer to the Soviet Union.

For the next decade, Saudi Arabia and Egypt came to constitute the main poles of two opposed camps within the Arab world, which engaged in what the late Malcolm Kerr memorably described as the "Arab Cold War."[33] These camps in turn came to be closely aligned with the United States and the Soviet Union. By this process, a regional cleavage with its own logic and specificity was subsumed into the great Cold War divide. As I argue in chapter 4, this grafting of the Cold War between the United States and the Soviet Union onto preexisting Middle Eastern rivalries and conflicts significantly exacerbated those conflicts in many cases. At the same time, the involvement of the Americans and the Soviets in internecine local quarrels provided opportunities for Middle Eastern "clients" to extract support from their superpower patrons, which the latter sometimes were obliged to extend against the better judgment of key policymakers.[34]

Saudi Arabia's value to the United States was soon to emerge in yet another sphere: the ideological arena. For among the key convergences of the Cold War era in the Middle East was that between the Soviet Union and not only states like Egypt but leftist and Arab nationalist movements in their various forms, including Nasserism, the Baʻth Party, multiple varieties of Arab socialism, the different Arab communist parties, and other radical parties and groups. Although this Soviet-Arab coalition seemed united by anticolonialism, a commitment to state-led development, contempt for "bourgeois democracy," and some other shared values, it was in fact a profoundly uneasy agglomeration of forces. There were deep divergences and suspicions, and sometimes open conflicts, between its very disparate component parts, and between many of these parties and the various Arab regimes on the one hand, and the Soviet Union on the other. Thus, almost immediately after the Iraqi revolution of 1958, the Communist Party in Iraq found itself at odds with the Nasserists, Ba'thists, and other Arab nationalists, which rapidly developed into a lasting conflict that only became more bitter and sanguinary as time went on. The Egyptian regime and the Soviets eventually were obliged to take sides with their respective squabbling Iraqi protégés, while keeping their bilateral relations as normal as possible.[35] Notwithstanding the problems that eventually emerged between would-be allies, for a time, in the mid-1950s through the early 1970s, this grouping of Arab leftists and nationalists appeared to be a formidable coalition, particularly when aligned with a growing number of nationalist Arab regimes and with the USSR. Indeed, in the struggle within the Arab world, the Arab cold war, this coalition seemed to be a winning one, as it proclaimed that it represented the future in the battle against the backwardness of the assorted traditional monarchies and conservative regimes associated with the United States.

The radical wave in the Middle East seemed to place the United States and its allies in a highly unfavorable position. To this apparently unbalanced situation, Saudi Arabia brought the powerful ideological weapon of Islam. This was something the Saudis were uniquely positioned to do, given the centuries-old alliance between the royal family and the rigidly orthodox Wahhabi religious establishment, and given the kingdom's special place as the location of two of the three most holy places in Islam, Mecca and Medina. Particularly after the much more competent and more pious and ascetic King Faisal took over from his profligate older brother Sa'ud in 1962, Saudi Arabia focused much more intensively, and more plausibly, on Islam as the backbone of its resistance to the self-proclaimed "progressive" Arab regimes. It sponsored various Pan-Islamic entities, among them what eventually became the Organization of the Islamic Conference, as a counterweight to the Pan-Arab bodies and parties dominated by Egypt. It spent its oil wealth liberally on spreading the kingdom's puritanical and dogmatic Wahhabi form of Islam and on other forms of religious propaganda, building mosques, religious schools, and Islamic centers all over the world. Finally, Saudi Arabia gave refuge to Islamist political activists persecuted by secular Arab nationalist regimes in Egypt, Syria, Iraq, and elsewhere. These included notably members of the outlawed Muslim Brotherhood, some of whom had already been spotted by Western intelligence agencies as potentially useful proxies in the Cold War struggle with the radical Arab protégés of the Soviet Union.

Saudi Arabia's employment of Islam as an ideological tool thus proved useful to the United States and its allies among the conservative forces in the Arab and Islamic worlds, which at this time, in the mid-1960s, seemed largely on the defensive in the face of the Soviet-backed "progressive" Arab regimes. Indeed, Islam eventually became an important part of the American ideological arsenal in the Cold War, used by U.S. intelligence services not only in the Arab countries but also in Pakistan and South Asia, in Southeast Asia, in Soviet Central Asia, and in other parts of the Islamic world. It may seem hard to believe today, given the current demonization of radical, militant political Islam in American public discourse, but for decades the United States was in fact a major patron, indeed in some respects *the* major patron, of earlier incarnations of just these extreme trends, for reasons that had everything to do with the perceived need to use any and all means to wage the Cold War.[36]

There was of course a price attached to this Cold War–driven approach, not least in terms of the ideals and principles that Americans like to believe their foreign policy is based on. While the Soviet Union generally aligned itself with authoritarian nationalist regimes, American policy backed absolute monarchies in Saudi Arabia, Iran, and the Arab Gulf states (with the exception of Kuwait), and other nondemocratic, authoritarian regimes in Jordan, Tunisia, Morocco, Pakistan, and elsewhere from the late 1940s until the 1970s as part of this same Cold War strategy. In so doing, the United States laid little or no stress on the promotion of democracy, constitutionalism, or human rights in the Middle East. Indeed, the United States had previously helped to subvert Middle Eastern democracies by actions such as supporting the Husni Zaim coup against the constitutionally elected president Shukri al-Quwatli in Syria in 1949, organizing with Britain the overthrow of Iran's democratically chosen prime minister Mohammad Mosaddeq in 1953 and imposing an autocratic regime under Mohammad Reza Shah, and providing Lebanese president Camille Chamoun with the funds to bribe his way to achieving a parliamentary majority in the 1957 elections.[37] Chapter 5 examines in more detail the deleterious impact of both American and Soviet Cold War policies on the growth of democracy in the Middle East. In some cases when the United States subverted democracy in the region, Islam served as a screen or as an ideological adjunct, as in Iran, for example, where some elements of the religious establishment became part of the American-supported anti-Mosaddeq coalition in 1953. Needless to say, this went down very well among the absolutist, antidemocratic elites of the conservative states the United States was aligned with, who were generally ostentatiously pious Muslims (although this outward appearance was sometimes scandalously far from the sordid reality).

The long-standing inattention of American policymakers to the promotion of democracy and human rights in the

Middle East (and often their outright disdain for these things), and their aggressive sponsorship of radical Islamic groups and trends, are both significant in light of the Bush administration's claim that its policies aimed to spread democracy in the Middle East, and in view of the global war on terror that it launched. This "war" in fact has amounted in the main to a diffuse and incoherent campaign against a broad and quite disparate range of largely unconnected regimes and militant, radical Islamic political movements. Some of these groups, like al-Qaʻida, are lineal descendants of ones the United States was allied with for decades, often until the administration of George W. Bush's father. The now conveniently forgotten Cold War alliance between the United States and these Saudi- and Pakistani-backed Islamic movements and forces was only belatedly to produce some of its most bitter fruits in Afghanistan, and thereafter in the smoking ruins of U.S. embassies in East Africa, the World Trade Center, and the Pentagon, long after the Cold War was over.

During much of the Cold War, this alliance with a politicized, militant, and often extreme form of Islam was seen as doing yeoman's service for American policy in the Middle East and beyond. Islam as an ideological tool was particularly crucial in rallying conservative forces in the Middle East and beyond at a crucial phase of the Cold War, notably at the height of the civil war in Yemen from 1962 to 1967. In this conflict, Egyptian troops and air power backed the Republicans, and Saudi Arabia and its conservative regional allies supported the royalists financially and militarily in a desperate seesaw struggle on the southwestern borders of the Saudi kingdom. Behind both sides in this conflict stood their superpower patrons, the United States and the Soviet Union. The banner of Islam and American backing (with support from the British) indeed became the cement that brought together a disparate coalition throughout the Arabian

Peninsula and the Gulf. It included Yemeni royalist and tribal forces, the governments of Jordan and Oman, which faced their own radical domestic oppositions, and, farther afield, the governments of Pakistan and Iran under the shah. Included as well in this American-led coalition were various groupings and parties, among them elements of the underground Muslim Brotherhood in Egypt, Syria, and Iraq. As part of this sub rosa regional conflict, while Saudi Arabia supported its allies in the Yemeni civil war with weapons and money, Jordan and Iran sent military advisors and some military units to the neighboring Dhofar region of Oman to fight against a radical Marxist guerilla movement there that opposed the sultan's regime and the British advisors who propped it up, while British troops fought to hang on to Aden and South Yemen against a tenacious insurgency.[38] On the other side, disparate radical groups and Arab nationalist regimes, such as those of Egypt, Algeria, and Iraq, as well as the Soviet Union, gave extensive military support to the Yemeni Republicans, the Popular Front for the Liberation of Oman and the Arabian Gulf fighting in Dhofar, and the South Yemeni insurgents.

As the forces aligned with the United States proclaimed their defense of the Middle East against atheistic communism and its secular Arab nationalist allies, a particular form of militant political Islam thus provided an ideological banner and a critical rallying point. Islam was to continue to provide a lasting focus for a number of these allies, playing a significant role in American, Saudi, and Pakistani regional policies until the instrumental employment of radical Islam as a tool of policy reached its apogee during the Afghan war against the Soviet occupation from 1979 to 1988. This was many years after the high tide of radical Arab nationalism (and allied Marxist currents) had ebbed in the wake of the crushing defeat inflicted by Israel in June 1967 on two of the leading paragons of militant Arabism,

Egypt and Syria, and after a number of Arab countries, led by Egypt, had abruptly ended their alignment with the Soviet Union. I will return later in the book to some of these developments and to the unpleasant outcome of the Afghanistan experience for most of those concerned.

THE ARAB-ISRAELI CONFLICT
AND THE COLD WAR

The events of the Arab cold war described above were only one example of the many important ways in which the larger American-Soviet Cold War had a major impact on the Middle East. The alignment of each of the superpowers with one or another side in the Arab-Israeli conflict is probably a better-known example. For several decades starting in the 1960s, and until the very end of the Cold War in 1991, the United States was the primary backer of Israel, while the Soviet Union was the main supporter of most of the Arab states engaged in the conflict, to the point that uninitiated observers may have assumed that it had always been thus. This fixed alignment did not, however, go back to the earliest phase of the Arab-Israeli conflict, the Palestine war of 1948–49. In fact, in that crucial formative period, both the United States and the USSR were ranged on the same side (albeit for different reasons): they both voted in the UN General Assembly in 1947 to give the Jewish minority in Palestine 55 percent in a partition of the country, both raced to recognize the independence of the new Jewish state that resulted from that decision on May 15, 1948, and both helped surreptitiously to arm Israel during the war that ensued. Soviet arms, delivered through Czechoslovakia in the summer of 1948, were in fact crucial to Israel's ultimate military victory.

The main reason for the United States taking the position it did, against the professional advice of the State Department and the Pentagon, was simple, and was summed up in President Truman's words quoted earlier: "I'm sorry, gentlemen, but I have to answer to hundreds of thousands who are anxious for the success of Zionism; I do not have hundreds of thousands of Arabs among my constituents."[39] The Soviet position, which shifted from anti-Zionism to support of the creation of Israel in a few short months, owed a great deal to Stalin's obsessive concern about the power of Britain in the Middle East, which he did not seem to realize was waning rapidly, his suspicions of what he saw as Britain's Arab clients, including Transjordan, Iraq, and Egypt, and his mistaken belief that a Jewish state might align itself with the USSR.[40]

Israel and the Soviet Union drifted apart soon afterward, with Israel moving closer to the United States during the Korean War, and the Soviet Union eventually developing closer relations with Arab countries that sought to free themselves from direct and indirect control by the old European colonial powers. Thereafter, Britain and France became the main arms suppliers to Israel, which used their Centurion and AMX-13 tanks and Super Mystère and Mirage fighters to win its next two wars against Arab states. These were the Suez War against Egypt, which Israel fought in alliance with the British and French in 1956, and the June 1967 war against Egypt, Syria, and Jordan. Crucially, France also provided Israel with the wherewithal to produce nuclear weapons, which it did surreptitiously starting in the mid-1950s, a far-reaching measure that fundamentally changed the strategic balance in the Middle East, tipping it even further in Israel's favor.[41]

The tripartite Anglo-French-Israeli invasion of Egypt in 1956 marked another moment when, rather than being ranged on opposite sides, the United States and the USSR found themselves strange bedfellows, both opposing the aggression of the two old colonial powers and their Israeli ally against Egypt.

Their alignment came at one of the high points of the Cold War, when Soviet forces were engaged in bloodily suppressing the Hungarian uprising, and the United States and the Western powers were loudly decrying Soviet brutality while doing little to help the Hungarian rebels. Over Suez, however, the two superpowers took the same position, of opposing the tripartite attack on Egypt, albeit—as in 1948—for different reasons. The Soviets were happy to be able to point to Western imperialist aggression while they put down a rising in their own imperial backyard. Meanwhile, President Eisenhower was furious at Britain and France for acting without consultation, for doing so with overtly neocolonial motives, and for distracting world public opinion from Soviet bad behavior in Eastern Europe. The subtext of American displeasure was that Britain and France did not know their place in the new world of the Cold War, where there were only two superpowers, and all important decisions on the western side of the East-West divide were made in Washington.[42]

The Suez War was to be the last time until the end of the Cold War that the superpowers found themselves on the same side of the Arab-Israeli conflict. Soon thereafter, the Arab cold war began, the Eisenhower administration's sympathy for the Egyptian regime of Gamal Abdel Nasser, never very deep, was exhausted, and the American-Soviet rivalry ratcheted up even further in the Middle East. The Eisenhower Doctrine resulted from this escalation. It was in fact directed not just at the Soviet Union but at Arab states with which the USSR was aligned, like Egypt, which in the Manichaean vision of Secretary of State John Foster Dulles were seen implicitly as being "controlled by International Communism."[43] The Soviet Union had been supplying Egypt with arms since 1955 (the original arms deal here, too, was made via Czechoslovakia), and soon was supplying Syria, Iraq, and other Arab countries as well. Thereafter the

USSR provided aid for the construction of Egypt's Aswan Dam, after the United States reneged on its commitment to do so. The United States was arming Saudi Arabia, Iran, Jordan, and other allies, and by the 1960s had begun to supply Israel with weapons. At the outset, in the late 1950s, the United States surreptitiously allowed West Germany to ship surplus American-manufactured M-48 tanks to Israel. This arms-supply relationship became more overt in the subsequent administrations of John F. Kennedy and Lyndon B. Johnson, as the former sent Hawk antiaircraft missiles, and the latter A-4 Skyhawk attack bombers, to Israel.

It was the 1967 war, however, that marked both the full alignment of the United States with Israel and the beginning of Israel's heavy reliance on American weapons systems, starting with the top-of-the-line F-4 Phantom fighter-bombers supplied by the Johnson and Richard M. Nixon administrations. The massive dependence of Israel on billions of dollars annually in U.S. military and economic aid came a few years later, following a subsequent Arab-Israeli conflict, the October 1973 war. By this time, the United States had come to see Israel as its most valuable ally in the Middle East region in the global struggle with the USSR and its proxies. It fitted perfectly into the Nixon administration's strategy of "Vietnamization," or finding local proxies to serve U.S. interests, and was seen as more valuable even than Iran under the shah, as was shown by American willingness to deliver to Israel weapons that neither Iran nor NATO allies received.[44]

Policymakers in the Johnson and Nixon administrations were obsessed by a scenario in which they saw the USSR and China as pinning the United States down in Southeast Asia at little cost to themselves, via what they myopically perceived as their Vietnamese proxies. They looked to Israel to even the score against the Soviet Union's proxies, Egypt and Syria, at little direct cost to the United States. The Soviets in turn could not allow themselves to be left behind. They upped the ante further after the 1967 war by writing off most of Egypt and Syria's debts for military equipment destroyed or captured by Israel during the war, and by delivering to them massive amounts of new arms, among them advanced new weapons systems, notably surface-to-air missiles (SAMs), including the SAM-2, SAM-3, and the new SAM-6.

The two superpowers raised the stakes higher and higher thereafter, notably during the strategically crucial 1968–70 War of Attrition along the Suez Canal, when the Egyptians, at enormous cost to their forces, pushed their air defenses to the edge of the Suez Canal, making possible a crossing of this enormous antitank barrier a few years later. During this fierce but little-known phase of the Arab-Israeli wars, Soviet pilots and advisors to Egyptian air defense crews were directly engaged in combat (several of the former were shot down by Israeli pilots and many of the latter were killed in Israeli air strikes), and the most advanced antiaircraft missiles and radar were sent to Egypt. Naturally, the United States countered with deliveries of top-of-the-line military equipment to Israel.[45]

Finally, in the 1973 war, Nixon and Dr. Henry Kissinger (originally Nixon's national security advisor but by 1973 secretary of state) ordered the airlift of massive quantities of military equipment to Israel when its stocks were in danger of running out. This escalatory sequence from 1967 until 1973 was driven, incidentally, as much by the clients on both sides as by the competition between their superpower patrons, as Israel refused to negotiate seriously with Egypt in spite of American remonstrance, and the Egyptians insisted on a military option in spite of the deep reluctance of the Soviet military.[46] Throughout this six-year period, both superpowers progressively sent their respective allies more and more advanced weaponry, and became more directly committed themselves. In the final stages of the 1973 war, the United States placed its armed forces worldwide on a general nuclear alert, DefCon 3, in response to reports that several Soviet paratroop divisions had been placed on alert, and that the USSR was shipping nuclear warheads to its forces in the Mediterranean.[47] The Soviets were reacting to the refusal of Israel to obey a UN-mandated cease-fire, as its troops continued to roll toward Cairo after crossing the Suez Canal. In a message to Nixon, Soviet Communist Party general secretary Leonid Brezhnev demanded a joint superpower intervention to end the war, failing which the Soviets threatened to intervene unilaterally themselves. They were apparently on the point of doing so when Kissinger raised the ante by ordering a nuclear alert, and at the same time belatedly called a halt to the Israeli advance. Though this event has had less attention than the Cuban Missile Crisis a decade earlier, here again the superpowers had seemingly been brought to the brink of a nuclear confrontation, but this time by their proxy competition in the Arab-Israeli arena.

By this point, the Cold War rivalry as played out through the Arab-Israeli conflict had clearly taken on a dynamic of its own. This can be seen in the behavior of Richard Nixon and Henry Kissinger and in the actions of their Soviet opposite numbers. Nixon and Kissinger's objective was to expel the Soviets from Egypt and to win that country over to the side of the United States. Their goal incidentally fitted in perfectly with the aims of Egyptian president Anwar Sadat, who was eager, together with his military high command, to get out from under the Soviet thumb and receive the American support he eventually did win. The Soviets' aim was to retain their foothold in the region at all costs. Much of their large military presence in Egypt by this point—over twenty thousand "advisors"—was in fact involved in maintaining a naval base under exclusive Soviet control that was used to keep track of the movements of U.S. submarines carrying submarine-launched ballistic missiles (SLBMs) in the Mediterranean.

For both superpowers, these and other Cold War aims were far more important than the ups and downs of the Arab-Israeli conflict, or than peace between Arabs and Israelis. Partly in consequence of the single-minded concentration of both of the superpowers on besting each other, that conflict came no closer to final resolution for the duration of the Cold War. There were a number of efforts toward such a resolution, most of them desultory: a brief single session of a peace conference at Geneva in 1973; three disengagement agreements negotiated by Henry Kissinger, two between Egypt and Israel and one between Syria and Israel; an American-Soviet joint communiqué of 1977 calling for a comprehensive Middle East peace settlement to be negotiated at a multilateral peace conference; and an Egyptian-Israeli peace treaty that emerged after President Jimmy Carter's 1978 mediation at Camp David. Yet in spite of these initiatives, no resolution of the conflict was achieved. In chapter 4, I expand further on these points, and argue that, in effect, achieving advantages in their rivalry with one another ultimately was far more important to the superpowers than was peace in the Middle East, which consequently got relatively low priority in their efforts in the region. Even with the Cold War long over, peace between Arabs and Israelis has not been achieved to this day, in part because for what is now the sole Middle Eastern hegemon, the United States, pursuing other aims has apparently so far taken precedence over this objective.

A LEGACY OF BETRAYAL
AND ABANDONMENT

There are numerous other instances of how the overarching Cold War rivalry shaped and distorted outcomes in the Middle East, beyond interstate relations. Decisions on economic devel-

opment, domestic policies, the balance of forces between political parties, majority-minority relations within states in the
region, and many other things, were affected and often distorted by the machinations of the Soviets and the Americans in
their unceasing rivalry with each other. To single out one case
among many, consider the tragic example of how the Kurds in
Iran, Iraq, and Turkey became pawns in regional rivalries that
came to be overlaid with the confrontation between the superpowers. The episodes of this ill-starred story began with the
proclamation of the Kurdish Mahabad Republic in January
1946, when Soviet troops were still occupying northern Iran,
including Iranian Kurdistan. This initiative marked the establishment of the first autonomous Kurdish entity in history, one
that was initially warmly supported by Stalin, and soon afterward just as coldly abandoned by him.[48] One of the key leaders
of the Mahabad Republic, its defense minister, the Iraqi Kurdish leader Mullah Mustafa Barzani, escaped and ended up in
the Soviet Union. He returned in 1958 to his native Iraq, where
his Kurdish Democratic Party launched a series of revolts
against different governments in Baghdad, including a major
uprising, with Iranian, American, and Israeli support, against
the Ba'th regime in 1974–75. This ended with the betrayal of
the Kurds in the 1975 Algiers agreement between Iran and Iraq,
with the collusion of Henry Kissinger. The United States had
blessed this Iran-Iraq accord, which entailed the United States
and Iran abandoning their support for the ongoing Kurdish
revolt against the Iraqi regime, a revolt that these two powers
had helped instigate. Thereafter, Kissinger (whose first book
betrayed his cynical conservatism in its unalloyed admiration
for Metternich, Castelreagh, Talleyrand, and other luminaries
of the post-Napoleonic age of reaction in Europe) told an ap-
palled aide: "Covert action should not be confused with missionary work."[49]

A more recent episode of this depressing story of the Kurds

was the Iraqi regime's slaughter with gas and by other means of thousands of Kurdish villagers in the course of the Iran-Iraq War of 1980–88, during which the superpowers played both sides of the street in their tireless efforts to gain advantage over each other. Thus the United States and its allies encouraged the Iraqi Ba'thist regime to go to war with the Islamic revolutionary government in Iran, supplying Iraq with the means to engage in gas warfare against Iran (and also its own Kurdish population),[50] while the administration of President Ronald Reagan later surreptitiously contacted Iran as part of the illegal Iran-Contra conspiracy, delivering to it much-needed parts for Hawk SAM missiles.[51] The Soviets, meanwhile, were no less callous and self-serving, remaining the main arms suppliers of the Iraqi armed forces while also selling armored vehicles and missiles to the Iranians. In all of this, the Kurds were left to their fate by the two superpowers, which had both cynically exploited them against what they perceived as each other's regional proxies, and then just as cynically dropped them when they were no longer of any use. This recurring trope in Kurdish history, of adoption and then abandonment by great-power protectors, which had its precedent in similar behavior by the British at the end of World War I,[52] risks being repeated once again in northern Iraq, whenever the overextended power of the United States is finally obliged to retreat from that distant, landlocked region.

Even as the Iran-Iraq War that so devastated the Kurds and both countries involved was starting, the Soviet Union made a fateful, and ultimately fatal, decision to invade Afghanistan in order to prop up a crumbling pro-Soviet regime. In so doing, it sent the Red Army across a Cold War line that had not been crossed since the end of World War II, and set off alarm bells all over the Western world, and especially in the United States. The Carter administration, already battered by the humiliations attendant on the Iranian Revolution, decided to respond vigorously by supplying various forms of support to anti-Soviet Afghan guerillas, the mujahideen, in a bid to bleed Soviet forces. However, partly because of his administration's perceived weakness in the face of challenges in Iran and Afghanistan, Carter was succeeded in the White House by the much more assertive Reagan administration, which saw in Afghanistan an opportunity to do much greater harm to the Soviet Union. Indeed, Afghanistan opened for the Reagan team the long-sought prospect of bringing down the entire "evil empire." The Reagan administration included a number of the most vigorous proponents of the aggressive prosecution of the Cold War since the days when John Foster Dulles headed the State Department in the mid-1950s. In some senses they were more aggressive than even Dulles had been: for all his messianic anticommunist bluster, Eisenhower's secretary of state had been committed to the Cold War doctrine of containment propounded by the pragmatic George Kennan.[53] By contrast, many of the neoconservatives in the Reagan administration favored a radical strategy of "rolling back" communism, a belligerent approach that had never become established doctrine in Washington, not even at the height of the Cold War. Now that the most viscerally anticommunist administration since that of Herbert Hoover was in office, rollback of communist regimes or regimes perceived to be under Soviet influence, whether in Africa, Central America, or Afghanistan, became its policy. The incoming administration had picked the right moment in 1981, and in Afghanistan it picked the right place.

Activating the old radical Islamist allies with which it had worked in various nooks and crannies of the Cold War and the Arab cold war, the CIA under William Casey, with the support of the Saudi and Pakistani intelligence services and those of other countries, soon helped to field a well-armed, -supplied, and -financed force of Afghans, together with Arab volunteers and others whom it brought in from all over the Islamic world. It eventually proved to be more than a match for the Soviet occupation forces and their Afghan allies, who went down to a defeat even more staggering than that inflicted on the United States in Vietnam. The defeat was particularly shocking because it occurred in a country adjacent to the Soviet Union. But after the bloodied Red Army crossed the bridges and mountain passes back to the Soviet Union in 1988, the lethal, divided, and ill-disciplined mujahideen movement created by these Cold Warriors eventually fractured and metastasized into forces that continued to engage in an endless war that engulfed Afghanistan. That war still rages there, today largely directed against the United States and its local allies. Other networks that grew out of the thousands of Arab and other Muslim volunteers brought to Afghanistan by the American, Saudi, and Pakistani intelligence services developed into al-Qaʻida. All of these brutal, nihilistic, and violent organizations and forces are ghosts of the Cold War, bastard children born of the blowback of a now conveniently forgotten era.

Soon after the Soviet Union was defeated in Afghanistan and after the Iran-Iraq War ended in mutual exhaustion, the Soviet empire in Eastern Europe and the rest of Eurasia began to crumble from within. The Soviet Union itself finally disappeared in 1991. It was undoubtedly sapped by its disastrous intervention in Afghanistan, and by exorbitant military expenditures to match the Reagan strategic arms buildup, but most experts agree that the Soviet system was probably ripe for collapse in any case.[54] The Cold War was over, but its tragic sequels, its toxic debris, and its unexploded mines continued to cause great harm, in ways largely unrecognized in American public discourse. In a very real sense, the tragic outcome of 9/11 represents one of these sequels, the evil work of the distant but very real ghosts originally conjured up by the United States to wage the last phases of the Cold War. The Cold War is over, and the Soviet Union is no more, but those ghosts are still with us. They can perhaps only be fully laid to rest, and their malice overcome, if we recognize that their true origins are not as foreign as they are sometimes made out to seem.

UNANSWERED QUESTIONS

So to re-pose the questions with which I began, was the Cold War just a prologue to the current unfettered hegemony over the Middle East (and the rest of the world) that the United States was only able to exercise once the Soviet Union was out of the way? Or was the Soviet Union's power exaggerated in American perceptions and public discourse, was it in fact less of an obstacle to American domination of the Middle East than it may have seemed to some, and was the United States always more dominant, globally and in the region, than it may have appeared? My inclination is toward concluding that the power of the Soviet Union in the Middle East and elsewhere was often exaggerated in the contemporary American view. One indication of the imbalance between the two is the fact that the Middle East, like most of the other major arenas of Cold War rivalry, was immediately adjacent to the USSR. There were no such Cold War battlefields in the immediate vicinity of the United States, with the exception of Cuba and, for a brief period in the 1980s, parts of Central America. Thus, from soon after 1945, it was the United States that was containing the Soviet Union and stationing forces and strategic weapons all around its frontiers and those of its satellites, and not vice versa, only one of many indices of the great disparity of power between the two superpowers in favor of the United States.

Of course, the United States has, and has always had, the luxury of a greater degree of isolation from the rest of the world than any other great power in history. Unlike Russia, it does not have, and has never had, powerful neighbors on its borders or off its shores. Moreover, except for an abortive Soviet attempt to deploy IRBMs and IL-28 medium-range bombers in Cuba in 1961, foiled by President John F. Kennedy during the Cuban Missile Crisis, the Soviet Union was never able to place land-based or airborne strategic weapons in close proximity to the U.S. mainland. The United States was able to do this with the most lethal of strategic weapons, nuclear weapons, in a great arc surrounding the Soviet Union from the very first moments of the Cold War, in 1945–46, with some of these weapons based in the Middle East. Indeed, some historians have argued that the dropping of two atomic bombs on Japan was at least in part aimed as a warning to the USSR of the overwhelming strategic capabilities at the disposal of the United States.[55]

Even after the USSR detonated its own atomic bomb in 1949, shifting the strategic balance somewhat in its favor, it had no assured delivery system for nuclear weapons until the deployment of intercontinental ballistic missiles (ICBMs) in the mid-1960s. Thereafter, both powers soon became capable of destroying one another many times over. These are all indications, nevertheless, of the great superiority of the United States over the USSR, a superiority that was most importantly based on the United States' far greater economic power, and its postwar dominance of the European and Japanese economies, which together produced more than the Soviet economy, little more than a decade after World War II. While the Soviet Union had a formidable heavy-industrial base (although it had been gravely damaged during World War II) and a massive arms industry, both were dwarfed by those of the United States, whose economy had been raised by the stimulus of war production from the doldrums of depression to unheard-of heights of productivity.

To be sure, the USSR also had certain advantages. By its very location it dominated the Eurasian landmass, and it had vast land armies, led by combat-hardened commanders. It had an initial ideological advantage in Europe because of the presence of strong communist parties there. It had a similar advantage in much of the developing world in the face of the persistence of European colonialism. I have suggested, and will discuss further in later chapters, how this ideological edge operated in the Middle East, although it now appears to have been of relatively limited significance in the long run. Yet, although the USSR was a great power, by far the greatest after the United States, in many respects it was not truly a superpower, lacking the global reach that the United States enjoyed with its fleets and air forces and with its far-flung military bases. This is not to speak of the enormous strength of the interlocking and interdependent capitalist economies that the United States thoroughly dominated through the financial system centered on Wall Street and the International Monetary Fund and the World Bank, which it put into place after World War II and which gave absolute economic primacy to Washington and New York.

All of these American strategic advantages can be seen operating in the Middle East, where a quiet struggle was waged, first in the Mediterranean, when in the 1960s the U.S. Navy initially based Polaris SLBM-carrying submarines targeting the USSR there, and the Soviets sought naval and air bases in the region to counter them. These advantages could be seen operating again in the 1970s when the United States' deployment of longer-range Poseidon SLBM-carrying submarines also targeting the USSR turned the Persian Gulf, the Arabian Sea, the Red Sea, and the Indian Ocean into a similar theater of naval competition for both superpowers. As I will show in more detail in chapter 4, in the Middle East and elsewhere the United States was taking the initiative by stationing lethal strategic weapons in the backyard of the USSR, not vice versa. Thereafter, the United States was able to use its formidable economic power to help wean Egypt and other Arab states away from their former Soviet patrons, with generous promises of aid.

Thus, I would argue that while the struggle for influence in the Middle East seesawed back and forth, and at times looked desperate to some in Washington, it was the United States that ultimately always had the upper hand strategically. This became apparent with the "defection" to the American side of formerly radical Arab nationalist regimes like that of Egypt under Sadat in the 1970s, and later that of Iraq under Saddam during the Iran-Iraq War. Moreover, for all the fevered rhetoric in 1950s Washington about countries in the Middle East being controlled by "international communism," these Arab regimes and their elites were never drawn ideologically to the USSR. Quite the contrary, all of them were deeply, fundamentally anticommunist, and none were committedly anticapitalist (the sole exception in the entire Middle East for the entirety of the Cold War was South Yemen). Even where communist parties had a role in the domestic politics of Middle Eastern countries, as in Iran, Iraq, Sudan, and to a much lesser extent Lebanon, Syria, Jordan, and Egypt for very short periods, communists were never even close to being in control of these countries. The attraction of most Middle Eastern rulers to both sides in the Cold War was purely based on naked power, and as it became apparent to Middle Eastern elites that the United States was far more powerful and far richer than the Soviet Union, they eventually tended to gravitate toward Washington. Even the revulsion caused by Washington's constantly increasing bias in favor of Israel was not enough to alienate many Arab governments. We have seen this in the case of Saudi Arabia. It was equally true of Jordan, Morocco, Tunisia, and other reliably pro-American regimes. After Sadat's "apostasy" in leaving the pro-Soviet camp in 1972 and thereafter, it was increasingly clear that there were no longer any red lines in this regard, and that the United States could have its Israeli cake and eat whatever it wanted in the Arab world too.

I will leave to the conclusion of this study of the Cold War in the Middle East the final question of whether the George W. Bush administration's unilateral and interventionist policies in the region, starting with invasion, occupation, and regime change in Iraq, will come to be seen as an aberration and an anomaly, and whether in consequence we will see the pendulum swing back to a less assertive, less aggressive, less intrusive American policy in the Middle East following Bush's departure from office in January 2009. Alternatively, were the occupations of Afghanistan and Iraq the beginning of a new era in American hegemony in the Middle East, an era of even more naked direct intervention than in the past? I will try to show that the answers to these questions are rooted in a thorough understanding of how the current position of the United States in the Middle East evolved in response to the Soviet challenge over the four and a half decades of the Cold War. These questions are therefore best answered after an examination of that challenge and the evolving response, and their impact on the Middle East, to which we now turn.

II

OIL AND THE ORIGINS
OF THE COLD WAR

Historians are notorious for their preoccupation with beginnings, with origins, with the starting points of historical periods. Different scholars point to different moments as marking the beginning of the Cold War. However, there is general agreement about the first indications in the Middle East of the confrontation between the United States and the Soviet Union that dominated the succeeding decades. These were linked to a series of apparently grave crises that took place in 1945 and 1946 along the southwestern perimeter of the newly expanded sphere of Soviet power, drawing in the major wartime allies, the USSR, the United States, and Great Britain. These crises involved Iran, Turkey, and the adjacent Balkans, and started in the closing stages of World War II, continuing immediately after the war ended and through 1947, by which time the Middle East had been fully drawn into the Cold War.

These linked Middle Eastern and Balkan flare-ups, together with others at the same time in eastern and central Europe, were among the first signs that the precarious wartime amity between the three major allies might not be long-lived, and are generally considered to be among the most important markers of the beginning of the Cold War. They aroused deep suspicions in the United States and Britain as to Soviet intentions, while the actions of the Americans and the British and their responses to Soviet initiatives in these regions were in turn causes for serious alarm in Moscow.

President Harry S. Truman's address of March 12, 1947, to a

joint session of Congress about these developments, which came to be known as the Truman Doctrine, was a key turning point in the Cold War as a whole. It was also the culmination of the sequence of events that began with these 1945 great-power confrontations over Iran, Turkey, and the Balkans. This speech focused on the crises involving Turkey and Greece in particular, and warned of the dangers developments there posed to the Middle East. Truman told Congress that if the United States did not extend military and financial aid to both countries in confronting domestic communist forces and the Soviet Union (although the latter was never mentioned by name in the speech) "confusion and disorder might well spread throughout the entire Middle East."[1]

This address, delivered less than two years after World War II ended, marked a notable evolution in the position of the United States in two respects. The first was vis-à-vis the Soviet Union, which was now being described publicly by the president as a rival and potential enemy. Truman's address was one of the first major landmarks of the Cold War, and showed clearly that a full-blown direct and indirect confrontation between East and West was already well under way in the Middle East. Second, this speech constituted the first time an American president had designated the Middle East as an area that was crucial to the national security interests of the United States. It thus signified that American power had become global and extended to areas never before considered vital to decision makers in Washington or to the American public. In consequence, Turkey and Greece, and later on other Middle Eastern states, became dependent on the United States, and in some measure became client states of this nascent superpower.

The United States and the Soviet Union had already become deeply engaged in the Middle East at an early stage of their participation in World War II. Although other great powers (including tsarist Russia) had throughout their modern history regarded this region as being of considerable strategic importance, it is ironic in view of their later deep involvement in the Middle East that in the immediate pre–World War II period neither the foreign policy of the Soviet Union nor that of the United States laid particular stress on the region. This was the case at least until the two powers were drawn into World War II by surprise attacks in June and December 1941, respectively. Before that, leaders of both countries appeared far more concerned with events in Europe and East Asia, notably the frightening military rise of Nazi Germany and the growth of expansionist Japanese militarism. For both, the Middle East was by comparison a foreign-policy backwater through the end of the 1930s.

This situation changed dramatically immediately after the Soviet Union and the United States were attacked and thereby brought into World War II. Soon after the German conquests of the Balkans and Crete in early 1941, the Middle East and adjacent areas became the theaters of some of the war's most decisive and strategically important military operations. This became even more the case starting with Hitler's 1942 Stalingrad and North African campaigns, which for a time became the focal points of the war with Germany. These two major offensives eastward, combined with covert Nazi subversion in Syria, Egypt, Iraq, and Iran, and efforts to woo neutral Turkey, constituted an attempt at a vast pincer movement, with its focus on the Middle East and the neighboring region to the north of it between the Black Sea and the Caspian. Should the Wehrmacht—which was undefeated until this point in the war—have been successful in this great gamble, Hitler's armies would have controlled the southern Soviet Union, nearly the entire Mediterranean and Black Sea basins, and most of the Middle East. They would have been in a position to dominate the Suez Canal and with it the shortest route to India. The possibility of such an extremely dangerous strategic situation emerging in 1942 naturally obliged American, British, and Soviet leaders and military commanders to concentrate their attention on this region from an early stage of the war. The critical situation in the Middle East clarified in the most urgent possible way the vital strategic position of the region for those who might have been previously unaware of it. Given that they had focused relatively little on this area in the prewar era, the key American and Soviet strategists who directed their countries' war efforts had to adapt quickly. The lessons they learned during this difficult year of the war were to inform their thinking throughout the Cold War.

From the moment the Western powers and the Soviet Union began to focus seriously on the Middle East at this point in World War II, the region's strategic importance to them was almost self-evident, and its continuing prominence thereafter during the Cold War was easy to understand. The region lay at the junction of three continents; it bordered four major bodies of water, the Mediterranean, the Black Sea, the Caspian Sea, and the Indian Ocean; and it lay immediately to the south of the borders of Russia, Ukraine, the Caucasus, and Transcaspia. For all these reasons it had long attracted the ambitions of would-be global powers, even if in the decades before World War II neither American nor Soviet policymakers had seemed particularly concerned with it. As soon as the war began, however, the region's geographic characteristics quickly attracted the attention of strategists in both Washington and Moscow.[2] The great German offensives just described, finally blunted by the Soviets at Stalingrad and by the British at El Alamein in North Africa, and the great victories for both that followed, had the effect of further underlining the region's already considerable strategic importance for leaders in Moscow, London, and Washington.

But something other than its intrinsic strategic importance

and the fact that early on in World War II the Middle East was clearly a focus of the grand strategy of the Axis powers drew the attention of Cold War policymakers in the United States and the USSR to this region. Even before the outset of the Cold War, an uncannily symmetrical simultaneous interest in Middle Eastern oil was shown by American and Soviet leaders at the highest level, although the oil question has won relatively limited attention from historians by contrast with other elements of the broader strategic picture. Considerable concern about establishing access to the oil resources of the Middle East was indeed manifested while World War II was still raging, and while both powers were focused on Germany, rather than each other, as a rival. While linked to long-standing strategic factors that had been brought to the surface in the course of the war, such as control of the Black Sea, the Mediterranean, and the route to India, the interest in access to oil involved an entirely new emphasis, at the same time as it was linked to traditional approaches of both powers. It is a minor irony that at the outset of what was soon to become the atomic age, an earlier form of energy was to play such a prominent role in the confrontation between the two nascent superpowers.

The fact that as early as 1945 both the United States and the Soviet Union were paying considerable attention to Middle Eastern oil does call for some explanation. Both powers were major producers of oil, the world's two greatest, both had considerable reserves, and both had traditionally enjoyed self-sufficiency in oil production. Indeed, in 1941 the United States was the world's largest oil producer, with 63 percent of world production, with the USSR second, with 10.7 percent.[3] In this respect they were in a far better position than all their great-power rivals during the first half of the twentieth century. Germany, France, Japan, and Italy had limited or no domestic sources of oil, even as the development of air and land transport and of various new forms of military technology drastically increased demand for this vital commodity and made it considerably more strategically important than ever before. Even the great British Empire was dependent upon faraway supplies of oil in distant and unstable lands, notably Iran and Iraq.

World War II, however, had further underlined the crucial and growing strategic importance of oil, which was coming to play a more vital role in warfare than it ever had before. Now not only fleets of ships, as in earlier conflicts, but also growing fleets of trucks, tanks, and planes were completely dependent upon oil products for propulsion. The armies of all the powers still used railways and animal transport, but their increasingly crucial mechanized forces were entirely dependent on oil by-products, as were their air forces and navies. This vital nexus was increasingly apparent to all Allied war planners. It was clear in particular to American military strategists, who by 1944 directed a major proportion of the U.S. Army Air Force's strategic bombing offensive against oil production, storage, and transport facilities in Germany and Japan and the countries under their occupation.[4] Thus in June 1944, the man in charge of the European portion of this bombing campaign, the commander of the USAAF Strategic Air Forces in Europe, Gen. Carl Spaatz, issued an order to his commanders that the "primary strategic aim of the U.S. Strategic Air Forces is now to deny oil to enemy air forces."[5] By this point a valuable lesson about the strategic importance of oil in wartime had clearly been learned by the top levels of the American military command. It was learned effectively: by the end of the war, American bombing of German oil facilities had been so devastating that on both the eastern and western fronts, German panzers could not move and the Luftwaffe could not fly for lack of fuel.

If both American and Soviet leaders and strategists came to understand the vital importance of denying oil to their enemies in order to achieve victory, their own frightening wartime experiences gave both of these allies reason to be concerned about their own oil supplies in the future. The Nazi offensive southeastward toward the Caucasus in the spring and summer of 1942 had been directed in large part at depriving the USSR of its fuel supplies from the rich Baku oil fields, the country's main source of oil. Had the great 1942 Wehrmacht assault that was finally brought to a halt at Stalingrad succeeded, it might have crippled the Soviet war effort by depriving it of oil, and perhaps changed the course of the war. Similarly, had the southern arm of the German pincers, led by the Afrika Korps commanded by Field Marshal Erwin Rommel and including Italian forces, managed to break through the British defenses in North Africa, not just Egypt and the Suez Canal but also the oil fields and refineries of the Middle East, on which a large part of the Allied war effort in that region depended, would have been vulnerable.

Meanwhile, the massive German U-boat offensive of 1942, directed in large measure against Allied tankers in the Atlantic and the Caribbean, if successful could have had a similar effect of cutting off the fuel supply across the Atlantic to Britain and for Allied operations in the entire European theater. Thus during the early years of the war, each of the three great victorious powers had suffered a serious scare relating to their own oil supplies and facilities.[6] Britain had been conscious of its vulnerability in this regard since the moment before World War I when it took the momentous decision to make its fleet (previously fueled by coal readily available at home in the United Kingdom) dependent on Middle Eastern oil supplies.[7] Such issues were new to American and Soviet war planners, however. Moreover, by 1945 both the United States and the Soviet Union were aware that their economies' rapidly growing need for oil, stoked by increased wartime demand, might soon outstrip their respective domestic supplies. In the case of the United States, by 1945 demand for refined petroleum products was already beginning to exceed supply (if one does not count production in Mexico, Venezuela, and the Caribbean).[8]

This was the crucial background to uncanny parallel moves relating to Middle Eastern oil made by the leaders of both countries at the very end of World War II. Thus, on his way back from Yalta, the ailing President Franklin D. Roosevelt met on February 14, 1945, with the Saudi Arabian monarch ʿAbd al-ʿAziz ibn Saʿud, on the deck of the heavy cruiser USS *Quincy* in the Great Bitter Lake, in Egypt's Suez Canal.[9] We have seen that Saudi Arabia was already linked to the United States by the oil accord signed in 1933 with ARAMCO. This consortium formed by Standard Oil of California (later joined by a number of partner companies, most of which had originally been parts of the old Rockefeller-owned Standard Oil empire that had been broken up decades earlier by federal trustbusters)[10] had enabled the powerful U.S. oil industry to break a near complete British stranglehold on Middle Eastern oil dating back to before World War I. Saudi Arabia's oil reserves were already known to be great, and by 1945 Saudi production had outstripped that of Bahrain and was approaching that of Iraq, which it surpassed the following year, becoming second only to Iran in the Middle East.[11] By 1945 Saudi oil production had already begun to be of considerable help in the war effort.[12]

The gravely ill American president, who looks visibly worn in photos of the encounter,[13] was taking part in this unprecedented meeting with the ruler of a small, faraway country for many reasons.[14] As was suggested in chapter 1, these included the fact that starting in 1943, American military planners began to be interested in basing rights for U.S. aircraft in eastern Saudi Arabia (which were soon afterward to be acquired at Dhahran). Moreover, we have seen that Saudi Arabia was one of only two countries in the Middle East not subject directly or indirectly to the colonial control of the European powers, meaning the United States might be able to obtain exclusive basing rights there, parallel to American companies' exclusive oil concessions.

The meeting took place essentially, however, because the war had taught the president and his advisors the crucial strategic importance of oil, and because it was already beginning to be clear to them how great the oil reserves of Saudi Arabia were. President Roosevelt himself, an assistant secretary of the navy during World War I, undoubtedly already knew a great deal about how vital oil was even before World War II impressed its strategic importance on everyone in a decision-making capacity in Washington. In any case, less than two months after this meeting, Roosevelt was dead, but with this personal contact he had inaugurated a crucial direct connection with the Saudi regime at the highest level.[15] The close link between the power of the United States and the leaders of a country in a strategic position, a country that contains the world's largest proven reserves of oil, has continued until this day, despite repeated ups and downs. These have occurred over issues relating to Palestine and Israel, and most recently about the Saudi role in support of Islamic militants in Iraq and elsewhere in the two decades following joint American-Saudi sponsorship of such militants in the war against the Soviet occupation in Afghanistan. Nevertheless, the relationship initiated by Roosevelt and Ibn Sa'ud has had incalculable importance for the subsequent global capabilities of the United States, due to the pivotal role in the world oil market of Saudi Arabia's oil wealth, and to Saudi Arabia's conscious direction of a huge proportion of its oil revenues into the American economy, whether by the purchase of treasury bonds, real estate, weapons, or other products.

STALIN'S MATCHING MOVES ON OIL

In an odd coincidence, a few months after the American president's meeting with Ibn Sa'ud, in June 1945, Roosevelt's opposite number at Yalta, Marshal Josef Stalin, signed a decree ordering Soviet geologists and oil technicians to enter Iran (which at that time was still under occupation by Soviet, British, and American troops) and to begin exploring for oil in the Soviet-occupied northern part of the country.[16] Earlier, in 1944, the Soviets had asked the Iranian government for a five-year concession to explore for oil in the country's northern region around the Caspian Sea. This request had been refused by the pro-British, but increasingly nationalist, Iranian government of the day.[17] In defiance of this refusal, the Soviets went ahead in a surreptitious fashion with the oil exploration ordered by Stalin in the northern areas of the country controlled by their occupation forces. In the event, no oil was found by the Soviets, nor have any significant quantities ever been found in the north of the country: all of Iran's known reserves are in the south, along the Gulf. Nonetheless, these Soviet initiatives were unprecedented for a country that since the Bolshevik Revolution had endeavored to be economically self-reliant to the point of autarky. They testify both to the newfound power of the USSR at the end of World War II and to the changed role of oil in the calculations of the Soviet leadership. After the 1944 effort to obtain an oil concession had been turned down by the Iranians, Stalin was in effect upping the ante in 1945 by ordering Soviet geologists to search secretly for oil in Soviet-occupied northern Iran, without the permission of the Iranian central government in Tehran.

Iran at that stage was by far the largest oil producer in the Middle East. The entirety of its oil production had been completely controlled by a state-controlled British company, the Anglo-Iranian Oil Company (AIOC), since Britain had won an exclusive concession in 1901, secured by businessman William Knox D'Arcy, to explore for and exploit oil resources throughout Iran (except in the five northern provinces bordering Russia). This sweeping concession, extracted from the weak Iranian monarchy of the day, gave the British company extraordinarily advantageous terms, and allotted to Iran only a miniscule 16 percent share of the profits and an even smaller proportion of total oil revenues. In the 1930s the new, more independent Iranian government of Reza Shah Pahlavi had tried to bring the AIOC under greater Iranian control and to get a larger share of oil profits. The British company, backed by the might of the British imperial government, proved completely intransigent, categorically refusing the Iranian demands. Such a humiliating failure and the imperious arrogance of the British left a bitter memory in the minds of Iranian patriots that was to fuel a later Iranian government's expropriation of the British-owned company in the early 1950s.

In 1945, however, there was a new factor in Iran, where Russia and Britain had dueled for influence for over a century: American troops had been stationed there since 1942 to help send Lend-Lease supplies to the USSR, and American oil companies had just begun making efforts with the Iranian government (constantly stymied by the efforts of the British, who still retained great influence over the Iranian government) to secure oil concessions in Iran.[18] Nevertheless, the oil exploration ordered by Stalin primarily constituted a direct challenge to British predominance over the Iranian oil industry, which since 1901 had been concentrated exclusively in British hands in the southern regions of the country. It was a challenge as well to the nationalist Iranians, who for decades had been highly sensitive where matters relating to their country's oil were concerned, and who were already chafing over the presence in Iran of troops from Russia and Britain, part of a recurring pattern of intervention by the two countries going back for many decades.

The launching of oil exploration ordered by Stalin was followed two weeks later by even more far-reaching orders from the Politburo of the Central Committee of the Soviet Communist Party to its top party official in Soviet Azerbaijan, Mir Bagirov. The Soviet Azeri party chief was ordered in early July 1945 to begin to organize a separatist movement in Iranian Azerbaijan, as well as launching similar activities in Iranian Kurdistan and other regions.[19] Orders went out from Moscow a week later to bring leading Azeri communists to Baku for consultations, to support the creation of an Azeri Democratic Party, and to promote separatist movements in Iranian Azerbaijan, Kurdistan, and other regions.[20] By September, Iranian Azerbaijan had escaped central government control, and in November proclaimed itself an autonomous republic, while in Iranian Kurdistan, the Kurdish Mehabad Republic was established in December 1945 and was formally proclaimed in January 1946. Both of these newly created autonomous regions, in Iranian Azerbaijan and Iranian Kurdistan, were protected from the intervention of troops of the Iranian central government by Soviet occupation forces.

Beyond these clandestine and overt Soviet moves, the Soviet Union showed a noticeable reluctance to remove its troops from Iran after the war was over and they were expected to leave according to the treaties governing the presence of all Allied forces in the country. Britain was similarly loath to withdraw its forces, which were also obligated by treaty to withdraw within months of the war's end. Britain eventually did pull out its troops, while by the end of 1945 the United States had promptly withdrawn its much smaller noncombat contingent. Together, the USSR's clandestine efforts at oil exploration and its support of separatist movements, combined with foot-dragging on the withdrawal of Soviet troops, provoked the Iranian-Soviet crisis of 1945–46. Given the sensitivity of these issues, this rapidly turned into one of the first major postwar crises between the

USSR and the West. In Washington and London there was deep concern, both because of the importance of Iran in terms of its strategic position and oil resources and because of fear that these Soviet moves might be part of an aggressive postwar pattern. Both powers protested directly to the Soviets, and raised the matter in the new forum of the United Nations.

Soviet troops eventually withdrew from Iran in May–June 1946 under intense Iranian and Anglo-American pressure. Thereafter, the USSR again asked for an oil concession from a new Iranian government, which was inclined to grant it, but it was once again refused, this time by the Iranian Majlis, or Parliament, which was growing in strength and asserting its prerogatives after foreign troops had left the country. Meanwhile, once Soviet troops had withdrawn, the Soviet-backed autonomous Azeri and Kurdish Mahabad republics, the last fruits of the 1945 Politburo directives, could finally be put down by Iranian troops without Soviet interference in November and December of 1946. Autonomous Iranian Azerbaijan and Kurdistan were thereby reunited with Iran. The Iran crisis marked an inauspicious beginning to postwar relations between Iran and its powerful neighbors, as well as to relations in the Middle East between the Soviet Union on the one hand and the United States and the United Kingdom on the other.[21]

A few observations are in order in light of these parallel moves by the two rapidly emerging superpowers as part of their newborn competition in the Middle East. Much has rightly been made in the historiography of the early Cold War of the jockeying for strategic position in this vital region by the United States and the Soviet Union. Stress has been laid in traditional Western historiography in particular on these aggressive Soviet moves in Iran. Much has also been made of the parallel crisis resulting from the postwar Soviet demand for bases near the Turkish Straits and for frontier revisions in favor of the Soviet

Union in the areas of Kars and Ardahan in the northeastern corner of Turkey (which will be discussed later), and simultaneous moves in the Balkans, notably external support for the Greek communists in their civil war with the British-backed royalists. These are seen as constituting a pattern of aggressive moves by Stalin, parallel with others in Eastern Europe, which were foiled only because of a resolute response by the West. In the case of Iran, we now know that American military planners certainly feared a Soviet push southward into the oil fields of Iran and Iraq in case of war, and were pessimistic about their ability to hold either in the face of a determined Soviet offensive.[22] Given the growing appreciation in Washington of the importance of Middle Eastern oil, these were very serious concerns. American policymakers meanwhile were aware that a Soviet naval presence at the Turkish Straits would have opened the Mediterranean to the Soviet fleet, especially Soviet submarines. Beyond this, a communist victory in Greece would have meant the spread of Soviet influence into the Aegean and well beyond those areas in Eastern Europe that had been effectively conceded to the USSR by Roosevelt and Churchill at Yalta.

In fact, serious strategic concerns were at play for both sides. It has been argued persuasively that the Soviet Union's actions in Iran, notably support for the Azeri and Kurdish autonomy movement, and the reluctance to withdraw its occupation forces, were motivated by a desire to push its defensive perimeter as far south as possible. This was because the planned Dhahran air base and other Western air bases in the Middle East could be used by the U.S. Strategic Air Command to bomb southern Russian targets, notably vital and highly vulnerable oil facilities and heavy industry moved eastward and southward from the western parts of the Soviet Union during the war.[23] The concern was not entirely fanciful: American strategic planning in case of war with the USSR did call for bombing of oil and other industrial facilities in the south of the country from bases in the Middle East, which was almost the only direction from which they could be reached by the heavy B-29 bombers of the day.[24]

It may well be the case that each of these perceived Soviet moves, in Iran, Turkey, and the Balkans, should be understood somewhat differently from how they are presented in the standard historiography. At Yalta and before, Stalin had agreed with Churchill to accept British dominance over the Greek government (in return for Stalin being granted a free hand elsewhere), and it was not the Soviets who upset this cozy division of spheres of influence. It was primarily independent Yugoslav support directed by Marshal Josip Broz Tito (who even at this early stage was not taking orders from Moscow) that sustained the Greek communists, not the support of Stalin. Indeed, the Soviet leader counseled compromise with the right-wing government in Athens, and later impassively stood aside and watched the Greek communists being crushed by British- and American-supported royalist forces, and their partisans killed and shipped off to prison camps.[25]

And at least insofar as a request for revision, in the USSR's favor, of the Montreux Treaty governing passage through the Turkish Straits was concerned, Stalin was acting in keeping with a tacit understanding reached at Yalta with the Americans and British in response to their inability to use this waterway to send desperately needed supplies to the USSR in the most difficult days of World War II. It was in his demands on Turkey for the reversion to the USSR of its post–World War I territorial concessions to Turkey (which is to say the handover to Russia of provinces that had earlier been seized from the Ottoman Empire and were returned to Turkey after the revolution by the Bolsheviks), and his meddling in Iranian internal affairs that Stalin's behavior was the most indefensible.

Stalin can undoubtedly be said to have been following in the footsteps of the tsars in bullying both Turkey and Iran, taking advantage of the USSR's newfound power. However overbearing they may have been, his government's demands on Turkey and interference in Iran may also have been a defensive reaction to the USSR's demonstrated vulnerability along its southern frontiers during World War II. If this is the case, it was prompted as well by Stalin's long-standing fear of moves by the Western powers in this region, where his own career as a revolutionary started. More specifically, the Kars-Ardahan region abutted the Soviet port of Batum, where major Soviet oil facilities were located, and thus, as in Iran, this attempted push southward may have involved an attempt to create a buffer around the strategically sensitive area of the southern Soviet Union. In any case, once rebuffed by the Turks over the issue of frontier revisions, the Soviets dropped the matter, which was not mentioned again after the spring of 1946.[26]

Stalin's aggressive initiatives were in turn interpreted by Churchill (who had first entered British public life as an MP in 1900 when the Conservative statesman Lord Salisbury was still prime minister) as a continuation of the old Anglo-Russian rivalry over these regions dating back to the high epoch of the Eastern Question, the competition between European powers for domination over the Ottoman Empire and adjacent regions.[27] And even after Churchill left office in 1945, there seems little doubt that his deep and enduring suspicions of Russia, and his virulent anti-Bolshevism, were shared by key members of the government of Prime Minister Clement Attlee, who succeeded him. As I suggested in chapter 1, it also seems clear that these attitudes helped to influence the thinking of many American decision-makers who were new to dealing with this part of the world, and gave a patina of respectability to the existing anticommunist prejudices of others in the United States, especially formerly isolationist Republicans.

Nevertheless, for all the enduring strategic elements that

were at work here, the focus by both the United States and the Soviet Union on Middle Eastern oil was a new factor, and marked the beginning of a novel phase for both. Rarely had the foreign policy of either resource-rich power previously been so closely linked to attempts to achieve exclusive control over such resources outside their own territory (although the American oil industry had long dominated the oil production of the Western Hemisphere, and aggressively pursued opportunities elsewhere, including its striking success in Saudi Arabia in 1933).[28] The two new superpowers' parallel moves regarding Middle Eastern oil, the defensive sensitivity of the Soviets regarding their own nearby domestic oil resources, and the projected targeting of the latter by United States strategic planners, were all clear signs of the dawning of a new age of competition for world dominance. They marked an extension into the postwar era of both sides' newly enhanced strategic concerns and fears regarding what is today called "energy independence," fears born of their traumatic experiences involving threats to their own oil supplies in World War II.

The United States and the Soviet Union were in fact both acting in the Middle East (and elsewhere) in ways that marked significant departures from their previous practices. Since the foundation of the Republic, American statesmen, fortified by the injunctions of the founders and framers, had traditionally disdained involvement in the entangling alliance systems and balance-of-power calculations of the "Old World."[29] This did not for a moment stop the United States from playing a predominant, often overbearing, and sometimes nakedly imperialist role in the nineteenth and twentieth centuries in its own hemisphere, especially in the Caribbean, and it did not in the least inhibit American industry, trade, and finance from expanding worldwide. Nor did it prevent an expansion of American naval and economic power into the Pacific with the forcible "opening of Japan," the colonial seizure of Hawaii and the Philippines at the end of the nineteenth century, and the capture of a large segment of the China trade.

However, although the United States had become a great power, and indeed in some respects a hegemonic power, in the Western Hemisphere and the Pacific long before World War II, it was barely acting like a major power on the rest of the world's stage. Even President Wilson's decision to bring the United States to enter World War I alongside Britain and France and against Germany had been undertaken as an exception to previously accepted patterns of disdain for European entanglements. Moreover, in order to overcome the isolationist instincts of large segments of the American people, this exceptional action had to be clothed by Wilson in the loftiest of ideals, and portrayed as a crusade for democracy and self-determination for oppressed peoples. This was the case irrespective of both the severe limitations intended by Wilson on his Fourteen Points (he never meant them to be extended to the colonized countries, for example),[30] and of the less-than-idealistic outcomes of the war as they were later hammered out at the Paris Peace Conference, at Versailles, and afterward. Wilson's unprecedented initiative, which briefly turned the United States into not just a world power but in some respects the most formidable power of its day, had been followed almost immediately by the rapid withdrawal of American troops from Europe. Soon afterward, the United States returned to its traditional position of semi-isolationism regarding Europe and much of the rest of the world, in spite of its demonstrated economic and financial power, a stance that lasted throughout the 1920s and 1930s.

The presidency of Franklin D. Roosevelt, and more immediately the outbreak of World War II, marked a completely new departure for the United States. Before Pearl Harbor, at Roosevelt's instructions, the United States launched a major military buildup and began extending vital aid to Britain, whether in the form of destroyer sales, the extension of Lend-Lease assistance, American destroyers convoying ships part of the way across the Atlantic to Britain, or financial support. Attacked at Pearl Harbor by Japan on December 7, 1941, and soon afterward subject to a declaration of war by Nazi Germany, the United States responded by upping war production to unprecedented heights and launching a truly global military campaign, sending troops, fleets, and planes from North America to five continents. Thereafter, as the war ended there was no complete withdrawal of American troops and no return to isolationism as after World War I: far from it. Although many troops were withdrawn as the size of the U.S. armed forces shrank after the war's end, numerous new American military bases spanning the globe, which were originally established to prosecute World War II, were kept in place, and base rights were requested in a host of new areas. The shrinkage of the size of the U.S. military at war's end, especially the army, was not paralleled by the removal of U.S. forces based in far-flung places like South America, Morocco, Libya, Saudi Arabia, Korea, and China, not to speak of Western Europe and the territories of the defeated enemy powers that remained under occupation. And the navy and the air force, although reduced from inflated World War II levels, retained much of their strength.

Suddenly, starting with World War II, the United States began to behave in every way like a traditional great power on the world stage, and not just in the Western Hemisphere and in the Pacific. It had the wherewithal to do so. At war's end American production constituted half of world GDP. The United States had "almost doubled its GNP during the conflict: by 1945, it accounted for around half of the world's manufacturing capacity, most of its food surpluses, and almost all of its financial reserves."[31] By contrast, all of the traditional Western European powers and Japan, as well as much of the rest of the world, were economically prostrate, the military establishments of most had been smashed, and vast swaths of the Soviet Union had been devastated by the war. Given these facts, and given the vast size, reach, and potency of the American armed forces, particularly those elements most suited to power projection, the navy and the air force, not to speak of America's sole possession of atomic weapons, the attraction of wielding such immense power to those responsible for the task in Washington must have been great. Moreover, Roosevelt and other American policymakers took away from the slide into a second world war the determination to use American power to prevent the recurrence of another such catastrophe. The new activism was clothed in a rhetoric very much suited to a great power, suggesting that after fighting and winning two world wars, the United States had global "responsibilities" it could not shirk. And like every traditional great power with global capacities for nearly two centuries, the United States began to take an intensive interest in the strategic Middle Eastern region. That interest was greatly accentuated by the presence there of what were known to be vast unexploited deposits of oil, the heightened strategic importance of which had just been emphasized by wartime events.

The Soviet Union was acting in new and different ways as well after World War II. All around its vast periphery, the USSR was now flexing its newly developed muscles in a fashion not seen in most regions since the Bolshevik Revolution and the subsequent civil war, when revolution in much of Europe seemed a possibility and the Red Army under Leon Trotsky was sweeping into Poland. Thereafter, for the better part of two decades an inward turn had been marked by Stalin's slogan of "Revolution in one country," and an attempt to develop the Soviet economy in the direction of self-sufficiency, while Soviet foreign policy overall had been marked by belligerent defensiveness and suspicious caution.

Although this was generally true of Soviet policy, it only

applied in part to dealings with countries to the south of the USSR. Soviet relations with the states of the Middle East after the end of the Russian Civil War had been characterized by an effort to give the appearance of a sharp break from the heavy-handed imperialist practices of the tsarist regime. Generations of Russian rulers had bullied and seized territory from Iran, the Ottoman Empire, and Russia's other southern neighbors. Even as the newly formed Soviet Union in effect re-created the tsarist empire at home in a new and different form, through the imposition of Soviet Socialist Republics on the subjugated peoples of the former Russian domains, in its foreign policy and economic dealings with Turkey, Iran, and Afghanistan in particular, the young Soviet regime was careful to take an entirely new tack.[32] This started immediately after the revolution with Trotsky, the first commissar for foreign affairs, publishing the tsarist secret treaties, including those between Russia and Britain and France for the partition of the Ottoman Empire. It continued with a series of bilateral treaties negotiated in 1921 with Turkey, Iran, and Afghanistan, whereby the Soviet Union renounced all tsarist concessions extracted unfairly from these countries, returned border regions earlier seized from the Ottoman Empire, and promised noninterference in their internal affairs.[33] Followed by other similar treaties that reinforced this emphasis on equitable relations, these accords were by and large respected for two decades by a Soviet Union still weak from the civil war, foreign intervention, and the tumultuous internal upheavals caused by Stalin's brutal rule. Lenin and his colleagues and successors thereby secured Turkey, Iran, and Afghanistan as friendly buffer states to the south. At the same time, they prevented any possible continuation of post–World War I British efforts to use these countries as springboards for anti-Bolshevik intervention.

With the new dangers and new opportunities World War II revealed to Stalin and the leadership in Moscow, and with the new power the war offered them, the Soviet Union, too, began a series of radical and far-reaching departures in its foreign policy, in particular toward the countries to its immediate south. As we have seen, Iran, whose territorial integrity the USSR had promised to respect in a series of interwar treaties with that country, was invaded and occupied in a coordinated effort by Soviet and British forces in June 1941. The two powers removed Reza Shah and installed his pliable young son Mohammad Reza Shah on the throne. The newly allied powers had feared that Iran under Reza Shah would align itself with the Axis in the wake of Hitler's invasion of the Balkans and Russia and the ongoing Nazi military successes in North Africa. London and Moscow made common cause in Iran once again, as they had so many times in the past, in spite of the rivalries between them. As in its World War I occupation of Ottoman territory in Iraq adjoining the Iranian oil fields, and in its raising in 1916 of a local force called the South Persia Rifles commanded by British officers from the Indian army and tasked with dominating southern Iran,[34] Britain was also determined to control and protect the vital oil supplies it obtained from Iran and other parts of the Gulf region.

The Soviet Union and Britain had another reason for this occupation: it made it possible to turn Iran into a corridor for the shipment of millions of tons of vital military supplies to the USSR. These supplies, mainly American in origin, were crucial to the Soviet Union's capability to resist the Nazis.[35] The corridor through Iran was all the more necessary since, with the Mediterranean and Black Sea having become war zones, the Turkish Straits closed to naval vessels by Turkey under the terms of the 1936 Montreux Treaty, the Baltic controlled by the Nazis, and convoys to Soviet Artic ports subject to constant German submarine and air attack from bases in the North Sea and Norway, Iran was indispensable as a supply route.[36] Soon after Pearl

Harbor, U.S. military forces joined what became a tripartite occupation of Iran.

None of these pressing reasons for Iran's occupation by the three great powers made foreign military domination of their country any easier to stomach for the country's population. Iranians were always leery of British and Russian intervention in their country, which had occurred multiple times in the twentieth century alone. Nor did these reasonable-sounding wartime pretexts for intervention change the fact that Soviet policy toward Iran had changed radically from its relatively benign course between 1921 and 1939. As we have just seen, it changed still more radically at war's end, with the Soviet effort to obtain oil concessions from Iran, and other forms of pressure on that country, including the Soviets dragging their feet on the withdrawal of their troops, and their clandestine support for Kurdish and Azeri separatist movements and for the Iranian Communist Party, the Tudeh.

TURKEY AND SOVIET "ASPIRATIONS"

Soviet policy changed toward Turkey as well. In the wake of the founding of the Turkish Republic, Moscow had established reasonably good relations with Kemal Atatürk's republican regime, marked by the March 1921 treaty and four later ones in 1925, 1927, 1931, and 1933, and it maintained them throughout most of the interwar period.[37] However, in 1939, just as World War II began, the Soviet Union had tried in vain to obtain from Turkey revisions in its favor of the 1936 Montreux Treaty governing passage through the Turkish Straits. Beyond this, Turkey's neutrality during the first years of World War II (which masked the initial subtle tilt of important elements of the Turkish Republic's politico-military establishment toward the Axis powers), and its closing of the Turkish Straits to the shipment of war material to the USSR, clearly had angered the Soviets by the end of the war. Typically, Stalin forgot none of this, and in 1945 he was in a far stronger position than he had been in 1939. Already at the Potsdam meeting of the wartime allies, the Soviet leader had gotten Truman and Churchill's assent to a revision in favor of the Soviet Union of the terms of the Montreux Treaty.

This was followed at the end of the war, as we have seen, not just by an insistence on revising the Montreux Treaty in the Soviet Union's favor, but by Soviet demands for bases in the region of the Turkish Straits and for significant frontier revisions in the areas of Kars and Ardahan in eastern Turkey. The latter demand would have meant a return to the frontiers established under the tsars through annexations of Ottoman territory, and a reversal of the new Bolshevik regime's generous border reversions to Turkey that had been sealed by the Soviet-Turkish treaty of March 1921. Albeit ostensibly motivated by the bitter lessons of World War II, these aggressive demands for territory and for bases on the straits looked like nothing other than a reversion to old tsarist positions. In any case, they indicated quite a radical shift in Soviet policy toward Turkey. As in its policy in Iran at this time, the Soviet Union too was beginning to act like a traditional great power in the Middle East, and appeared to be reverting to the imperialist approach of the tsars regarding the states to its immediate south.

Two explanations stand out: one is that, as in Eastern Europe, the Soviet Union was taking advantage of its newfound postwar power to stake out long-standing claims that it had been too feeble to make earlier, claims that in some respects went beyond what the tsars had tried to do. This is said to reveal an inherent Soviet—or Great Russian—imperialist southward drive, one that had somehow been cleverly masked for decades or had been hidden by the initial weakness of the Soviet regime. Among the evidence adduced for this interpretation is language that emerged from the Molotov-Ribbentrop negotiations in Berlin in November 1940 for a Nazi-Soviet pact in the wake of Moscow's failure to negotiate an alliance with London and Paris. There the Nazi leaders proposed in a draft treaty that, as part of a partition of the world into spheres of influence with Japan, Germany, and Italy, the Soviets should focus their territorial aspirations on the areas to their south, "in the direction of the Indian Ocean."[38] Soviet foreign minister Vyacheslav Molotov concentrated on other issues in his discussions with German foreign minister Joachim von Ribbentrop, and the Soviets thereafter rejected this draft, and later responded with one of their own that focused on the matters of primary concern to the Soviet leadership, having to do with the central questions at issue in Europe between the USSR and Germany. Insofar as spheres of influence were concerned, this Soviet counterdraft located "the center of aspirations of the Soviet Union south of Batum and Baku in the general direction of the Persian Gulf."

Much has been made of the terminology used in these drafts, but such analyses ignore the fact that, as the political scientist John Campbell astutely pointed out decades before the Soviet archives were partially opened, first, the Soviets had behaved with exemplary restraint toward their southern neighbors for a two full decades before this, for a variety of reasons, not just weakness. Moreover, he notes, during the Berlin talks, Molotov showed that the Soviet leadership was much more concerned about Western Europe and the Balkans than the Middle East or the vague Nazi proposals about the Indian Ocean. He suggests further that the Soviets saw that these proposals were intended by the Nazis to distract them from what both they and the Germans considered most important: Europe and the Balkans. Moreover, Campbell points out, the Nazi proposals were rejected by the Soviet side, the Soviet counterproposal was itself vague and meant nothing more than a general interest in

Iran and Turkey (to which the Soviets did in fact turn their attention immediately after the war), and it was in any case rejected by the Nazis, and perhaps was meant to be rejected.[39]

More persuasive than this reliance on a supposed smoking gun that is actually quite cold is new and concrete evidence that has emerged since the partial opening of the Soviet archives about Soviet interest in the Middle East, and in Iran and Turkey in particular, toward the end of the war and in the immediate postwar period, some of it cited at the beginning of this chapter. While, as has already been pointed out, this evidence shows that these Soviet policies involved browbeating and pressuring both countries and intervening in their internal affairs, in a manner reminiscent of the worst behavior of the tsarist era, they also involved a striking departure by the Soviet Union from its previous policies. They reveal as well a profound sense of insecurity regarding the vulnerability of the USSR from the direction of the Middle East. This appears to provide a more convincing explanation of the USSR's shift to more aggressive behavior toward its southern neighbors than tenuous overinterpretations of a few phrases plucked out of abortive texts produced during the Molotov-Ribbentrop negotiations.

In helping further to explain this major shift, some of the new evidence from the archives is quite revealing, particularly a lengthy dispatch from Nikolai Novikov, the Soviet ambassador in Washington, to his superiors in Moscow in September 1946.[40] The document has been compared to George Kennan's famous "Long Telegram" sent from Moscow several months earlier. Kennan's lengthy dispatch deeply influenced thinking in Washington about the implacably hostile nature of Soviet behavior, and of the need to contain the Soviet Union.[41] An anonymous version published in Foreign Affairs a year and a half afterward under the title "The Sources of Soviet Conduct," shaped and crystallized American elite perceptions of Soviet policy.[42] Given the closed nature of the Soviet system, and the relative paucity of documentation, it is impossible to say with any assurance whether Novikov's cable had this kind of influence in the Kremlin. However, at least one historian has judged that a major shift in the Soviet approach toward the United States "was heralded by a confidential report from the Soviet Ambassador in Washington, Nikolai Novikov, on U.S. foreign policy trends."[43]

In his cable of September 1946, Novikov is explicit in seeing the United States as "striving for world supremacy," as asserting that it had "the right to lead the world," as having "plans for world dominance," and as preparing "the conditions for winning world supremacy in a new war." Novikov could not have been blunter: the United States was putting intense pressure on the Soviet Union in service of a plan for global hegemony. In his analysis Novikov stressed the significance of the expansion of the U.S. military and of its new global role. He noted the thirteen-fold expansion of the proposed military budget for fiscal year 1948–47 by contrast with that of 1938, the creation for the first time in American history of a peacetime army based on a draft, the postwar plans for the establishment of nearly five hundred new U.S. naval and air bases inside the United States and worldwide, and the maintenance of a fleet that was the largest in the world and far larger than that of Britain. He noted that all of this "indicates the offensive nature of the strategic concepts of the commands of the U.S. army and navy," and concluded that "a decisive role in the realization of plans for world dominance by the United States is played by its armed forces."

Beyond these general propositions about the expansiveness and aggressive nature of American power, Novikov pointedly stressed the vital importance of the Middle East to American strategic planning. He focused at length on American-British rivalries, and acutely noted how they related to competition for domination of the oil resources of that region. He pointed out the "thorough penetration of the Mediterranean basin and the Near East, to which the United States is attracted by the area's natural resources, primarily oil." Novikov noted that "in recent years American capital has penetrated very intensively into the economy of the Near Eastern countries, in particular into the oil industry." He went on to give extensive details of American efforts that had produced "American oil concessions in all of the Near Eastern countries that have oil deposits." The Soviet ambassador to Washington noted that although it had started its efforts to obtain such concessions in the region only in 1928,[44] the United States already controlled 42 percent of all proven reserves in the Middle East, excluding those of Iran. He added that "the American oil companies plan to build a trans-Arabian pipeline to transport oil from the American concession in Saudi Arabia" to the Mediterranean, a reference to the Tapline, completed by ARAMCO in 1947 with a terminus at Zahrani, near Sidon in Lebanon.

Having focused in his treatment of the Middle East largely on American-British rivalries and on American oil interests in the region, Novikov concluded his lengthy discussion of the Middle East ominously with reference to visits of American warships to eastern Mediterranean ports, and efforts to obtain basing rights there for the U.S. fleet: "These incidents constitute a political and military demonstration against the Soviet Union. The strengthening of U.S. positions in the Near East and the establishment of conditions for basing the American navy at one or more points on the Mediterranean Sea (Trieste, Palestine, Greece, Turkey) will therefore signify the emergence of a new threat to the security of the southern regions of the Soviet Union." In addition to signaling the importance of the penetration of the Middle East by American oil interests, Novikov was clearly warning his superiors in Moscow about what he saw as the dangers in this region and elsewhere in terms of "the siting of American strategic bases in regions from which it is possible to launch strikes on Soviet territory."[45]

It is impossible to say whether this cable did in fact have an impact in Moscow similar to that of Kennan's "Long Telegram" in Washington, or whether it was simply a reflection of some of the views that Novikov shared with his immediate superior, Soviet Foreign Minister Molotov, and therefore presumably those of Stalin. In either case, it is highly indicative of how much interest top Soviet officials were showing in the Middle East immediately after World War II, the high degree to which matters relating to oil seemed significant to them, and their deep concerns about the potential of this region as one from which threats to the security of the Soviet Union might emanate. There is little indication that any of these factors diminished in the Cold War decades that followed.

In some respects these interests and concerns of Novikov, and presumably of Molotov, Stalin, and his colleagues in the Soviet leadership, mirrored those of their American opposite numbers. Moreover, it is uncanny that in their confidential communications with their respective capitals, both Kennan and Novikov lay great stress on Iran and Turkey as potential points of contention between the two powers and Great Britain at almost the same moment. In pointing in his "Long Telegram" to areas of potential conflict with the advance of Soviet power, Kennan indeed refers to the Middle East first: "For the moment, these efforts are restricted to certain neighboring points conceived of here as being of immediate strategic necessity, such as Northern Iran, Turkey, possibly Bornholm. However, other points may at any time come into question, if and as concealed Soviet political power is extended to new areas. Thus a 'friendly Persian Government' might be asked to grant Russia a port on Persian Gulf."[46]

For all these similarities, there were of course also important differences in how the two powers regarded the Middle East. While at the end of World War II, as we have seen in this chapter and the last, Stalin tried clumsily and in vain to achieve a strategic foothold and access to Iranian oil, by then the United States had already achieved both of these things, and clearly had no intention of relinquishing them. While the Soviets saw American initiatives in the Middle East as part of a move toward world hegemony, and as directly threatening the security of their homeland, the Americans saw Soviet moves there as aggressive threats not to their national security in the narrowest sense, but rather to their increasingly powerful posture in this region and to the resources it contained, which were so vital to America's newfound dominant position in the world. The oil of the Middle East had by this point become central to the thinking of policymakers on both sides of the new iron curtain. It constituted a new factor for them to take into account, and increased further the already great strategic importance of the Middle East to both superpowers.

III

THE MIDDLE EAST AND THE INTERNATIONAL SYSTEM

The Middle East attracts, and for a very long time has attracted, an inordinate share of people who are obsessed. This is true whether they are obsessed with God, with themselves and their own narratives, or with something else. Those obsessed with one area or aspect of the Middle East often lose sight of larger patterns that may in fact determine or explain outcomes throughout this region and beyond. Thus, for example, those who focus obsessively on Israel, Palestine, or the Arab-Israeli conflict tend to see their object of interest as unique, as sui generis, and as too important and too driven by its own complex internal dynamics to be profoundly affected by any broader patterns. This chapter examines one of these larger patterns that sometimes determined (and often still determine) outcomes, specifically how the Middle East as a whole has fitted into and was affected by the overall international system as that system has evolved over time. I will concentrate here on the impact of the international system before and especially during the Cold War, as well as in the years that have followed. The next chapter will examine another of these patterns: how the bipolar international system that emerged during the Cold War severely exacerbated several protracted regional conflicts, while the succeeding chapter argues that this Cold War system affected, and in many ways deeply distorted, internal developments in several countries of the Middle East.

I begin with four main points about the place of the Middle East in the international system. These points focus particularly on how this system has shifted over the past century or so from being a primarily European system to, increasingly, an international one, dominated during the Cold War by two superpowers, and since then by the United States. It is a system that may or may not have become more of an international community in the process.

The first point is that until about the middle of the twentieth century, the Middle East was an important arena for the operation of the traditional European state system, but Middle Eastern states were not fully accepted as part of that system, although one of them, the Ottoman Empire, for centuries controlled large areas of southeastern Europe and of the Mediterranean and Black Sea littorals. In this respect, this region resembled South Asia and North America in the eighteenth century, and Africa and China in the nineteenth century. All these areas were scenes of intense European rivalry, but states there, even highly organized, long-established, and powerful states like the Ottoman Empire, the Mughal Empire, and China under the Ch'ing dynasty, were not considered legitimate or full parts of the European system of states. This had to do not so much with power as with the fact that this was an essentially *European* system (including eventually colonial settler states like the United States and Australia that came to be inhabited mainly by populations that originated in Europe). Europeans did not consider non-Christian states without European settler populations to be part of this system, even if they were largely in Europe, like the Ottoman Empire. In some cases major states, like many in West Africa, were not even considered by Europeans to be "real" states. When this essentially European system later became the core of what developed into an international one, from which the bipolar Cold War system developed, some of these attitudes, with the racist overtones they implied, persisted in a variety of ways.[1]

The second point is that in the twentieth century there was a nominal change in the position of some of the peoples in the Middle East in the international system. This was partly a result of the post–World War I and post–World War II expansion of the European state system into a somewhat more broadly based international order, via the full inclusion in it of the United States, Japan, Latin American countries, and later the Soviet Union. It was a result as well of the restructuring of this system into something more closely resembling an international community through the establishment of generally accepted legal norms codified in the Covenant of the League of Nations, the United Nations Charter, and other international conventions and treaties. In stages after the two world wars, and with a speed that was accelerated partly because the Cold War rivalry helped further weaken the already loosening grip of the old colonial powers, certain Middle Eastern (and other) peoples obtained independent statehood and their states joined this "community of nations." The result was a major change in the complexion of world affairs. The adhesion of these newly independent Middle Eastern states to the international order was not part of a universal process encompassing all the peoples of the region. It took place in some measure at the discretion of the victors of these world wars, or as a result of dissension between them. Some Middle Eastern peoples, such as the Armenians, the Kurds, and the Palestinians, were unable to achieve independent statehood, or to follow on this path.[2]

A third point is that in spite of these restructurings and transformations of the European interstate system into a somewhat more inclusive and fully international system between the world wars and during the Cold War, the Middle East remained almost continuously a major arena where the ambitions and rivalries of the great powers played out. These powers continued to strive to dominate the region, although which of them emerged as ascendant changed over time. In this respect, it may have appeared that even after the two world wars and the onset of the Cold War, little had changed from the old days of the Concert of Europe that emerged after the Napoleonic Wars, the Eastern Question, and the "sick man of Europe" (a derogatory European way of referring to the Ottoman Empire in its last decades). Then, states and peoples in the Middle East were essentially objects, but were generally not allowed to be subjects, of international relations. Over time, however, some things did change, or appeared to change, as the bipolar Cold War system occasionally allowed certain powerful Middle Eastern states like Egypt, Israel, Iran, Turkey, Iraq, and Syria to play one superpower off against another, or to exploit the rivalry between them to obtain benefit. Meanwhile other, smaller, weaker states generally suffered as a result of the regional polarizations that were exacerbated by this rivalry. The end of the Cold War put a stop to such limited opportunities as the bipolar Cold War era had offered. Under the sway of a unipolar system dominated by what initially appeared to be an unchallengeable single superpower, the United States, in some ways the Middle East appeared to have returned to the old days when its states, weak and strong, were largely dominated from without. I will examine in this and subsequent chapters the extent to which these appearances coincided with reality.

Finally, in the interwar and Cold War periods, and in the nearly two decades since the end of the Cold War and the rise of the current unipolar world system, the international system and international institutions, rather than restraining the dominant power or powers from expanding their dominion in the Middle East, have often facilitated this dominion. The degree to which the United States has been free to operate unilaterally and without restraint from other powers or international institutions like the UN, in Iraq and Palestine in the first years of the twenty-first century, is a striking example of this situation. The current American position in the Middle East should make us think carefully about the degree to which today anything that resembles the ideal vision of an "international community," regulated by international law and conventions, exists independently of the influence of the dominant power or powers in the international system. This seems to have been true whether this system was multipolar, as it was before 1945, bipolar, as it was during the Cold War, or unipolar, as it has been ever since.

For well over two centuries after the formation of the modern state system that emerged with the Treaty of Westphalia in 1648, the Middle East[3] was generally considered to be outside of this system. Their exclusion meant that the states of the region were not considered to be on a par with European states, nor were they treated in terms of the same rules and norms. The Middle East was nevertheless a crucial arena of European wars and diplomacy in the late eighteenth century and well into the nineteenth, mainly involving Russia and Austro-Hungary. The Ottoman Empire was drawn into the Napoleonic Wars by none other than Napoleon himself, through his invasion of Egypt in 1798. In consequence, the empire at times served as a diplomatic arena, as a battlefield, and as a junior ally in the quarter-century-long European conflict that began with the French Revolution. However, the Ottoman Empire was not a party to the Peace of Paris or the Congress of Vienna, where those wars were ended and where a new European system, one with pretensions to being an international order, was put into place.

Interestingly, one of the main architects of that new system, the British foreign secretary Lord Castlereagh, while at the Congress of Vienna in 1815, originally intended that the Ottoman Empire be subject to the "general accord and guarantee" that he envisaged be directed against any power that disturbed the peace of the European continent. This was one of many precursors of the ideas for a new global interstate order that were later embodied in the Covenant of the League of Nations and the United Nations Charter.[4] Nothing came of the proposal for such a guarantee, which aroused the suspicions of a British Parliament wary of involving Great Britain in a broader system that might restrain its freedom of action and limit parliamentary prerogatives.[5] In consequence, the Ottoman Empire and the rest of the Middle East remained on the margins of the European state system. Nevertheless, we find here the beginnings of a pattern, whereby the Middle East is an active arena for the major powers in the international system but does not form part of that system, and whereby Middle Eastern states are not treated as full parties to an international order that in time encompasses them.

There were other mileposts along this path: they included the Treaty of London of 1840, to which the Ottoman Empire was a party but which was crafted entirely by the European powers led by Lord Palmerston; the 1878 Congress of Berlin, whereby European statesmen like Otto von Bismarck and Lord Salisbury imposed onerous terms on the Ottoman Empire; the London Ambassadors' Conference of 1913 to resolve issues resulting from the Balkan Wars, which laid down the outlines for the post–World War I great-power partition of the Ottoman Empire, primarily via concessions for railways;[6] and the 1915–16 Sykes-Picot accords and the 1917 Balfour Declaration, whereby European powers arrogated to themselves the right to dispose of Arab lands as they saw fit, with no attention whatsoever to the interests and wishes of the peoples affected. All of these measures, and many others, however, including the 1920 Treaty of Sèvres, which unsuccessfully proposed the partition of Turkey, could be seen as examples of the bad old European secret diplomacy that the fresh wind of Wilsonian idealism was supposed to sweep away, with its "open covenants of peace, openly arrived at."[7] We know that this did not happen, and nowhere was this more apparent than in the Middle East: there, the traditional behind-the-scenes realpolitik of the great powers ultimately prevailed, notwithstanding the fleeting influence of President Wilson on the new structure of the Middle Eastern state system that was fashioned at the Paris Peace Conference.

The actual nature of the League of Nations Mandate system as it worked in practice was one of the most egregious examples of outcomes in the Middle East being determined by the cold calculus of power politics rather than idealistic Wilsonian rhetoric. In the Middle East in general, and in Palestine in particular, great-power interests rather than the principle of self-determination or the wishes of the indigenous peoples concerned dictated the nature of the form of governance that was imposed on them by the League of Nations. British foreign secretary Arthur James Balfour, one of the primary architects of both the League of Nations and of its Mandate system, and author of the famous declaration that bears his name, was brutally frank in a confidential 1919 memo. In it, he described the hypocrisy of Britain and the other great powers in ignoring the commitments regarding Syria and Palestine embodied in the Covenant of the League of Nations and earlier Allied pledges:

> The contradiction between the letter of the Covenant [of the League of Nations] and the policy of the Allies is even more flagrant in the case of the "independent nation" of Palestine than in that of the "independent nation" of Syria. For in Palestine, we do not propose even to go through the form of consulting the wishes of the present inhabitants of the country, though the American [King-Crane] Commission has been going through the form of asking what they are. The four Great Powers are committed to Zionism. And Zionism, be it right or

wrong good or bad, is rooted in age-long traditions, in present needs, in future hopes, of far greater import than the desires and prejudices of the 700,000 Arabs who now inhabit that ancient land.

In my opinion that is right. What I have never been able to understand is how it can be harmonized with the [Balfour] declaration, the Covenant, or the instructions to the Commission of Enquiry.

I do not think that Zionism will hurt the Arabs; but they will never say they want it. Whatever be the future of Palestine it is not now an "independent nation," nor is it yet on the way to become one. Whatever deference should be paid to the views of those who live there, the Powers in their selection of a mandatory do not propose, as I understand the matter, to consult them. In short, so far as Palestine is concerned, the Powers have made no statement of fact which is not admittedly wrong, and no declaration of policy which, at least in the letter, they have not always intended to violate.[8]

In fact, as historian Margaret MacMillan, among others, has argued, Wilson's Fourteen Points, and in particular those relating to national self-determination, were far more ambiguous and equivocal than many took them to be, especially when it came to the Middle East.[9] Moreover, neither Wilson nor other Western statesmen necessarily had a clear idea of the nature of the peoples and nations involved in the Middle East. Wilson seems in any case to have intended his concept of self-determination to apply primarily to European peoples, and only secondarily to those of the Ottoman Empire, and he clearly did not mean for them to apply at all to peoples under colonial rule. Whatever Wilson's intentions, and however his words were interpreted by colonized peoples the world over, the leaders of the great colonial powers allied with the United States, notably Great Britain and France, did everything possible to prevent these principles from applying to their colonies and semicolonies.

Nevertheless, in certain fundamental ways, it was intended by the victorious Allied powers who constructed the new international order symbolized by the Fourteen Points, the Versailles Peace Conference, and the League of Nations, that this new order would deal differently with the Middle East than had the old European state system. The Middle East was adjudged by the victors of the Great War to be deficient, among other things, in not having states organized along the national principle. The victors proposed to remedy this deficiency by creating new nation-states there, as they did in Central and Eastern Europe, regions judged to be similarly deficient. They did not do so, of course, in accordance with the wishes of the peoples concerned. Had they, the Middle East might have been quite different in the twentieth century. The region might conceivably have witnessed less conflict, although since the development of many Middle Eastern national identities at this time was still at an embryonic stage, more conflict might also have been the result.[10] There would also very likely have been fewer nation-states in the Mashriq (the eastern Arab world), as well as possibly an Armenian and a Kurdish state.

For all the flaws of the process as it worked out in practice, many of the states that exist today in the Middle East—notably Iraq, Israel, Lebanon, Syria, and Jordan—were direct products of these great-power interactions, and of the eventual implementation of the Wilsonian principle of self-determination. It is open to question whether these existing states were constructed out of already existing "nations," or whether new nations have since grown up inside these states and others that were arbitrarily conceived by the Allied powers in Paris in 1919, and put into place within thoroughly artificial frontiers by the

Mandate system that these powers thereafter erected. In any case, all remain independent nation-states today.

Equally important, at the same time as several entirely new states were being conceived in Paris, as already mentioned, other independent states did not see the light of day: notably Kurdistan, Armenia, and Palestine. Their disposition was left to an uncertain future, although both Armenia and Kurdistan were promised independence by the victorious Allied powers in the Treaty of Sèvres after World War I (and Armenia is today an independent country, on a fraction of the ancestral homeland of the Armenians), and the Palestinian people were promised a state decades later by the United Nations General Assembly. In two of these three cases of peoples who in the end were ignored by the great powers—those of Kurdistan and Palestine—the final disposition of their countries, and indeed their future as peoples, is still very much in question.[11]

Given the continuing commitment to colonialism of the victorious great powers that dominated the Paris Peace Conference, yet another category of states was effectively denied representation in the new international community that they created: the existing colonies and protectorates of these European powers. The people of Egypt, for example, understandably believed that in view of the principles enunciated by President Wilson they should be entitled to send representatives to the peace conference in Paris in order to achieve their freedom from British occupation. For that purpose, their leaders organized a delegation (in Arabic, *wafd*, for which the dominant political party in Egypt for the next three decades was named) of leading political figures to go to Paris to plead their case. Like subject peoples in the Middle East and other parts of the colonized world, the Egyptians were denied that right by the British, who summarily exiled the members of the delegation to Malta, provoking a huge popular uprising known in Egyptian historiography as the Revolution of 1919. Colonized peoples the world over felt a similar sense of disappointment at the frustration of their initial expectations raised by the Fourteen Points and at their exclusion from the Paris Peace Conference. This frustration led directly to massive popular anticolonial uprisings in the spring of 1919 in India, Korea, China, and elsewhere.[12]

The only Middle Eastern state allowed a place at the table at the Paris Peace Conference was the isolated, backward, and lightly populated Hijaz, which in light of the Arab revolt against the Ottomans in alliance with Britain was adjudged to be one of the Allied and Associated powers. This aroused the fury of the Egyptians, who saw themselves as heirs to a great civilization, possessing at the same time all the modern prerequisites for independence, but who were barred by the British from sending representatives to Paris, while the Hijazis were fully represented. The representative of the Hijaz, Amir Faisal ibn Husayn, considered himself to be both the plenipotentiary of his father, Husayn ibn ʿAli, the king of the Hijaz, and the king of Syria, a post to which he had been elected by the Syrian Parliament. Faisal was allowed to participate in the proceedings in Paris, but only as an emissary of his father and as a representative of the Hijaz, not as king of Syria. This was emblematic of the way the "new" international community dealt with the Middle East: in an arbitrary fashion little different from that of the old European state system. The League of Nations Mandate formula that was thereafter applied to several parts of the Middle East combined many of the worst features of the old European colonialism with the amateurishness and high-minded ignorance that characterized so much of Wilson's diplomacy. Speaking about the concept of self-determination, Wilson himself said at the Paris Peace Conference: "When I gave utterance to those words, I said them without the knowledge that nationalities existed, which are coming to us day after day."[13]

The post–World War I settlement in the Middle East created states within what were often completely arbitrary borders (including thousands of miles of straight lines in the frontiers of Jordan, Iraq, Saudi Arabia, and Syria that slice through communities, natural features, trade routes, and economic zones) which were drawn solely for the convenience of the British and the French. Some of these borders have been continuing sources of conflict over more than eighty-five years. This settlement exacerbated existing regional problems and created entirely new frictions, many of which have lingered until the present day. There is much discussion of some of these frictions in circles completely innocent of any knowledge of Middle Eastern history, as if they were "age-old," whereas in their current form they are essentially the result of a state structure recently imposed from outside the region. I will touch on some of these problems newly created by the grasping ambitions of the colonial powers in chapter 4, with specific reference to Lebanon.

The postwar settlement also did nothing to rein in the competition of the great powers in the region. Britain and France, allies during World War I, for decades thereafter maintained in the Middle East that attitude of cordial contempt for each other that had been such a striking feature of their relations for so many centuries, and that still lingers today, particularly among the British. Thus Britain in 1925–26 gave refuge to Syrian rebels against the French, who repaid the favor in 1937–39 by sheltering Palestinian rebels against the British. Toward the end of the interwar period, other great powers entered the fray, as fascist Italy and Nazi Germany challenged Anglo-French hegemony in the Middle East. As we have seen in chapter 1, the region thereafter became one of the major battlefields of World War II, as it had been of World War I. It was again reorganized as a result of the postwar restructuring of the world order. The new post–World War II order, which initially appeared as if it might reflect

a new cooperative ethos, symbolized by the wartime cooperation of the Allies, and their new creation intended to organize
international affairs, the United Nations, rapidly came to be
dominated by the Cold War.

THE COLD WAR AND THE INTERNATIONAL
ORDER IN THE MIDDLE EAST

The United Nations, which was the primary fruit of the postwar
restructuring of the international order, grew out of the alliance
of victorious powers in World War II—indeed, this wartime alliance of the United States, the Soviet Union, Great Britain, and
other powers called itself the United Nations well before the creation of the organization of that name.[14] The new United Nations organization included several newly independent Middle
Eastern states, some of which were helped to achieve their independence by the victors in the war. But again, as after World War
I, some entities saw the light as independent states, while other
Middle Eastern peoples, like the Palestinians and the Kurds, or
the peoples of French-controlled North Africa and the British-
controlled peripheries of the Arabian Peninsula, did not obtain
the benefit of statehood or independence, and remained under
occupation or colonial tutelage or dispersed among existing
states. The colonial status of those Middle Eastern states remaining under European rule was not long-lasting, however.
The influence of the two new post–World War II superpowers,
the United States and the Soviet Union, their opposition to
colonialism, and their Cold War rivalry all helped to erode old-
style colonial domination, which was already under pressure
from the national movements of the colonized peoples. The result was the independence of more states in the Middle East,
and their joining the international system, as symbolized by
their membership in the United Nations. This was one of the

little-recognized indirect benefits of the Cold War in its earliest phases: the American-Soviet rivalry helped considerably in the dissolution of the centuries-old European colonial empires the world over.

A new factor in the Middle East in the wake of World War II was the region's growing centrality to the two new superpowers as their rivalry developed into the Cold War. It is clear that East and Southeast Asia were hotter arenas of open conflict between the superpowers and their proxies than was the Middle East, as was evidenced by the Korean and Vietnam wars, while Europe always remained in many ways the central arena of the Cold War. Nevertheless, the Middle East was also an important early Cold War battleground, as I have shown in the preceding chapters, the first time it had been a primary area of attention for either the United States or the Soviet Union. It was one of the first sites of friction between the superpowers, starting with the crises immediately after the end of World War II involving the USSR and Turkey over Kars, Ardahan, and the Turkish Straits, and that over the Soviet-supported autonomous Republic of Azerbaijan and the Kurdish Mahabad Republic in northern Iran. The region was the focus of the Truman Doctrine of 1947 (specifically its northern tier of Turkey and Iran, which was essential to the U.S. strategy of containment of the USSR), and of the Eisenhower Doctrine of 1957. American attempts to incorporate the states of the region into the military alliances that were central to containment included plans for the abortive Middle East Command and the Middle East Defense Organization, and then the Baghdad Pact and its successor, the Central Treaty Organization, which will be examined in chapter 4. These plans had a powerful destabilizing effect on the internal politics of several Middle Eastern states and on inter-Arab and regional politics for nearly a decade.

Later on, the Middle East was one of the foci of the Nixon

Doctrine of 1969, for which both Iran and Israel were central Middle Eastern pillars. This erection of privileged regional powers into local policemen for the interests of the United States too had a destabilizing effect, as did the efforts of the Soviet Union to counter this strategy via mobilizing and organizing its own clients and allies in the region. As I have already mentioned, the Middle East was the scene of repeated international crises over the Arab-Israeli conflict that produced superpower confrontations, including in 1956, 1967, 1968–70, 1973, and 1982. The 1973 crisis resulted in a grave confrontation between the superpowers in support of their respective clients, and led to Soviet threats to intervene militarily in Egypt and to a global American nuclear alert. Early in the Cold War, bases in the Middle East became crucial to the strategies of both superpowers because of its proximity to the southern frontiers of the USSR. In consequence, intermediate-range ballistic missiles and bombers, and then submarine-launched ballistic missiles, were stationed in and around the region by the United States, and the Soviet Union established naval and air bases there to counter this strategic threat and to expand its local influence. All of these developments will be further discussed in chapter 4.

Another characteristic of the region during the Cold War era was that it became a major concern of the new United Nations, which took upon itself the disposition of Italy's former colony of Libya and of Britain's former League of Nations Mandate of Palestine, and played a role in the decolonization of several other Middle Eastern states. Beyond this, 25 percent of the resolutions passed by the United Nations Security Council over more than a quarter of a century after 1948 were devoted to one single Middle Eastern issue, the Palestine question and its various ramifications, as compared to all other issues and all other regions of the world combined.[15] Clearly, the United Nations and the international community it purported to represent were deeply involved in Middle Eastern affairs.

What is striking about all the attention paid by the United Nations, and the League of Nations before it, to the Middle East is how closely the involvement of what was nominally an international community tracked with and reflected the policies and outlook of the era's dominant power or powers. Thus the Mandate for Palestine promulgated by the League of Nations in 1922 to provide guidance for Britain in its governance of this territory incorporated verbatim the terms of the Balfour Declaration issued unilaterally by the British cabinet five years earlier. It was no more than a recasting in nominally international terms of a unilateral policy decision taken earlier by the British cabinet. The Mandate indeed consisted essentially of an extrapolation and amplification of the terms of the Balfour Declaration relating to "the establishment in Palestine of a national home for the Jewish people." In neither the Balfour Declaration nor the Mandate for Palestine were the words "Arab" or "Palestinian" utilized, nor was there any reference to the overwhelming 90 percent majority of the population of the territory who were Arab, except in describing them negatively and in a backhanded fashion as "existing non-Jewish communities in Palestine." This 90 percent Arab majority were described in the Mandate as having neither national nor political rights; only "civil and religious" ones.[16] Thus, the language adopted by the League in the terms of the Mandate for Palestine perfectly reflected the utter obliviousness of the British to Arab national claims in Palestine. This obliviousness continued at least during the first two decades of their control over Palestine, until the 1936–39 Palestinian national revolt finally forced British policymakers to take grudging account of these claims.[17]

It is true, as the historian Susan Pedersen has shown,[18] that the Permanent Mandates Commission of the League of Nations occasionally had different ideas than did the British Colonial Office as to how Palestine should be governed. In most cases, these ideas were even more sympathetic to the Zionists than were those of the British, although on occasion some members of the commission expressed disquiet about Britain's treatment of the Palestinian Arabs. Nevertheless, it cannot be said that the League measurably changed or hindered the course of British policy in Palestine during the two decades when it was nominally responsible for supervising Britain's execution of its mandatory responsibilities there. British concerns and interests indeed largely determined the behavior of the League toward all of Britain's Middle Eastern mandates, as did those of France regarding its mandates in the region. In other words, the new "international order" embodied by the League of Nations affected only slightly the behavior of the dominant powers of the day.

The way in which the United Nations dealt with the Middle East differed somewhat from the approach of the League. This was a result of the much-changed international situation, specifically the Cold War and the wave of post–World War II decolonization. It was a result as well of the structure of the United Nations, which in important respects did not resemble that of the League of Nations. Unlike the latter, the new UN included all the major powers, and it had many more member states and a slightly more functional form of organization, with a powerful Security Council and an occasionally effective General Assembly. Finally, it was a function of the new Cold War architecture of international relations dominated by the United States and the Soviet Union, both of which had had a limited involvement with the League of Nations. For this reason, and in spite of changed international circumstances, the United Nations tended to reflect, as had the League, the interests of the dominant powers in the international system, which in the post–World War II era were increasingly the United States and the USSR. Because of the veto power of the permanent members in the Security Council, that body could only take action, in the Middle East or elsewhere, when all of them were in concurrence.

In practice this meant that the Council was able to act relatively frequently in the Middle East during the first decade or so after World War II, before Cold War rivalries became all consuming, and while both superpowers were still concerned with diminishing British influence in the region. It was able to take action somewhat less frequently thereafter.

There was relatively limited friction over the Middle East at the United Nations between the United States and the USSR at the very outset of the Cold War, except for early tensions concerning the northern tier of Turkey and Iran. At this early stage both superpowers often seemed more concerned (for different reasons) with eliminating the residual—albeit still considerable —British imperial presence in the region than with dealing with each other. It is often forgotten that the United States and the USSR were on the same side as far as the conflict over Palestine was concerned in 1947–49: they both opposed Britain and supported the partition of Palestine and the establishment of Israel. In this sense, the new era symbolized by the United Nations did not differ significantly from the old one symbolized by the League of Nations: the November 29, 1947, General Assembly resolution to partition Palestine reflected the views of the dominant great powers, the United States and the USSR, rather than those of the still overwhelming Arab majority of the population of Palestine. Soviet military support, via arms supplied through Czechoslovakia, was essential to Israel's resounding ultimate victory during the first Arab-Israeli war of 1948–49. The position of the superpowers was similar in 1956, when, in spite of the high tension between them over the Soviet invasion of Hungary, both the United States and the USSR opposed the Anglo-French-Israeli attack on Egypt. Indeed, as we have seen, it was not until after the 1967 war that the superpowers became fully and rigidly aligned on opposite sides of the Arab-Israeli conflict. Meanwhile, the Cold War became even more entrenched in the

Middle East, and its impact came to be reflected at the United Nations, which increasingly became a forum for the superpowers to wage their propaganda war with one another.

Over time, however, largely because of the growth of the power of the nonaligned bloc at the UN, the increasingly hegemonic United States was either obliged to find means to subordinate the United Nations to its policies, or had no choice but to bypass it entirely. Subordination notably took the form of the United States repeatedly using its veto power in the Security Council in support of Israel to paralyze the efforts of the world body.[19] Sometimes the United States achieved the same end more subtly, as on the last day of the June 1967 war, when U.S. ambassador Arthur Goldberg suddenly asked for a recess in the urgent Security Council meting called to vote on an already-agreed-upon draft cease-fire resolution. This was intended to halt the Israeli army's offensive after it had overcome the resistance of Syrian troops in the Golan Heights and was moving rapidly through Quneitra toward the Syrian capital. The nominal purpose of this recess was for Goldberg to "consult with his government," but in fact it was meant to stall the United Nations Security Council, and to give Israel more precious time to continue its advance toward Damascus just a bit farther, to the intense frustration of the Soviets and their Arab allies.[20] Something similar happened in 1973, as is discussed in chapter 4. We have much more recently seen another egregious example of these stalling tactics, this one in the post–Cold War era, once again subordinating the United Nations to American purposes, in the delay imposed by the United States on Security Council consideration of a cease-fire in Lebanon during August 2006. This constituted yet another transparent American effort to enable Israel to continue a military offensive and achieve more of its strategic objectives.

Insofar as the tactic of bypassing the United Nations was

concerned, the Rogers Plan of 1968–70 for a cease-fire on the Suez Canal and the launch of Egyptian-Israeli negotiations, Secretary of State Henry Kissinger's shuttle diplomacy of 1973–76, and the Camp David Accords of 1978 were all part of an essentially unilateral U.S. approach to Arab-Israeli negotiations that largely ignored the UN, and indeed any multilateral forum, or any other major power. As we will see in more detail in chapter 4, the primary objective of these efforts was to achieve exclusive influence for the United States and to freeze the Soviet Union out of peacemaking, and ultimately out of the Middle East. These efforts were essentially unilateral, although Kissinger did agree to convene a purely symbolic single session of the Geneva Conference on Middle East peace including representatives of the USSR and the United Nations in December 1973. This was no more than an empty piece of playacting. Thereafter, Kissinger again deliberately ignored the Soviets and the UN (although Soviet foreign minister Andrei Gromyko attempted to make his country relevant by repeated visits to the area) and returned immediately to the unilateral American shuttle diplomacy that produced two Egyptian-Israeli disengagement accords and the Syrian-Israeli disengagement agreement between 1973 and 1976. This shuttle diplomacy was meant primarily to establish the paramount position of the United States in the Middle East at the expense of the Soviet Union, and weaken the latter, rather than to resolve fully the Arab-Israeli conflict. This is true although in both cases these accords solidified and made more permanent UN-established cease-fires. Proof that resolving the larger Arab-Israeli conflict was not a priority for Kissinger can be found in his studiously avoiding giving serious attention to those aspects of it involving Lebanon and Jordan. Most notably, he never addressed the question of Palestine, which is the core issue of the entire conflict. Regarding these essential matters, Kissinger engaged in crisis management when necessary, but he made no serious effort to deal with them in a manner that would have furthered a just permanent resolution of the overall conflict.

Before, during, and after Kissinger's stewardship of American policy, the United Nations thus served the interests of both superpowers when they were in accord on halting a major or minor round of Arab-Israeli violence. Otherwise, it was largely ignored by the United States, which was gradually acquiring a dominant position in the region and was determined to monopolize and control peacemaking efforts in ways that enhanced American influence and diminished that of the USSR. It did so irrespective of whether that facilitated the achievement of a lasting peace between all the parties concerned. It was argued by some during the latter decades of the Cold War that to be lasting, Middle Eastern peace would have to be comprehensive and involve the United Nations. Moreover, they argued, given the ties of several key Arab states to the Soviet Union and the latter's power and influence in the region, it would be impossible to achieve a comprehensive settlement without the Soviets, who with their Arab friends urged such a comprehensive approach. Nevertheless, American policymakers tended to avoid such a settlement, for several reasons. Among them were the intensity of the rivalry between the superpowers, the hostility of Israel to the UN and to any multilateral forum with the Arabs in which it believed it would be at a disadvantage, and in particular the desire of the United States to expand its own growing regional dominance. Whether it was achievable or not, a comprehensive settlement was never reached during the Cold War, nor has it been up to this day. I will come back to other aspects of how the Arab-Israeli conflict was affected by the Cold War in the next chapter.

THE INTERNATIONAL SYSTEM IN THE
MIDDLE EAST SINCE THE COLD WAR

These two contrasting American approaches to the United Nations and the international community—subordination and bypassing—could be seen at work during the last phase of the Cold War, and also after its end. This was the case during the last two Gulf wars, that of 1991 to expel Iraqi forces from Kuwait, and that of 2003 leading to the current American occupation of Iraq (the first Gulf war, it is often forgotten, was that between Iraq and Iran from 1980–88). In the former instance, the United States essentially made a unilateral decision as to what action to take. It then took advantage of the winding down of the Cold War, the imminent dissolution of the USSR, and the hostility that the odious regime of Saddam Hussein inspired in virtually all its neighbors and most of the rest of the world, to fashion a United Nations–sanctioned coalition to drive Iraqi troops out of occupied Kuwait. Although the UN was involved, it was in a strictly subordinate capacity. The Kuwait campaign was very much an American-directed, American-controlled effort, albeit operating under the flag of a Security Council resolution. American monopolization of decision making was made much easier by the weakness of the declining Soviet Union and by its incapacity to project power into the Middle East (although Middle East expert Yevgeni Primakov made a last-minute trip to Baghdad as an envoy of Soviet leader Mikhail Gorbachev in a futile effort to avert war).[21] In the waning stages of the Cold War, the United States both had a large measure of freedom of action and was able to obtain international sanction for its efforts.

By contrast, after the end of the Cold War in a situation where there was no longer another superpower confronting it, in its 2003 invasion and occupation of Iraq, the United States was obliged to bypass a recalcitrant Security Council, where it would probably have faced three vetoes from permanent members: those of Russia, China, and France. It thus went to war (together with Britain and a few other allies) without any formal international endorsement. The United States thereby acted in violation of the UN Charter and international law, but otherwise without the slightest practical hindrance. Since then, the United States has obtained much of what it wanted regarding Iraq from a bullied and compliant United Nations in the way of Security Council resolutions blessing and legalizing some of its unilateral (and illegal) actions ex post facto. This included one such resolution (UN Security Council resolution 1546) stating in effect that the U.S. occupation of Iraq was not an occupation. It asserted as well that an Iraqi government that had virtually no control over most of the most important decisions made in its country (these were made in Washington and by the U.S. Embassy in Baghdad) was sovereign, and could freely request the maintenance of U.S. forces, now placed under a nominal UN mandate.[22] Over time, that government, while still almost entirely dependent on U.S. forces, has begun to exhibit a small degree of independence from its American patrons, although nothing it had yet done at the time of writing in August 2008 made it appear fully "sovereign."

The Iraq campaign was one of a sequence of efforts following the events of September 11, 2001, whereby the Bush administration proclaimed that it had the right and the obligation to engage in vigorous unilateral actions, launching wars and actively intervening militarily in the Middle East and its peripheries, like Afghanistan, acting together with ad hoc coalitions of allies put together for each occasion. A few years after 9/11, however, it appeared to some observers as if Washington might be following a more multilateral approach in the Middle East. Certainly, other powers like France, Germany, Russia, and China, which were vigorously opposed to the 2003 war in Iraq, drew lessons from that bitter and divisive episode and the harshness of the Bush administration's response to their criticisms, and thereafter became much more careful to avoid overtly opposing the United States in the Middle East. There was even a degree of multilateral cooperation in some areas of the region, such as with France over Lebanon or with the European Union over Iran's nuclear program, although much of it was on the ad hoc basis favored by the Bush administration, and these efforts were anything but comprehensive, often rigorously excluding Russia and China, and still treating as pariahs major Middle Eastern powers like Syria and Iran.[23]

Even when the United States did act in a more multilateral fashion as in these cases, however, its new policies often went along with others emerging from the strong ideologically grounded drive of the Bush administration. Thus, while U.S. undersecretary of state Nicholas Burns was sent to meet with the Iranians together with European envoys in July 2008, the first such high-level contact since the Iranian Revolution, the Bush administration continued to try to weaken, isolate, and destroy those Middle Eastern forces, such as Hamas and Hizballah, that it defined as "terrorist" and thereby as irreconcilable enemies, and that were seen as proxies for Iran and Syria. At the same time, there was no halt to efforts by the administration to free its actions abroad of any limitations, whether legal, congressional, or international.

How little had changed in the Bush administration's single-minded pursuit of the Moby Dick of Middle Eastern terrorism was demonstrated with crystal clarity in early August 2006 over Lebanon. Then, in rejecting an immediate UN cease-fire in its support of an expansion of the Israeli offensive against Lebanon, this administration's isolation and unilateralism, and its unheeding stubbornness, were as great as at any time in the past. Indeed, the Bush administration's go-it-alone tendency in the face of expert advice and common sense has rarely been more in evidence than over its obsession with Hizballah in Lebanon, then and later. The shambles of its wrongheaded policy over Lebanon culminated in 2007–8. A confrontational American approach unwisely supported by Saudi Arabia and Egypt (together with the dangerous brinkmanship of other regional actors like Iran and Syria) gravely inflamed the situation in that country to the point that it appeared by mid-2008 as if Lebanon were headed toward a renewal of its civil war in the midst of spiraling regional rivalries. Thereupon, as ominous sectarian clashes in Beirut and other parts of the country escalated in May 2008, almost overnight the hard-line American approach was effectively sidelined. The United States was left mutely and helplessly on the margins, as Qatar and the Arab League eventually won the support of all regional actors (notably Syria, Iran, Egypt, and Saudi Arabia) and brought about an accord between all the Lebanese factions. This produced a coalition government that included Hizballah, seen in Washington as the terrorist arch-villain of the piece.

Irrespective of the ultimate success or failure of this Qatari peacemaking effort, the very fact that it took place against the wishes of the superpower that had been trying for years to impose its preferred outcomes in Lebanon at the expense of its regional enemies was striking. Equally striking was the unconcern of both Israel and Syria for American wishes as they began negotiations around the same time via the intermediary of Turkey, while Israel engaged in similar indirect negotiations over prisoner exchanges and other issues with Hizballah and Hamas, and France in July 2008 made an effort to broker the inauguration of Syrian-Lebanese diplomatic relations and to further Israeli-Syrian negotiations.[24] All of this was in direct contravention of Bush administration dogma about not negotiating with terrorists or their state supporters.

Even if those observers who perceived a somewhat greater willingness to coordinate American policy with that of other states were correct, however, the Bush administration's grudging and sporadic acquiescence to multilateralism in its waning days did not by any means amount to its acceptance of the idea that an international community truly exists, let alone its willingness to allow American actions to be constrained in any way by such a community or by international legal norms. This was visible in the stubborn resistance of the top ranks of the administration (but not the U.S. military) to the Supreme Court decision that it must apply the norms laid down by the Geneva Conventions and by relevant U.S. laws to detainees held at Guantánamo Bay and elsewhere. Indeed, the Bush administration's entire approach conformed perfectly to the words of Henry Cabot Lodge speaking in the Senate against the League of Nations treaty in 1921, as quoted by Alan Brinkley: "I would keep America as she has been—not isolated, not prevent her from joining other nations for . . . great purposes—but I wish her to be master of her own fate."[25] Not isolationist like Lodge, but rather aggressively interventionist, the Bush administration had an utterly unilateral vision of the international order. This was anything but a communal vision. It was one deeply congenial to George W. Bush and those who were closest to him, notably Vice President Dick Cheney, former secretary of defense Donald Rumsfeld, and Secretary of State Condoleezza Rice.

The Bush administration's abhorrence for the very symbol of the international community, the United Nations, was shown by one of the president's choices as ambassador to that body, John Bolton. Bolton expressed his utter contempt for the United Nations in saying that it would not matter a bit if its headquarters lost several stories (imagine the outcry if someone were to say the same thing about the Pentagon or any other U.S. government building). In this respect, Bolton perfectly and brutally reflected the real attitude of his masters in Washington. It was to the credit of the Senate, in an exceedingly rare assertion of its constitutional prerogatives in the face of the Bush administration's expansive interpretation of presidential powers, that it refused to confirm Bolton when he first came before that body, although he eventually took up this post for the duration of a congressional session under the terms of a presidential "recess appointment."

THE MIDDLE EAST AFTER BUSH

To conclude, the international order in the post–Cold War Middle East appeared to be in a shambles in the wake of the eight years of George W. Bush's presidency. This was the case whether in regard to Iraq, Lebanon, or what is still quaintly called the Middle East "peace process." Use of the latter term primarily serves the purpose of obfuscating reality, since no negotiating process of any sort went on for the better part of six years while the junior Bush sat in the White House. Indeed, during this time neither the United States nor Israel was willing to allow any serious negotiations to take place at all over any issue of substance between the two sides. Thereafter, although the Bush administration made halfhearted last-minute efforts toward peace between the Palestinians and Israelis, it was not surprising that they produced little in the way of results. In all of these areas of crisis in the Middle East, a determined effort was made by the Bush administration to monopolize all decision making in Washington, and to prevent peacemaking efforts at the United Nations, or by the so-called Quartet—the United States, the European Union, Russia, and the United Nations.[26] Insofar as the UN played any role in these and other Middle Eastern matters, it appeared to be one of pathetic eagerness to win the approval of the United States by hastening to do its bidding, as in Iraq after the American occupation was a fait accompli. Otherwise, the UN simply waited until the United States came around to accepting an international consensus, as with regard to the imposition of a cease-fire during the July–August 2006 conflict in Lebanon. Insofar as any tensions were defused in the Middle East during the last year of the Bush presidency, this was largely thanks to the good sense of the regional parties and to the credit of local mediators like Qatar, Turkey, Egypt, and France, all of whom acted in the teeth of American opposition and simply ignored the aggressive noises emanating from Washington.

In light of the stubborn unwillingness of the Bush administration to change its confrontational policies in the Middle East, or to allow other major actors or the UN to play an independent role, what emerged in its waning months in office was a growing willingness of actors in the region, including close U.S. allies, to attempt to resolve issues without the United States, and often against its expressed wishes. The Qatari/Arab League effort in Lebanon was one example. Another was the Turkish mediation between Israel and Syria, initiating the first serious negotiations between the two sides in eight years and directly contravening the Bush administration's rigid policy of isolating Syria. Similarly, Egypt brokered a lengthy negotiation between Israel and Hamas to reach a cease-fire in the Gaza Strip, while Israel and Hizballah negotiated successfully via European intermediaries for the exchange of prisoners and human remains. It may well be that none of these efforts will ultimately succeed, and it is certainly not possible to argue that they represent the beginnings of a new international order in the Middle East. If anything, they show the degree to which the failed policies of the Bush administration have led to the self-inflicted marginalization—perhaps temporary—of the greatest superpower in world history. What is remarkable about this outcome, even if it is a temporary one, is that it has eventuated after the

United States appeared to stake its post–Cold War claim to international dominance largely on the basis of its actions in the Middle East.

The Middle East has been and remains a crucial testing ground for theories about the organization of an international community, about the nature of the international system, about the role of international law and norms in interstate relations, and about the place in the world of what is currently, and will probably for a considerable time remain, its dominant actor, the United States. Are we in a new imperial era, and if so, what kind of empire is being erected?[27] How, if at all, did the vision of the world of George W. Bush and those who advised him differ from those of previous administrations?[28] Is this a period of growing or declining hegemony of the United States?[29] Is there more or less likelihood of other powers coalescing to hinder the sole hegemon, and are new powers rising to challenge it? Will the kind of regional efforts to find solutions to regional problems just described be more than a temporary interruption of the process of domination of the Middle East by external powers as outlined in this chapter? All of these questions are posed particularly acutely in the Middle East, which is still a crucial arena for the demonstration of global power, and for the waning rivalries of the past, as well as for the nascent ones of the future. I will consider answers to some of these questions in chapter 6.

The statements and writings of key figures in and around the Bush administration indicate that in their actions in Iraq, in Palestine/Israel, in Lebanon, and elsewhere in the Middle East, as well as in Afghanistan and central Asia, U.S. policymakers were fixated on the international system that they saw evolving in the future rather than that of the present. Basing themselves on approaches that developed and matured during the Cold War, they appeared to perceive that because of the strategic position and the energy reserves of the Middle East and central Asia, in the coming century both will be vital arenas in view of the potential revival of Russia and the emergence of new powers in Asia, most notably China and India.[30] These leaders clearly intended to avoid as much as possible any inhibitions or limitations on America's freedom of action in these regions.

At the same time, at their behest and in furtherance of this long-term vision of an imperial America dominating Eurasia and its resources into and through the twenty-first century, the United States engaged in the expensive process of digging in for the long haul with an extensive military presence in both the Middle East and central Asia, irrespective of public statements to the contrary.[31] Numerous "enduring bases"[32] have sprung up all over the larger region, notably in Iraq, the neighboring countries of the Gulf, and the Caspian and Transcaucasian area. The financial and political costs of such a massive long-term military presence seem to have provoked little reflection in Washington, whether among Democrats or Republicans, and little was said about it in the 2008 presidential campaign. Simultaneously, in the waning years of the Bush administration, the United States involved itself more deeply in the internal affairs of countries of this area, notably Lebanon and Palestine, but also including Syria, Iran, Libya, and several Gulf and central Asian states. It did so in a variety of new and radical ways, whether under the pretext of support for "democratization," or on the basis of old-fashioned realpolitik backing for pliant and useful local despots, or covert intervention against regimes described as hostile. The failure of most of these efforts did not appear to slow down the Bush team's ideological fervor right up to the end of the president's term.[33]

It remains to be seen how long it will take for reality to catch up with these boundless and in some cases delusional ambitions in Iraq and elsewhere in this vast and complex region, many of whose countries, from Afghanistan to Iraq, are characterized by a long-standing and rich history of fierce resistance to external domination. It also remains to be seen whether and how long such ambitions, acknowledged or not, will continue to animate the United States under a new administration. Notably, both U.S. presidential candidates in 2008 made a point of stating that the United States had to reinforce its presence in Afghanistan. However great the raw power of the United States, and however potent the ability of politicians to manipulate the media to obscure much of what actually happens in the Middle East and its environs, we can assume that irrespective of whoever takes office as president in January 2009, the cold reality of the unwillingness of most Middle Easterners and their neighbors the Afghanis to relinquish control of their hard-won sovereignty or their oil will eventually assert itself in the face of these unrealistic and unrealizable ambitions.

What seems clear, however, is that after many decades of efforts to foster an international community, and to establish legal norms for the behavior of states, the evidence, from the Middle East at least, is not terribly encouraging about the success of this endeavor. The Bush administration's activist and unilateral policy, relying largely on force and driven by a blend of old-style balance-of-power politics, and an even larger dose of old-style ideological messianism (ironically quite Wilsonian in some respects, with a touch of Trotskyite "permanent revolution" thrown in), was entirely at odds with any approach based on the idea of an international community of nominal equals, or of an international order grounded in law, which amounts to much the same thing. For the foreseeable future, and until it is explicitly disavowed and dismantled in its specifics by a successor administration starting in 2009, in 2013, or thereafter, this approach seems likely to continue to prevail in the Middle East, perhaps even more than elsewhere in the world, due to the extraordinarily extensive involvement of the United States in that region over the past few years.

SUPERPOWER RIVALRY AS A CATALYST FOR CONFLICT

The historian ... must constantly put himself at a point in the past at which the known factors still seem to permit different outcomes. If he speaks of Salamis, then it must be as if the Persians might still win; if he speaks of the coup d'état of Brumaire, then it must remain to be seen if Bonaparte will be ignominiously repulsed. Only by continually recognizing the possibilities are unlimited can the historian do justice to the fullness of life.

—JOHAN HUIZINGA[1]

One of the main purposes of this book has been to stress the largely unacknowledged importance of the Middle East in the strategic calculations of the United States and the Soviet Union during the Cold War. However, insofar as developments within the Middle East itself were concerned, while the superpower rivalry had a positive impact in a few domains, such as accelerating decolonization, it also had major lasting, and largely negative, effects. It had a particularly strong impact on disputes within the region, severely exacerbating the conflict between the Arabs and Israel, the series of wars and upheavals in Lebanon, and the war between Iran and Iraq, among other regional disputes.

These negative effects of the Cold War have probably been insufficiently recognized by analysts. Indeed, there is much portentous commentary, some of which purports to be scholarship, ascribing the primary responsibility for various cases of regional strife to what are described as age-old quarrels, ancient hatreds, and intractable divergences in the Middle East. These accounts are generally meretricious and shallow, for most conflicts in the region are in fact essentially fairly recent, dating only to the twentieth century, even if in some cases they have older roots. By contrast, it is rare to see full recognition given to the role played by the superpowers in worsening regional tensions in the Middle East. During the Cold War, both the United States and the Soviet Union often provoked war rather than peace, as well as retarding the spread of democracy and reinforcing the strong authoritarian tendencies that have existed in the region, in some cases since the dawn of recorded history. Sadly, nearly two decades after the end of the Cold War, some of these negative patterns are still continuing, indicating the lingering effects of the Cold War on the region—and the continuation of some Cold War practices there by the United States, the global hegemon and sole remaining superpower, and by a resurgent Russia—even after the dissolution of the USSR.

It is certainly the case that the Middle East was not the only region to be so affected. In many other areas of the world that became significant arenas of the Cold War, especially in the third world, the impact of the intense rivalry between the superpowers both severely distorted internal politics and intensified or complicated regional conflicts.[2] The extent of this impact was a function of the frigid intensity of the Cold War itself. For the Cold War was more than just a contention between great powers, such as the competition among the European great powers over colonies in the late nineteenth century, or the sometimes veiled rivalry between Britain and France in the Middle East (and elsewhere) before World War I and between the two world wars.[3] Unlike these earlier standoffs, the Cold War was a profoundly ideological and highly charged confrontation that fully mobilized both American and Soviet societies, and kept them on a virtual war footing for much of its length. In its earliest phases, through the 1950s, the confrontation was so intense that at times there seemed to be a danger that it might explode into a hot war, a third world war. If there was in fact any such danger, it may only have been prevented by the traumatic memory of World War II, and the existence of nuclear weapons on both sides (after 1949, when the USSR broke the American nuclear monopoly) and fear of the terrible consequences of their use.

We can thus understand the profound impact of the global polarization along Cold War lines on the domestic politics and regional rivalries of countries in major arenas of East-West rivalry, such as Europe, East Asia, and later Southeast Asia, as well as on the Middle East and other regions. In many European countries, political parties, trade unions, the press, and a variety of intellectual milieus became battlefields for influence between the superpowers, particularly in countries like France and Italy, where there were large and popular communist parties (which drew on their role in the wartime resistance to fascism to attract adherents). Some of these parties and unions became vehicles for the policies of their great-power patrons: communist parties (excluding the Yugoslav and later the Albanian parties) were from the outset largely controlled by Moscow. The United States financed parties like the Christian Democrats in Italy, and we know that a number of cultural and other forums (such as the Congress of Cultural Freedom, *Encounter* magazine, *Partisan Review,* and *Der Monat*) were subsidized by the CIA and long remained under its influence.[4] The Cold War blighted much of the political and intellectual life of Europe in profound and unique ways, as heightened fears of espionage and subversion poisoned life in the Soviet bloc, and haunted Western Europeans as well. Moreover, the entirety of the European continent from north to south was physically divided for over four decades by a largely impermeable boundary, an iron curtain, to reprise Churchill's fateful phrase, whose impact is felt to this day, within Germany and in the European Union as it absorbs former parts of the Eastern bloc.

In Asia, China, Korea, and Vietnam were also divided by similarly impermeable Cold War partitions. The first two of these that were solidified, if not created, by the Cold War are still in place today, and the third, along the 17th parallel in Vietnam, might still exist had the United States not lost the war it waged in Southeast Asia. Beyond this, South Korea was the scene first of a subterranean near–civil war along Cold War lines, with the Communists who could claim to have resisted the hated Japanese occupation on one side, and a regime dominated largely by business and military elements that had collaborated with the occupation on the other. Thereafter, North Korea's attack across the 38th parallel in June 1950 produced the first hot war of the Cold War era involving either of the superpowers and their proxies and allies.[5] The devastating effect of the little-known earlier internal conflict in South Korea,[6] and the almost total physical destruction wrought by the war itself, combined with massive casualties and repeated dislocations on both sides, scarred Korea for generations.

Similarly, the freezing of the decades-old civil war within China into a partition of the country between Communist and Nationalist China was in some measure a consequence of Cold War considerations. The Communists might have taken the island of Taiwan, as they did with Hainan Island in the spring of 1950, were it not for the belated American reaction driven largely by Cold War considerations. After the Communist takeover of China in 1949, the United States initially was not deeply committed to the Kuomintang government that had taken refuge on Taiwan. It was only after the outbreak of the Korean War in the summer of 1950 that the U.S. Seventh Fleet was first interposed between the island and the mainland. While Communist China eventually escaped from some Cold War strictures in the wake of Nixon and Kissinger's shrewd decision to play China against the USSR, this was only after the heavy-handed authoritarianism of the Chinese Communist regime had already been strongly reinforced by China's direct involvement in the Korean War, and by China thereafter being drawn into subsequent Cold War confrontations with the United States. The remarkable blindness of American policymakers through the 1960s to the manifest differences between the regimes in Moscow and Beijing was in some measure a consequence of the self-inflicted damage to American expertise on China as a result of McCarthy-era hysteria. It was part of a larger insensitivity to the differences between many national communist parties that was due to the heavy ideological blinders rooted in fierce anticommunism that were worn by many of those in positions of responsibility in Washington.

Although Japan was spared internal civil strife and outright war after 1945, the impact of the Cold War strongly affected that country's politics as well. The American occupation authorities were supremely concerned with turning Japan into a bastion against communism, just as they were in West Germany, while Moscow hoped to use the Japanese Communist Party for its own purposes. Thus the political process in Japan was distorted even more than might otherwise have been the case under a postwar American occupation. Moreover, especially once the Korean War began, Japanese industry was integrated into the American-dominated capitalist economy as part of the global confrontation with the Soviet bloc economies. This was done with little more attention than in Germany to the loyal role of the country's industrialists and bankers in supporting the militaristic regime that fomented and waged World War II.

East Asian regional alignments developed during the Cold War have only begun, in the early twenty-first century, to shift, although some of them are still in place, notably the alignment of Japan with the United States and of Stalinist North Korea with China, not to speak of the ongoing deep gulf between China and Taiwan. Moreover, long after the Cold War has ended, efforts at a rapprochement between the two Koreas—originally divided as a result of an American-Soviet deal on the eve of the Cold War—have still met with some reticence in Washington. All of these are lasting results of the enormous impact of the Cold War on regional conflicts in East Asia.

In Southeast Asia, the impact of the Cold War was also massive and lasting. This was notably the case in Vietnam, Cambodia, and Laos, where first France backed by Washington, and then the United States itself, waged decades-long, costly, and ultimately futile wars. They were both fighting against a Communist North Vietnamese regime that their leaders purported to see as no more than another tentacle of the international communist octopus, ignoring its anticolonialist and nationalist component. As in Korea, the devastation, the casualties, and the dislocation wrought by these two Indochinese wars constituted only part of the cost of the countries of Southeast Asia being sucked into the East-West rivalry. The political and social polarizations attendant on this larger conflict and the wars it produced helped to tear apart these societies, in particular that of Cambodia, whose ruler, Prince Norodom Sihanouk, desperately tried and failed to prevent his country from being drawn into the maelstrom of the American war in Indochina. Intensive American bombing and American and North Vietnamese ground interventions in Cambodia in the end helped to produce the grotesque and murderous regime of Pol Pot. The Cold War also had a profound impact in other countries of the region like Malaysia, Thailand, and Indonesia. In the latter in 1965 and

1966, the Indonesian Communist Party was subjected to a ferocious CIA-backed repression that cost the lives of perhaps half a million of its members and sympathizers.[7]

The Cold War rivalry between the superpower giants had a similar impact on the internal politics and regional rivalries of South Asia, Africa, and Latin America, and had many similarly harmful consequences.[8] This impact is still felt long after the end of the Cold War in today's Afghanistan and Pakistan in particular. These two countries had the misfortune to be seen by both superpowers as primary battlefields in their competition with each other at the very end of the Cold War, with continuing tragic spillover effects on them and their neighbors, in the Middle East and elsewhere. Although these three regions have received less attention in the scholarly literature as arenas of the East-West rivalry than did Europe, East Asia, and Southeast Asia, the picture in all of them was largely the same as the ones I have just sketched out. Here, too, the superpowers aligned themselves with one or another faction in regional conflicts, supporting regimes of almost any nature that were willing to side with them (and sometimes, as with Ethiopia, Somalia, and Eritrea, changing sides more than once). Here, too, their heavy-handed intervention had a potent and generally negative effect on the internal politics of the countries concerned. In the cases of Afghanistan and Pakistan, for example, domestic politics, regional alignments, and alliances with external powers are to this day still deeply distorted by the lingering aftereffects of the Cold War, although this almost never appears to be recognized by policymakers or pundits.

THE MIDDLE EAST IN THE COLD WAR

How did the Middle East differ from other regions that were important Cold War battlefields in terms of the impact of the superpower rivalry on its internal and regional politics? And in what specific ways was the Middle East affected by the kind of pressures generated by the Cold War that have already been briefly mentioned?

The Middle East had at least three characteristics that made it quite different from other areas of the world insofar as the competition between the superpowers was concerned. The first had to do with its location. As earlier chapters have shown, this region was particularly important to both superpowers, first because it abutted directly on the vital southern flank of the Soviet Union. From the Soviet perspective, this meant that there was no buffer of satellite states as in Eastern Europe, nor a vast territorial expanse like that of eastern Siberia, to shelter the economically and strategically critical regions in the west and south of the country. In consequence, the Urals regions and the southern underbelly of the USSR, where much of the country's vital industries and oil resources were concentrated, and whose vulnerability had only recently been revealed during the first years of World War II, were directly exposed to American power. This was especially true of overwhelmingly superior American air power in the early years of the Cold War, and of American nuclear-tipped missiles in a later era. From the Western perspective, these same geographical realities meant that both the Middle East and adjoining seas were important as possible bases for offensive strategic weapons systems, like Jupiter intermediate-range ballistic missiles (IRBMs) and Polaris and Poseidon submarine-launched ballistic missiles (SLBMs).

The strategic value of the Middle East to the superpowers in this regard actually fluctuated over the course of the Cold War, with the ebb and flow of technological developments. We have seen in chapters 1 and 2 that immediately after World War II, the region provided bases for American strategic bombers carrying nuclear weapons targeting the southern USSR. In time, as strategic bombers with greater range came into service, bases for them in the Middle East ceased to be necessary. For a period in the late 1950s and the 1960s, American Jupiter IRBMs were based in Turkey (they were removed in the wake of the 1962 Cuban Missile Crisis, as part of a top-secret deal between John F. Kennedy and Nikita Khrushchev)[9] and the Polaris SLBM became a major weapons system in the American nuclear arsenal. This missile had a range that permitted it to reach targets in the southern regions of the USSR from the eastern Mediterranean, and as a result this sea briefly once again became a subject of intense strategic interest to both superpowers. For much of this period, American Polaris missile-launching submarines were based at Rota in Spain, while Soviet antisubmarine naval and air units tasked with shadowing these submarines were based at Alexandria in Egypt and at the Syrian port of Tartus. The American military was naturally preoccupied with this Soviet presence in the region, as was the Soviet military with that of the Americans. The resulting secret, silent underwater rivalry in fact was behind much of the maneuvering of the two superpowers in parts of the Middle East for about a decade.

During the 1970s, however, the Polaris SLBM was superseded by the longer-range Poseidon SLBM. A new generation of American missile-launching submarines carrying the Poseidon was thereupon deployed in the Indian Ocean, whence they had the range to strike previously unreachable targets in Soviet central Asia. In consequence, the areas bordering that ocean, including parts of the Middle East, like the coastal waters around the Arabian Peninsula, and ports like Aden, where Soviet naval vessels were based, replaced the Mediterranean as a primary strategic focus of both superpowers. Thereafter, with the deployment of the even longer-range Trident SLBM, which could be based even farther away from the USSR, the greater Middle East became a less vital arena in the strategic-weapons race between the superpowers. The strategic importance of the region to the superpowers in terms of the central nuclear balance between them was thereafter often conjunctural rather than constant.

At the same time as it served at times as a launching pad for weapons targeting the USSR, the Middle East was seen by Western planners as a source of strategic vulnerability. This was because the Soviet frontiers abutted directly on two key Middle Eastern countries that rapidly came to constitute part of the Western alliance system designed to "contain" the power of the USSR, both of them perceived as relatively weak and vulnerable in the early Cold War years: Turkey and Iran. Moreover, as we have seen, at the end of World War II Soviet troops were already in Iran and left only tardily, and the USSR (and to some extent its partners) still bore a grudge against Turkey for its very late adhesion to the Allied cause during the war. This concern was magnified by the increasing tendency of Western policymakers to see Stalin as reprising the southward drive of Russian power toward "warm waters." There was additionally an abiding fear of the massive Red Army, based on its crushing defeat of the Wehrmacht over the years 1942–45, which for Western forces in the Middle East translated into a concern about the ability of Soviet ground forces to drive rapidly south to the Gulf and the Mediterranean in case of war.

Their perceived vulnerabilities in the Middle East explain in part the concerns of both superpowers about this region, concerns that were perhaps more acute than regarding any other region of the world except Europe itself, where by May 1945 the Red Army had succeeded in pushing the effective frontier of Soviet power far to the west. Given the almost paranoid defensiveness of Stalin, and the age-old Russian anxiety about the country's vulnerability to attacks from all directions, it can be understood why the Middle East was so important to the

Soviets. By contrast, this sense of vulnerability, and its grave accentuation as a result of the fearsome initial successes of Hitler's drives eastward in 1941–42, was almost completely ignored in Washington and Western capitals as a motivation for Soviet actions. Instead, the enormous new military power of the USSR, the Red Army's grinding and relentless advance westward against the formidable Wehrmacht during the last years of the war, and the ideological hostility and apparent aggressiveness the Soviets exhibited in the wake of the war were held up as reasons to fear and contain the potentials of the Soviet Union in the Middle East.

There was a second, linked, aspect to the strategic importance of the Middle East besides its location on the southern flanks of the Soviet Union, one that I have also touched on in other contexts. This was the region's vital historic role as a passageway for East-West transit, whether by land, sea, or air. Put very simply, it was a vital corridor for movement between America and Europe on the one hand and South and East Asia on the other. The critical nature of this aspect had just been dramatically underlined by the events of World War II. Although this reality had been apparent to European strategic thinkers for at least a century and a half, at least since Napoleon's invasion of Egypt in 1798, it was newly prominent in the thinking of American strategic planners adjusting to the new postwar reality of the United States as a power with interests and military forces spread over the entire globe. At the same time as American planners appreciated the vital importance of the Middle East for the worldwide projection of their air and sea power, it also constituted a potential cork blocking the expansion of Soviet seapower and seaborne influence southward, a role this region had played vis-à-vis Russia since the eighteenth century. This was a fact of which American strategists quickly became aware, as had been European ones for over a century, and of which Soviet planners were as aware as had been those of imperial Russia.[10] Nor was the importance of the Middle East as a key arena for the operation of the international system discussed in the last chapter lost on American policymakers as they became more and more conscious of global realities and the increasingly dominant position of the United States in that system.

Third and finally, as I laid out in chapter 2, the countries of the Middle East contained, and still contain, most of the world's reserves of oil and gas. The extent of this area's hydrocarbon reserves was suspected but not fully known before World War II. Within a few years, after further exploration by Western oil companies, the full extent of the region's richness in this domain began to become apparent. Today, the Middle East contains 61.5 percent of the world's proven oil reserves, with 22 percent of the total in Saudi Arabia alone.[11] Given the two strategic considerations just mentioned, as well as the perceived insufficiency of Western Hemisphere oil reserves to meet the demands of the American economy, the need for oil to fuel the rebuilding of the war-devastated economies of Western Europe and Japan (a crucial Western Cold War objective), and the large profits of the multinationals that dominated the oil industry,[12] it can be seen why for the first time in history, events within the Middle East were a matter of abiding interest to American policymakers. And none of this was lost on Soviet policymakers, whom we have seen had their own strategic energy considerations, and understood perfectly the importance of Middle Eastern oil to the capitalist world economy.

Given these three reasons for the significance of the Middle East to both superpowers, it was thus not a coincidence that among the first major postwar moves by the Soviet Union outside the spheres allotted to it by wartime Allied agreement were its interventions in the internal politics of Iranian Azerbaijan and Kurdistan and its demands on Iran for oil concessions, both discussed in chapter 2. Nor was it a coincidence that the first major covert American intelligence operation abroad should have been in Iran in 1953, leading to the overthrow of the Mosaddeq government, which had nationalized that country's oil. Well before 1953, however, we have seen that both the United States and the Soviet Union had already become deeply involved in the regional politics of the Middle East, and in the internal affairs of several Middle Eastern countries, notably Iran and Turkey. The Middle East, while undoubtedly not as important in the calculations of either side in the Cold War as was Europe, nevertheless clearly had its own specificity, and was an area to which they devoted serious concern. In some respects, indeed, this region was of unique interest to them, and it was certainly not just another third world arena in their global rivalry.[13]

How then did this rivalry affect the Middle East over the course of the Cold War? I would begin by suggesting that its impact on the countries of the Middle East might have been particularly significant given a characteristic of the region that is not often appreciated: its long-standing and deep involvement in world politics, and the long-standing and deep involvement of great powers in its internal affairs. In the words of Princeton historian L. Carl Brown, "For roughly the last two centuries, the Middle East has been more consistently and more thoroughly ensnarled in great power politics than any other part of the non-Western world. . . . Other parts of the world have been at one time or another more severely buffeted by an imperial power, but no area has been so unremittingly caught up in multilateral great power politics." Brown concludes that in consequence "the Middle East is the most penetrated international relations sub-system in today's world," by which he means a system "that is neither effectively absorbed by the outside challenger nor later released from the outsider's smothering embrace," and which "exists in continuous confrontation with a dominant outside political system."[14]

In view of this perceptive observation, and of the devastating effects that such penetration has had on Middle Eastern politics, I will assess the impact of the superpower rivalry in the Middle East in two major domains: first, in this chapter, how the Cold War affected regional interstate politics, and second, in the following chapter, how it affected the internal politics of the countries of the region. Although these domains are interrelated in many ways, it is possible and indeed desirable to analyze them separately. In this chapter I will examine briefly three of the most important regional conflicts affected by the Cold War: that between the Arabs and Israel; the 1975–90 war in Lebanon; and the war between Iran and Iraq. The next chapter will follow with an assessment of the impact of the Cold War on the internal politics of a selected number of states in the region.

THE ARAB-ISRAELI CONFLICT

The conflict between Arabs and Israelis today involves two strands: one a sixty-year-old interstate dispute that overlays and masks the second, which is an older struggle that goes back to the beginning of the twentieth century between two nascent national movements, one Palestinian and one Zionist. In its current configuration this conflict was born, developed, and largely shaped in the Cold War era. Prior to World War II, the dispute was basically confined to the original territory of Mandatory Palestine between the Mediterranean and the Jordan, with occasional spillovers to neighboring countries. In this earlier pre–Cold War phase, it was essentially a struggle between two budding national movements: that of the indigenous Palestinian Arab population, and that of Zionist colonists, who were mainly settlers from Europe. As the League of Nations mandatory, Britain was the external power with preeminent influence on Palestine, in spite of the League's nominal responsibility for the country.[15] For at least the first two decades after World War I, Great Britain, the greatest imperial power of the age, used its power to support fully the aims of the Zionist movement, with devastating long-term results for the Palestinian Arab majority population of the country.

This configuration, like so much else in the world, changed fundamentally with World War II, which witnessed a phenomenal growth in the power of the United States and the Soviet Union, and the rapid diminution of that of Britain. These major shifts were soon reflected in the Middle East. By 1939 the Zionist movement, with the crucial assistance of Britain, had already created in Palestine what was a state in all but name. It thereafter succeeded in developing valuable links to both of the rising superpowers and to Transjordan, militarily the strongest Arab state. Meanwhile, the Palestinians failed to acquire any great-power support or reliable regional patrons. Moreover, outcomes in Palestine were increasingly affected by the growing influence of the United States over a weakened, impoverished, and overstretched British Empire. With the conclusive defeat by the Zionist military forces of the disorganized and poorly led Palestinians by the end of April 1948, and with the end of the Mandate a few weeks later and the entry (for several differing reasons) of four Arab armies into Palestine, this initial phase of the conflict ended. For decades thereafter, it became primarily an interstate dispute between Israel and the Arab states that was influenced not just by Britain but by a multiplicity of powers, preeminent among which were the United States and the USSR.

The new phase, characterized by a series of wars, every one of which Israel won resoundingly, began with superpower maneuvering over the end of the Palestine Mandate and the establishment of a Jewish state. This maneuvering presaged the predominant role both the United States and the USSR were thereafter to play in the evolution of the conflict. From the moment UN General Assembly resolution 181, calling for the establishment of a Jewish state in most of Palestine, was passed in

November 1947 with the support of the United States and the
Soviet Union (and the abstention of the United Kingdom), it
became clear that a new era had dawned in the Middle East.
It was apparent that the new "big boys on the block" intended
to call the shots. The two nascent superpowers thereupon competed for the favor of the new Israeli state. They raced to recognize it the moment it was established on May 15, 1948, and
extended differing forms of crucial initial support to it. Meanwhile, the Arab state called for by resolution 181 in less than half
of the territory of the Palestine Mandate was stillborn, with
much of its territory occupied by Israel and the remainder
controlled by Transjordan and Egypt. This result was in large
measure the consequence of collusion between the Zionist
movement and Jordan, and between Great Britain and Jordan,
none of which looked with favor on the establishment of an
Arab state in Palestine.[16] Nothing more was heard of this Arab
state from any of these powers, from the new superpowers (both
of which had voted for its creation), or from the United Nations,
whose General Assembly resolution had mandated its coming
into existence. It was by now becoming clear that for all the importance of Britain's residual role in the Middle East, the United
States and the Soviet Union were the ascendant powers in that
region. That new situation was confirmed by the outcome of the
subsequent regional crisis involving Israel and Egypt, over Suez
in 1956.

Ironically, in spite of their intensifying competition in the
Middle East, the two new superpowers remained on the same
side during the Arab-Israeli war that grew out of the Suez crisis.
It was a different side, however, as both countries had supported
Egypt in the face of the tripartite Anglo-Franco-Israeli aggression against it. This was partly because the Eisenhower administration throughout its time in office was wary of being
perceived as too close to Israel. The concern in Washington was

that such a perception might push nationalist Arab governments toward the Soviet Union. No such fear had affected President Truman in 1947–48 when he took decisions entirely in Israel's favor without any regard for Arab sensibilities, as was noted briefly in chapter 1. Concern about offending the Arabs further diminished with the Kennedy and Johnson administrations, which first began to supply Israel with a limited range of arms.[17] The aftermath of the 1967 war saw a full identification with Israel of the United States, which now replaced France as that country's primary arms provider, as the Soviet Union had been for leading Arab states since 1955.

Thus the 1960s witnessed the inauguration of what can be called the classic phase of the Arab-Israeli conflict, wherein the United States was fully aligned with Israel and the Soviet Union with the Arabs. Largely in consequence, interactions between Arabs and Israelis came to be deeply influenced by Cold War considerations. During this phase, certain Arab states like Jordan and Saudi Arabia remained close to the United States in spite of the stresses that being identified with the patron of Israel placed on their internal legitimacy. These "conservative" Arab states tended to play a limited role in the Arab-Israeli conflict by comparison with the "progressive" states aligned with the USSR, like Egypt, Syria, and Iraq (although all were involved in the larger Arab cold war of this period, which tracked closely with the Cold War between the superpowers). This polarized alignment remained in place until the end of the Cold War in 1990, and while little understood, it did much to shape the nature of the conflict between Arabs and Israelis.

The earliest phase of the Palestine problem before World War II was deeply influenced by the essential assistance offered by Britain to the implantation in Palestine of the Zionist movement and its parastate structures. However, the conflict was primarily driven by the struggle of the young Zionist movement to transform a predominantly Arab country into the Jewish national home, and by the strong resistance to the Zionist project of the nascent Palestinian national movement. As I have written elsewhere, the final outcome of this struggle was also deeply marked by the failures of the Palestinian leadership of the day.[18] In the initial stages of the subsequent post–World War II phase that was dominated by the new superpowers, external considerations became even more important. There can be little question that the establishment of the state of Israel in 1948 in 78 percent of the territory of Mandatory Palestine by the Jewish minority of the population at the expense of the Arab majority was mightily helped by the international support and legitimacy the Zionist project received in the wake of the shocking revelations of the Holocaust, and specifically by the backing of the United States and the USSR. While Zionist forces may have had the capability to conquer most of Palestine militarily unaided even before they actually began to do so on the battlefield in the spring of 1948, it was only the strong, overt backing of the United States and the Soviet Union that gave international cover and legitimacy, as well as indispensable material support, to this process. Indeed in 1947–48 the two superpower rivals' competition with each other for the favor of the new Jewish state operated to the great benefit of Israel, just as their competition for Egypt's favor later benefited that state at the time of the Suez War in 1956.

This apparent anomaly was a function not only of the competition between the United States and the Soviet Union, but also of the desire of each to see a diminution of the neocolonial power of Britain, which had a string of Arab clients in the region, from Egypt, through Transjordan, to Iraq. This is an underappreciated theme that I have already stressed, and will return to. The United States and the Soviet Union offered support to the Jewish state in 1947–48 partly because of domestic political and ideological reasons (very different in each case), and partly to prevent the other from obtaining sole advantage there. However, they also did what they did in order to weaken the regional position of Britain, which by 1947 had become hostile to the Zionist movement it had previously wholeheartedly supported, because a Zionist terrorist campaign was forcing an end to the British Mandate and to the possibility of a continuing British military presence in Palestine.

The opposition of the two superpowers to the tripartite Anglo-Franco-Israeli aggression against Egypt in 1956 was driven by some of the same motivations: the desire of each to prevent its rival from obtaining an advantage, and at the same time the desire to oppose the last gasp of old-style Anglo-French colonialism. The fact that the Suez War took place simultaneously with the 1956 Hungarian uprising against Soviet domination gave both superpowers further reasons for opposing the Suez adventure. For the Americans there was the hope of preventing what they saw as the foolishness of London and Paris in their Egyptian campaign from distracting from the spectacle of Soviet repression in Budapest. For the Soviets there was the obverse of this: the need to mask their own Eastern European neo-colonialism by highlighting that of the two Western powers in the Middle East.

By the time the Arab-Israeli conflict entered its classic phase of the alignment of the different sides with the two superpowers in the 1960s, external factors had become even more important. To a large degree this related to the strategically crucial issue of the supply of armaments to the contending parties. In May 1950, in the wake of the 1949 armistices that had brought the first Arab-Israeli war to an end, the United States, Britain, and France had issued the Tripartite Declaration, which ostensibly limited arms deliveries to the two sides.[19] In fact, this self-denying ordinance served only to guarantee the maintenance of the military superiority Israel had already achieved. At the same time, it did not prevent France from surreptitiously delivering to Israel advanced weapons systems or the nuclear technology that eventually enabled it to produce nuclear weapons. The so-called Czech arms deal of September 1955, in which the Soviet Union used Prague as an intermediary to supply armaments to Egypt, broke the Western monopoly of arms deliveries to both sides, and for the first time offered the Arab states the opportunity—thoroughly illusory, as it turned out—to achieve strategic parity with Israel.

From this point on, arms became a crucial component of the superpowers' means of exercising influence, although that influence at times revealed itself to be quite limited. The fact that France's delivery of highly sophisticated weapons systems like Mirage IIIC fighters failed to provide it with any influence over Israel's decision to go to war in June 1967 helped to lead French president Charles de Gaulle to cut off arms supplies to the Jewish state thereafter. For instead of listening to words of caution from the president of France, their main arms supplier at that point, Israel's leaders were waiting attentively for the green light they eventually got from Washington in the days before they launched their offensive of June 5, 1967. Some describe this light as yellow, but it makes little difference: a signal to attack without fearing the wrath of Washington was the one the Israeli leadership was waiting for and received.[20]

As a result of Israel's 1967 surprise attack, Egypt and Syria suffered the virtually total devastation of their air forces, almost entirely on the ground (which provoked the frustrated rage of some Soviet military advisors).[21] To replace these and other losses, Egypt and Syria requested high-tech aircraft and antiaircraft missiles, radar, tanks, and artillery, as well as a range of other equipment, from an initially reluctant Soviet Union. The specter of major Soviet client states being left defenseless in the face of an Israel armed and backed increasingly openly by Washington, and the equally embarrassing image of Soviet weapons being shown to be inferior to those provided by the West, led the Soviet leadership to acquiesce to most of these requests (though not initially for long-range MiG-23 fighters and certain other offensive weapons systems the Egyptians asked for), and soon copious quantities of Soviet arms were being shipped to both countries.

Several years prior to the outbreak of the 1967 war, Israel had already been allowed to acquire some relatively unsophisticated American military equipment, including surplus M-48A tanks (via West Germany) and Hawk antiaircraft missiles, while A-4E Skyhawk bombers were on order.[22] Now, in the wake of its spectacular 1967 triumph over Arab states that were mainly Soviet-armed, an already dominant Israel requested and received top-of-the line equipment from the United States. This included more Skyhawks, as well as the F-4 Phantom, the preeminent fighter-bomber of its era, and at that time the workhorse of the U.S. Air Force, Navy, and Marines in Vietnam, which began to be delivered to Israel in 1969.

In fact both superpowers had little choice but to deliver some, or sometimes all, of the military equipment insistently, repeatedly requested by the Egyptian, Syrian, and Israeli armed forces, even if Soviet and American policymakers and senior military officers were often skeptical about these requests. Those responsible in both the Israeli and Arab militaries were driven in their quest to procure more and more sophisticated weapons systems by the urgent need to provide supplies of arms for the nearly three-year-long War of Attrition that was raging by 1968. This conflict had started with Egyptian attacks on the Egyptian-Israeli cease-fire line along the Suez Canal, and eventually spread to the Jordanian, Syrian, and Lebanese fronts. It soon became apparent that in this situation of heightened confrontation, neither the United States nor the Soviet Union could afford to let its clients down, since by now the prestige of both superpowers was fully engaged. By this point, the Arab-Israeli conflict had developed into an intermittently hot war that had been largely subsumed into the Cold War between the United States and the Soviet Union. At the height of the War of Attrition, indeed, it was perceived as a potential global flashpoint: by July of 1970, President Nixon stated that the situation in the Middle East had become "terribly dangerous," adding that "it is like the Balkans before World War I where the two superpowers could be drawn into a confrontation that neither of them wants because of the differences there."[23]

Central to this enhancement of the global importance of the Arab-Israeli conflict was the fact that Israel's victory in 1967 had come to be seen as a victory for a U.S. proxy over those of the Soviets. This was an entirely novel way of framing the conflict, in view of the quite different ways it had intertwined with Cold War considerations over the preceding two decades. This new depiction of things was particularly welcome among many in Washington, where a besieged Johnson administration had been obsessed with the tenacity of the Soviet proxy it saw itself as grappling with unsuccessfully in Vietnam. Given the rigid worldview of official Washington and the frustrating inability of the United States to defeat what was seen there as a branch of "international communism" in Southeast Asia, many officials welcomed what could be described as a "victory" in the East-West conflict, even one by proxy. Several members of Johnson's circle of advisors, moreover, were both Cold War hawks and passionate supporters of Israel, like U.S. ambassador to the United Nations Arthur Goldberg, the president's national security advisor, Walt Rostow, and his brother, assistant secretary of state Eugene Rostow. For them, such a turn of events, which more closely allied the United States and Israel on a Cold War basis, was doubly welcome. Thus was inaugurated a degree of identification of American with Israeli interests that eventually superseded the connection with any other ally of the United States. This identification has survived and thrived over multiple administrations down to this day, even though its original Cold War pretext has long since faded away.

Although there was no similar identification of Soviet interests with those of the Arab states, the result was similar in some respects. For the pretensions of the Soviet Union to be a power equal to the United States caused the political leadership in Moscow to overcome the reticence of some of their own top military officers to engage in further adventures with the Arabs. In the view of some in the Soviet military hierarchy, the Arab states had already allowed two complete Soviet-supplied arsenals to be destroyed nearly unused: one by Israel, Britain, and France in 1956, and another by Israel in 1967.[24] The Soviet leadership overrode this reticence with the argument that as a superpower that aspired to parity with the United States, the USSR simply could not allow an American proxy to humiliate Soviet ones in the immediate vicinity of the country's southern borders.[25] The Soviet military high command incidentally was not always more reluctant than the political leadership to see the USSR involved in Arab-Israeli issues, and there were intriguing shifts over time in the positions on these issues of the various leading figures and the different institutional actors within the Soviet system.[26]

As the political scientist Alvin Rubinstein has shown, incorporation of the Arab-Israeli conflict into the Cold War rivalry paradoxically meant in practice that what he called the "influence relationship" between Soviet and Arabs went both ways, and was not just a matter of superpower patrons imposing their will on weak and pliable clients, as was often assumed. Far from being able to issue diktats, the patrons now needed the clients even more than before, now that this formerly local conflict had been integrated into a larger one, the global Cold War, which was vital for the superpowers. Quite frequently, indeed, Rubinstein argues, the Arab client got more of what it wanted from this relationship than did the Soviet patron, as the tail often wagged the dog.[27] Needless to say, the same thing was also often true for the patron-client relationship between Americans and Israelis.[28] Some would argue that up to the present day the Israeli tail often continues to wag the American dog, even though the Cold War is long since over.[29]

Perhaps the first example of the truth of Rubinstein's observation was the launching by the Egyptians, against the strenuous advice of their Soviet military advisors, of the campaign against Israeli occupation forces dug in on the east bank of the Suez Canal starting in 1968, which came to be known as the War of Attrition. This artillery and air offensive, together with occasional commando raids, provoked a massive Israeli response, primarily in the form of furious air and artillery bombardments that devastated and emptied of their population the Egyptian cities of Port Said, Port Fuad, Ismailiya, and Suez along the canal. Israel also fortified its positions on the east bank of the canal into a formidable barrier called the Bar-Lev Line. The War of Attrition, which lasted from 1968 until 1970, eventually enflamed all the other Arab fronts with Israel, and had other effects, to be discussed in chapter 6.[30] This in turn led to sporadic, unfocused, and initially unsuccessful UN, American, and Soviet mediation to attempt to end the fighting and move the parties toward a negotiated political settlement of the Arab-Israeli conflict. According to the accounts of Egyptian officials, improving their bargaining position through military means to make possible such a settlement with Israel—rather than outright victory in war—was always their basic intention in launch-ing the War of Attrition, although this was often belied by their warlike rhetoric.[31] The fact that in the teeth of bitter opposition from some radical "rejectionist" Arab states, Egypt joined Jordan in accepting UN Security Council resolution 242 of November 22, 1967, which mandated a peace settlement through negotiations (and which Israel refused to accept for nearly three years), indicates that there is some validity to this claim.

In the end, the War of Attrition and the Rogers Plan, put forward by American secretary of state William Rogers for a ceasefire and negotiations (which actually did halt the fighting along the canal in September 1970), combined with mediation by UN envoy Gunnar Jarring and Soviet foreign minister Andrei Gromyko over the same years, failed to resolve the problem that Egypt faced, namely Israel's 1967 occupation of the Sinai Peninsula, or to bring about a lasting peace. This occupation, the presence of hundreds of thousands of refugees from the cities along the Canal Zone in Cairo and other Egyptian cities, and the need to keep the entire country on a war footing for year after year, had become Egypt's primary foreign policy and domestic concern. After the death of President Gamal Abdel Nasser in September 1970, subsequent efforts by Egypt to initiate negotiations with Israel via the intermediary of the United States and the UN also failed. War was, in consequence, again inevitable, in spite of the fact that Anwar Sadat, who had now become Egypt's president, showed himself willing to go quite far in the direction of a separate peace with Israel (which his predecessor Nasser had always resisted), if by so doing he could end the occupation of the Sinai. Sadat proclaimed 1971, his first full year in office, the "year of decision," hoping to force a negotiated settlement of the conflict.

Newly released American documents show that Secretary of State Rogers was rebuffed by Israel in May 1971 when he presented the Israeli government with an Egyptian proposal that would have produced much the same outcome—a separate Egyptian-Israeli peace—as was later obtained via the successful 1977–79 peace negotiations between Egypt and Israel. However, these later talks only took place after the costly 1973 war, which brought the superpowers to the brink of nuclear confrontation.[32] These same newly declassified documents show that President Nixon and national security advisor Henry Kissinger, obsessed with the rivalry with the Soviet Union, actively undercut Rogers's efforts, demanding concessions from Egypt regarding its relationship with the Soviets as a precondition for American brokering of such a separate bilateral Egyptian-Israeli peace accord.[33] Peace in the Middle East, in other words, was less important to the White House than advantage over America's superpower rival. This was not the last time this was to be the case for either side engaged in the Cold War rivalry.

Although he did not get what he wanted from Rogers or the Israelis, Sadat got the message from Washington. Partly in response to intense American (and Saudi) pressure on Egypt to cut its ties to the Soviet Union (and also because of the Egyptian military's intense frustration with delays in the supply of needed equipment and with the arrogant behavior of Soviet military personnel), in 1972 Sadat expelled Soviet military advisors.[34] With them went Soviet combat forces that were stationed in Egypt for a variety of purposes, ranging from defense of the Egyptian interior against Israeli air attack to tasks that had nothing to do with Egyptian interests, like air and sea surveillance of American SLBM-carrying submarines. The exodus of perhaps twenty thousand Soviet military personnel served two purposes for Sadat. It constituted an effort to move Egypt closer to the United States in spite of the failure of his 1971 initiative brokered by Rogers and UN mediator Gunnar Jarring. It was also necessary preparation for the launching of a war to liberate the occupied Sinai Peninsula, which the Egyptian leadership now saw was inevitable, since Israel had spurned Egypt's 1971 political overtures.[35] Sadat and his advisors felt they could not go to war with Soviet forces and advisors on their territory, both because this presence might inhibit Egyptian actions and because it might incriminate the Soviets in the taking of a purely Egyptian decision to launch the war.

Given the two-way influence relationship analyzed by Rubinstein that I have discussed, it should be no surprise that after Sadat had ordered the humiliating expulsion of Soviet military personnel from Egypt, the Egyptian leader had no compunction in demanding that Moscow provide new and highly sophisticated weapons systems to enable his forces to launch a crossing of the Suez Canal. This was an operation of which Moscow, wary of jeopardizing its relationship with Washington and afraid that its Egyptian protégés might lose another war, did not approve. Faced with such effrontery, and quite miffed at Sadat, the Soviets nevertheless grudgingly delivered much of the requested weaponry, even though they knew that it would be used for a war the outcome of which seemed highly uncertain to them.[36] Just before this, the United States had found that in spite of delivering some of the most sophisticated weapons in its arsenal to Israel,[37] efforts by Secretary of State Rogers and the State Department to bring Israel to accept a negotiated settlement with Egypt were stonewalled by an Israeli refusal to consider Sadat's terms. Clearly both superpowers by this stage were so deeply committed to supporting their respective clients, and so involved in a proxy competition with each other in the Middle East, they had difficulty either in restraining these clients or compelling them to do much of what they wanted.

The limits on the capabilities of the superpowers to restrain their clients became further apparent when Egypt and Syria launched the October 1973 war. This was the last of the exclusively state-to-state Arab-Israeli wars. Thereafter, nonstate actors like the Palestine Liberation Organization (PLO) and, later, Hamas and Hizballah became the main combatants, although, during the 1982 war, Syrian forces were heavily involved for a single week of a ten-week war that was mainly waged by Israel against the PLO. This single instance over a quarter of a century ago was the last Arab-Israeli military conflict in which the military forces of any Arab state played any direct role.[38] In some respects, however, the October 1973 war was the most important of them all. It certainly was in terms of superpower involvement. The Soviet leadership feared the potentially negative outcome (and impact on their developing détente with the United States) of an Arab attack, even one like that planned by Sadat and Syrian president Hafiz al-Assad in 1973 with the limited objective of liberating territory occupied in 1967.[39] The Soviets could not persuade Sadat to show further patience after he had been subjected to domestic and Arab ridicule by proclaiming 1971 a "year of decision," when he had failed either to initiate negotiations or go to war. They were thus unable to restrain him from finally going to war.

In these less than ideal circumstances, Moscow went along, albeit reluctantly, with its clients in Cairo and Damascus, who proceeded to launch their October 1973 offensive. The attack achieved the desired effect of strategic surprise, but after initial rapid Egyptian and Syrian advances in Sinai and the Golan Heights, the situation changed as Israel counterattacked, first in the Golan and then later in Sinai. As the war turned sour for the Syrians and then for the Egyptians, the Soviets suddenly found themselves called upon to airlift vast quantities of weapons to replace heavy losses of equipment, notably surface-to-air and antitank missiles and armored vehicles. The United States was in an analogous predicament, as heavy Israeli aircraft losses to new Soviet-provided Egyptian and Syrian missile and antiaircraft artillery batteries, and losses of armored vehicles to new antiarmor weapons in the earliest phases of the war, forced a similar decision on Washington to that taken by Moscow. Soon thereafter, massive air resupply of critical items of military equipment (sometimes taken directly from Warsaw Pact and NATO stocks) was under way to the clients of both superpowers. In a new feature in the series of superpower confrontations over Arab-Israeli wars going back to 1956, there were constant direct communications throughout the crisis between Moscow and Washington (indeed Henry Kissinger, now U.S. secretary of state, was in Moscow part of the time during a late stage of the war, at Soviet request).

It was at this point that two important and enduring phenomena in the relations between the superpowers and their clients surfaced, revealing the crucially important effects of the Cold War on the Arab-Israeli conflict. The first, which was evident as the 1973 war drew to an end, was the way each superpower made mighty efforts to exploit the conflict to achieve advantage for itself at the expense of the other, and to prevent its rival from being able to portray an outcome in the Middle East as a triumph for its Cold War policy. October 1973 is indeed one of the most perfect illustrations of this phenomenon. In the very last days of the war, the two superpowers were simultaneously deeply engaged in resupplying their respective clients with weapons and ammunition even as Kissinger engaged in tense final negotiations with the Soviet leadership, while their forces worldwide were poised on a nuclear alert directed against each other.[40] This may have been the most serious standoff between the superpowers since the early days of the Berlin Wall and the Cuban Missile Crisis: a recent account based on the latest U.S. government documents that have been declassified called it "possibly the most serious international crisis of Nixon's presidency."[41]

The genesis of this dangerous development was deeply

rooted in the pattern I have already outlined of superpower one-upmanship over the Middle East. It came about because the Soviets were enraged to find that notwithstanding what they thought was a deal negotiated in Moscow with Kissinger on a standstill Israeli-Egyptian cease-fire, sealed with Security Council resolution 338 of October 22, 1973 (followed by a similar cease-fire resolution, resolution 339, on October 23), Israeli forces kept advancing southward on the west bank of the canal. In so doing they moved closer and closer to Cairo and to a full encirclement of the Egyptian Third Army, which they had cut off and trapped in its bridgeheads on the east bank of the canal. The Soviets were deeply suspicious of American complicity with the Israelis in this maneuver. This suspicion appears to be fully borne out by newly revealed confidential American documents showing that while in Tel Aviv before his return to Washington from Moscow, Kissinger did in fact encourage the Israelis to advance in direct contravention of his commitment to the Soviets. Just before leaving, he in effect gave the Israeli leadership further precious hours for their offensive, saying, "You won't get violent protests from Washington if something happens during the night, while I'm flying."[42] The Soviets were outraged that Kissinger appeared to be aiming at giving America's proxies an advantage on the battlefield when fighting ceased (which in fact is what happened).

In a blunt message to Nixon, Soviet leader Leonid Brezhnev demanded a joint American-Soviet military intervention to separate the two sides. Should this not take place, he warned that the Soviets might be obliged to intervene unilaterally with their military forces to impose a cease-fire, since UN resolutions to this effect were not being respected by the Israelis. Simultaneously, the Soviets began to move some of their forces, including paratroop divisions and nuclear tactical-missile warheads, movements that were instantly picked up by American intelligence monitoring, as the Soviets knew they would be. This provoked Washington to place American nuclear and conventional forces at DefCon3, the highest peacetime level of alert. This clear signal of American resolution was combined with menacing language from Kissinger: a message he sent to Moscow described Brezhnev's "suggestion of unilateral action as a matter of the gravest concern involving incalculable consequences."[43]

Having been brought by the actions of their clients, and by their own rivalry, to somewhere near the brink of nuclear war, both superpowers now stood down. The result was yet another UN Security Council cease-fire resolution, 340, of October 25, 1973, which this time was eventually respected by the Israelis, who by this point had already encircled the Egyptian Third Army and had achieved most of their objectives on the ground. The United States and the Soviet Union thus reached the level of a nuclear confrontation, essentially in order for each to show the other that it would not back down in what had by now become a central arena of the Cold War competition between them. This is an indication of just how high the stakes of this regional conflict had become for both sides. Just how high they were, and how serious this confrontation was, is often ignored by those who focus on the central strategic relationship between the superpowers, or classic standoffs like those over Berlin and Cuba. Thus, as experienced a policymaker as Richard Holbrooke could describe the Cuban Missile Crisis as "the world's only superpower nuclear confrontation."[44]

The second phenomenon, which emerged in the wake of the 1973 war but had recurred before this, was the strict subordination of the goal of achieving Arab-Israeli peace to what were seen in Washington and Moscow as much more important Cold War considerations. There had already been at least one important example of such a subordination in the years that followed the June 1967 war, when both the United States and the Soviet

Union chose to escalate quite drastically the arming of their protégés. The size and sophistication of both Arab and Israeli arsenals grew with alarming rapidity in consequence, to the point that the tank and air battles during the 1973 war were the largest since the battle of Kursk between the German and Soviet armies in 1943. The two superpowers in effect made a decision to ply both sides with armaments rather than cooperating in restraining their clients and aggressively seeking implementation of Security Council resolution 242 of November 22, 1967, which provided an agreed basis for a resolution of the conflict, and which both the United States and the USSR had voted for.

The contrast between each giant's competitive, muscular "military diplomacy" via arms supply, and their altogether feeble and unfocused statecraft in favor of a negotiated solution, could not have been more glaring for the six years between the 1967 and 1973 wars. Of course, at this stage of the conflict neither side could monopolize peacemaking and thereby obtain unilateral advantage (that ostensibly happy state was not far away for Kissinger and the United States). At the same time, they were far too wary and suspicious of one another to cooperate consistently. Stoking the arms race and therefore making regional war more likely, indeed inevitable, while ostentatiously flexing superpower muscle was in the end just so much easier for both sides. This irresponsibility in the pursuit of the narrowest form of unilateral interest complicated and deepened the conflict and contributed directly and massively to producing two of the most destructive of the Arab-Israeli wars: the nearly three-year-long War of Attrition ending in 1970, and the October 1973 war. One example during this period of the United States and the USSR placing Cold War advantage in the Middle East over the promotion of peace between Arabs and Israelis has already been described: the preference of Nixon and Kissinger, in 1971, for advantage vis-à-vis the Soviet Union, over the arrangements that were proposed by Sadat and were futilely brokered by UN mediator Gunnar Jarring and U.S. Secretary of State Rogers for a separate peaceful settlement between Egypt and Israel.

The period after the 1973 war witnessed perhaps the most egregious examples of this phenomenon, in the form of Henry Kissinger's vaunted Middle East shuttle diplomacy from the end of the October 1973 war until 1976. It is important to recognize that Kissinger had at least one important accomplishment on these exhausting trips: he defused the dangerous battlefield situation in the immediate wake of the 1973 war that had produced the October 1973 nuclear alert, and that threatened to lead to more war and to more superpower confrontations. He succeeded in doing this by negotiating first a disengagement agreement between Egypt and Israel, then one to halt continued fighting between Syria and Israel, both in 1974, and then another Egyptian-Israeli Sinai disengagement agreement in 1975. However, at the same time, and perhaps even more important to Washington, his actions had the effect of delivering Egypt fully into the American camp and removing it definitively from the Soviet one. This was clearly the primary objective of Kissinger and the two presidents he served, Richard Nixon and Gerald Ford. However, there was a cost to this achievement, which came at the expense of the possibility, however slim, of an overall comprehensive peace in the region: at no stage did Kissinger engage in multilateral talks or any other form of negotiations involving all the Arab parties and the Soviets.[45] Nor did Kissinger try to go any further with unilateral American efforts to make progress toward a final peace between Syria and Israel, or one between Jordan and Israel. He did not even contemplate dealing with the Palestinians. In all of these cases, unlike that of Egypt, no advantages for the United States at the expense of the Soviets could be expected. What the three disengagement agreements did, beyond the paramount achievement of winning over to American influence the largest Arab state, Egypt, was to calm the fighting and ease tension on the Egyptian and Syrian fronts with Israel: both have stayed almost entirely quiet in consequence for the subsequent quarter century. They did this without Kissinger even treating, let alone resolving, the core issues of the conflict, starting with the central issue of Palestine.

It has indeed been argued with some reason, at the time and since then, that notwithstanding any benefits they may have produced, this series of three American-brokered bilateral disengagement agreements (followed by the separate bilateral Egyptian-Israeli peace treaty negotiated in 1978–79 under the aegis of Jimmy Carter) had the effect of intensifying the conflict on other Arab-Israeli fronts, and contributing measurably to the consequent devastation of Lebanon. While they quieted the Israeli-Syrian front, and brought about a separate Egyptian-Israeli peace, these steps clearly did not end the overall Arab-Israeli conflict or bring real peace to that region of the Middle East. These were perhaps the most egregious examples of what had become an established American preference for quick advantage over the Soviets at the expense of efforts to establish a comprehensive and lasting peace involving all the parties to the Arab-Israeli conflict. The American predilection for separate deals keyed on Egypt to obtain Cold War advantage while ignoring other, more difficult issues inevitably meant that much war, death, and devastation lay in the future for Palestine, Lebanon, and Israel. But it did not prevent Henry Kissinger, and later Jimmy Carter, Menachem Begin, and Anwar Sadat, from winning copious laurels for their efforts at peacemaking between Israel and Egypt.

President Carter followed this pattern by securing further Cold War advantages at the expense of the possibility of a comprehensive Arab-Israeli peace. This is ironic, since in 1977, at the outset of his presidency, Carter launched the first good-faith

American push for a comprehensive Middle East peace settlement that involved the Soviets. It is worth noting that this first such effort by the United States came a full thirty years after the fighting in Palestine set off by the partition resolution of 1947 began the conflict in the interstate form it took until the end of the Cold War.

This major shift in American emphasis was driven by the realization on the part of Carter and his secretary of state, Cyrus Vance, that it was essential both for American interests and for world peace to resolve the Arab-Israeli conflict, and that in order to do so it was necessary to involve all the parties to it, and to deal with all of its aspects. It was clear to them that in these circumstances, there was benefit to be derived from bringing in the Soviets, who had close links with Syria and the PLO.

The outcome of this new willingness to search for a comprehensive peace and to engage the Soviets was the U.S.-Soviet joint statement of October 1, 1977, the first initiative that effectively united the superpowers in a practical search for a lasting solution in the Middle East. The statement committed both sides to seek a comprehensive resolution of the conflict through a conference at Geneva involving all the parties, including "representatives of the Palestinian people," and stressed that a key issue to be resolved was "the Palestinian question including ensuring the legitimate rights of the Palestinian people."[46] These were novel formulations for the United States, which had traditionally shied away from talking of Palestinian rights (and refused use of the term "legitimate national rights" for the Palestinians in this statement), preferring instead in the past to describe the Palestine question as no more than a refugee issue. Previously, the Palestinians had been rigorously excluded from consideration as a party to a settlement at the insistence of the government of Israel, supported by the United States. There was much else that was new in the 1977 joint statement by contrast with the policies of the Johnson, Nixon, and Ford administrations, most notably the willingness to involve the Soviets rather than to act at their expense. The new approach was not followed by Washington for very long, however.

In the end, Carter's novel effort toward a comprehensive settlement was not sabotaged by the United States, although there was vociferous domestic opposition both to the idea of a settlement involving the Soviets and to the new language about the Palestinians. This opposition came both from anti-Soviet hardliners and from political allies of Israel in Washington. Led by the hawkish senator Henry "Scoop" Jackson and aides of his, including Richard Perle, this alignment foreshadowed the later alliance between the neoconservatives and the Israel lobby, which flowered during the Reagan years and came to full, catastrophic fruition under the presidency of George W. Bush. The American-Soviet initiative was torpedoed not by these vocal and vituperative malcontents, noisy though their protests were, however, but rather by Anwar Sadat, aided and abetted by the new Israeli prime minister, Menachem Begin. The Egyptian president preferred (as he had since 1971) to try to arrange a bilateral deal with Israel quickly rather than be obliged to wait for all his disputatious Arab allies to arrive at a multilateral comprehensive peace settlement negotiated in the context of a reconvened Geneva conference. The Israeli government of Begin was of course happy to oblige in negotiating a separate peace with Egypt, even though as a price it had to evacuate the entirety of the occupied Sinai Peninsula, which Israeli governments had previously been loath to do. It did so nevertheless, since such a separate peace meant the definitive removal from the Arab-Israeli conflict of Egypt, the largest and most powerful Arab state. This guaranteed that Israel would come under no serious military pressure to settle with the Syrians and the Palestinians. The new Likud-dominated Israeli government was thereby freed to achieve its primary objective, of colonizing the West Bank with Israeli settlers, without hindrance.

The Carter administration finally went along with this hijacking of its policies, eager to take credit for the initiative launched in 1977 by Sadat, who, piqued by the American-Soviet joint statement, had secretly sent emissaries to meet with Israeli representatives in Morocco, and then dramatically flew to Jerusalem to address the Israeli Knesset. The ultimate results of this deviation from the path the Carter administration originally intended to take were the 1978 Camp David Accords and the 1979 Israeli-Egyptian peace treaty, and renewed conflict between Israel, Syria, and the Palestinians in Lebanon. By the end of his term, battered by events in Afghanistan (where the ill-fated Soviet invasion of December 1979 had renewed the chill of the Cold War) and revolutionary Iran, and under fierce criticism from supporters of Israel at home for trying to involve the Palestinians in peacemaking, Carter chose the path of least resistance where Arab-Israeli affairs were concerned. After an innovative beginning, he ended by following his predecessors in excluding the Soviets from the Arab-Israeli negotiating process, negotiating separate bilateral deals, and seeking unilateral advantage in the Middle East for the United States at the expense both of the Soviet Union and of the prospect of a comprehensive, negotiated settlement of the entire Arab-Israeli conflict.[47] The primary casualty of this policy, as in the past, was the slim possibility of a comprehensive just and lasting peace in the Middle East.[48]

The administration of Ronald Reagan continued, and indeed strengthened, the pattern of seeking East-West advantage at the expense of peace in the Middle East. This is just what might have been expected from a highly ideological group of policymakers who greatly intensified the competition with the Soviet Union in a number of spheres, from the arms race to

Afghanistan. Beyond this, the Reagan team sympathized deeply with, and indeed came to share, the Begin government's hard-line approach, which demonstrated a classical colonial mind-set in choosing to see the problem of Palestine entirely through the prism of terrorism.[49] The Israeli approach over time set the tone for more than two decades of disastrously superficial American approaches to a broad range of complex issues in the Middle East, reducing them all to the mindless shibboleth of terrorism. Aside from this poisoned legacy, the centerpiece of the Reagan administration's Middle East policy ended up being the disastrous American involvement in Lebanon, however, and so rather than deal with its actions in this context, I will do so as part of the discussion in the next section of the ruinous impact of the Cold War on the Lebanese conflict.

The last American administration of the Cold War period was that of George H. W. Bush, who with his secretary of state, James A. Baker, reverted to the initial approach of the Carter administration, once again involving the Soviet Union (and after its disappearance, Russia) in the search for a comprehensive solution involving all the parties to the Arab-Israeli conflict. Their initiative was made much easier by the decline and then the demise of the Soviet Union, which effectively ended the Cold War. This meant that although the USSR and later Russia were formally cosponsors of the Madrid peace conference, Soviet and Russian participation was only nominal in a process that in practice was wholly dominated by the United States. Nevertheless, this should not diminish the scope of the accomplishment of Bush and Baker. If Carter and Vance had been the first American statesmen even to attempt a comprehensive approach to all aspects of the Arab-Israeli conflict, Bush and Baker were the first to succeed in actually bringing all the key parties to the table and beginning the negotiating process on all the different Arab-Israeli tracks.

Sadly, the results of the Madrid process were aborted by the shortsightedness and lack of resoluteness of the Bush administration's approach in dealing with the Syrians and especially with the Palestinians, and then by its replacement by the Clinton administration, but Madrid was a significant achievement nonetheless. Never before, not when Britain dominated the region, nor during the Cold War era—which I have argued was a time of veiled American hegemony in many respects—had any power succeeded in getting all the relevant parties to the conflict over Palestine to accept a framework for the negotiating process, and to sit down together at one table, as Bush and Baker did at Madrid in October–November 1991. When and if serious Arab-Israeli peace negotiations resume in the future, they may well do so from the place where the Madrid conference stopped, in spite of the many flaws in the Madrid process.

In retrospect, it is clear that this moment of total American hegemony in the region and the world in the wake of the demise of the Soviet Union, and following the crushing defeat of Iraq in 1991 by an American-led alliance, provided a unique opportunity. This opportunity was greatly amplified by the effect of the first Palestinian intifada on Israeli (and American) public opinion, starting in December 1987. The uprising, a massive outburst of unarmed and largely nonviolent popular resistance, persisted for several years in spite of brutal repression. It ended the myth of Israel's "humane occupation," showed that the Palestinians would not accept their subjugation, and revealed to the Israeli people for the first time the full cost of their continued control of the West Bank and Gaza Strip. Had the George H. W. Bush administration not been poorly advised by deeply conventional and blindly pro-Israeli officials like the ubiquitous Dennis Ross,[50] and had it pushed aggressively and rapidly toward a permanent peace on the Palestinian and Syrian fronts at this decisive moment, the Madrid process might have produced a comprehensive, lasting settlement of the entire conflict. Instead, the only meager issue of the process was the Israeli-Jordanian peace treaty of 1994, and the much praised but ill-fated Palestinian-Israeli Oslo Accords of September 1993, both signed under the aegis of President Bill Clinton after Bush had left office.

Far from being a positive achievement, the Oslo Accords and their sequels have measurably worsened the situation on the ground, have so far allowed for another fifteen years of occupation, conflict, and suffering in Palestine, and have certainly not brought peace to either Palestinians or Israelis. Like all the (very limited) American efforts at Arab-Israeli peacemaking, these accords were nonetheless lavishly praised at the time by the American punditocracy, which characteristically ignored the decades-long Cold War context of constant American (and Soviet) aggravation of the conflict.[51] In spite of all the self-congratulation in Washington, D.C., in fact the Oslo Accords were essentially negotiated secretly between Israel and the PLO (quite incompetently on the Palestinian side)[52] with relatively little input from the United States. But they were nevertheless among the belated fruits of a long-standing American policy of placing advantage for the United States in the Cold War struggle with the USSR at the top of the Middle East agenda, effectively relegating Arab-Israeli peace to a secondary position, tipping the playing field heavily in Israel's favor and in the process severely exacerbating this conflict and several others, notably that in Lebanon.

THE WAR IN LEBANON, 1975–90

When speaking of any specific conflict or crisis involving Lebanon, whether those of the nineteenth, twentieth, or twenty-first centuries, it is always difficult to disentangle the roles played by international, regional, and local factors, since they have so often been interrelated and intertwined. As a highly "penetrated" system, to employ once again the apt term of L. Carl Brown,[53] Lebanon for nearly two centuries has been uniquely susceptible to external influences, which in turn have profoundly affected the country's politics. This was true of the 1860 civil war and massacres, the civil war of 1958, and many other episodes in the country's modern history. In this context, it is not always easy to discern the impact of the Cold War on the brutal Lebanese war of 1975–90. The task is made more difficult by the many actors involved in this complex conflict, and the different ways the conflict has been understood. Primarily a civil war to some, to others the conflict was the direct result of the flagrant intervention of external powers, whether the PLO, Israel, Syria, or myriad others.[54] It is common for some Lebanese and foreign analysts who subscribe to the latter view to ascribe all agency in Lebanon's problems to foreign powers, with the Lebanese themselves left blameless by this reading of Lebanese history and politics. Others assign the primary responsibility for these problems to deep and abiding divisions among the Lebanese, and to their constant pattern of appealing to outsiders to help resolve their differences. The high degree of penetration of the Lebanese system makes resolving this question conclusively one way or another very difficult.

It is nevertheless possible to discern the clear threads of superpower involvement in the war that started in Lebanon in April 1975, and continued through many different stages until 1990. This is easiest with respect to the first phases of the war, because they coincided with a regional and superpower polarization related to the Arab-Israeli conflict that had a clear and direct impact on Lebanon. April 1975 is significant not only because it marks the generally recognized beginning of the war, which was ignited by the massacre on Sunday, April 13, of twenty-seven Palestinians traveling in a bus through the Ain al-Rummaneh suburb of Beirut, dominated by the right-wing Phalanges Party, mainly supported by Maronite Christians, following an attack earlier that day on a church.[55] It is important also because it was when Egypt and Israel concluded the second Sinai disengagement accord brokered by Henry Kissinger.[56] This began a period of acute tension in the Arab world, as Syria and the PLO suspected, quite correctly, as it turned out, that Kissinger had no intention of involving them in any further peacemaking efforts, and that Sadat meant this agreement to be the first step toward a separate peace with Israel, leaving his erstwhile allies in the lurch.

The Soviets had by this point been progressively frozen out of Middle East peacemaking by the shrewd maneuvering of Kissinger, and feared (also rightly, as it turned out) that they were in consequence losing their privileged position in Egypt to the Americans. They were just as suspicious of Kissinger and Sadat as were the Palestinians and Syrians, and proceeded to reinforce their remaining clients' worst fears about the designs of the Americans and the perfidy of Sadat, in part to keep them close to Moscow.[57] This was the background to a conflict in Lebanon that initially pitted the Palestinians, their leftist and Muslim allies in the Lebanese National Movement (LNM), and Syria, all strongly supported by the Soviet Union and its East bloc allies, against right-wing Lebanese parties backed (very discreetly at first) by Israel, Iran, Saudi Arabia, and other states, and supported by the United States.[58]

This conventional Cold War alignment, and the conventional polarization of local and regional forces that went with it, did not last long. For by 1976 Syrian president Hafiz al-Assad had become concerned about the growing strength of the PLO-LNM alliance and its increasing independence of Syria. Most seriously, he feared the possibility that should the Palestinians and their Lebanese allies defeat the right-wing Lebanese parties (whose militias were organized as the Lebanese Forces [LF]), this might provoke Israeli intervention in Lebanon, which Israeli leaders repeatedly threatened. Such an outcome was intolerable to Syria, which would then have had to confront Israeli forces both to its south and its west. Thus Assad turned slowly against his former allies in the PLO-LNM alliance. He first ordered into action against this alliance Palestinian and Lebanese forces obedient to Syria. When that failed to stop the advance of Palestinian and leftist forces against those of the LF in the mountains east of Beirut, in June 1976 Assad finally ordered the intervention of Syrian troops to tip the balance against them.[59] An important element in this major transformation in the Syrian position was the brokering of Syrian intervention in Lebanon by the United States, which perceived a golden opportunity to turn one Soviet client against another and thereby weaken the Arab front aligned with the Soviet Union and against the developing American-Israeli-Egyptian axis.[60] Kissinger played a delicate game here, whereby he assuaged Israeli concerns about Syrian intervention in Lebanon and at the same time reassured the Syrians that there would be no negative Israeli or American reaction if Syrian forces intervened against the PLO and the Lebanese left and stayed north of an east-west line in Lebanon that came to be known as the Red Line.[61]

American policymakers killed a number of birds with this stone. First, they earned a certain measure of Syrian gratitude, in spite of Damascus's pique at the absence of American efforts to broker another disengagement deal with the Israelis along the lines of the second Sinai disengagement agreement of April 1975. Second, they broke up a coalescing bloc of Syria, the PLO, the LNM, and a number of Arab states like Iraq and Libya that were opposed to what were called "separate agreements" with Israel, meaning American-brokered deals that gained unilateral advantage for the United States while ignoring other fronts.

Third, they benefited from helping to turn Syria against the PLO, seen as the most irreducible Arab opponent of American influence and of Israel. Finally, and in some ways most important to Washington, they deeply discomfited the USSR, which saw two of its prime remaining regional allies at each other's throat, and which was thereby put into a thoroughly uncomfortable position.

The Soviets saw perfectly well the game Kissinger was playing, but could not prevent their ally, the Syrian regime, from acting in what it saw was its vital self-interest, even if this did grave harm to other Soviet allies and to the Soviet position in the region. So the Soviets effectively did nothing to halt the Syrian military intervention, and to rescue the Palestinians and their Lebanese allies from the plight they had in some measure gotten themselves into.[62] By the summer of 1976, the PLO and the LNM were besieged in Beirut and the region to its immediate south down to Sidon, cut off by an Israeli naval blockade and surrounded on all other sides without any real backing from the Soviet Union or any other major power.[63] They were at war facing the LF to the north, the Syrian Army to the east, and in the south the Israelis and the proxy force (called the South Lebanon Army) that they were already building up under a renegade Lebanese Army major, Saad Haddad.

The damage that this brutal initial 1975–76 phase of the war, which involved a whole range of external actors as well as Lebanese factions, did to Lebanon, and to the civilian population, Lebanese and Palestinian, was immense. Equally gravely, it set in motion fifteen years of sporadic but often fierce warfare that in the end destroyed large parts of Beirut, consumed the country, shattered its economy and society, and traumatized a generation. One searches in vain for signs that either of the superpowers (or any regional power), tried seriously to halt the carnage at this early stage. Instead, both worked assiduously to gain advantage at the expense of the other, with the Americans in the end making out far better than the Soviets.

A brief lull was finally worked out under Arab League auspices in the fall of 1976, as the Syrians, who had already achieved their basic objectives, were prevented by Saudi Arabia and other Arab states from finishing off the battered PLO and LNM. The respite was brief for Lebanon, however, as the war resumed in different forms and configurations in the succeeding years, with Syrian troops turning around and fighting against their erstwhile allies, the LF, in 1977, and Israeli forces invading to root out the PLO in the southern part of Lebanon in 1978. Sadat's 1977 visit to Jerusalem, the 1978 Camp David Accords, and the 1979 Egyptian-Israeli peace treaty served as the backdrop as the smoldering Lebanese conflict exploded periodically into renewed violence. These events once again polarized the region along Cold War lines, driving the PLO and Syria back into uneasy alignment with each other and with the USSR, and reinforcing the already strong American-Israeli-Egyptian axis. Both of these Cold War–derived groupings found in Lebanon a convenient battlefield.

It would be possible to chart in similar detail how American and Soviet policies driven by Cold War imperatives exacerbated the Lebanese crisis over the next several years, but one more illustration will suffice: the 1982 Israeli invasion of Lebanon and its immediate sequels. It would probably be an exaggeration to say that the 1982 war in Lebanon was a direct result of the renewed Cold War chill that was produced by the Soviet invasion of Afghanistan, and the American response to it, most notably under the new Reagan administration, with its full complement of vintage Cold Warriors. Nevertheless, the much more adversarial relationship between the superpowers, especially in the first years of the Reagan administration, considerably facilitated the decisions of the Begin government and its dominant figure,

Defense Minister Ariel Sharon, to invade Lebanon, with the aim of uprooting and destroying the PLO, eliminating Syrian influence, and creating a Lebanese puppet regime. Gen. Alexander Haig, Reagan's first secretary of state, was much taken by Sharon, by the evidence of his own autobiography, and gave the Israelis the green light they wanted for this ambitious scheme.[64]

What was quite striking in this situation, in which the United States and its powerful ally were telegraphing their aggressive intentions in Lebanon (it was an open secret in Beirut, Washington, and elsewhere in the spring of 1982 that Israel would invade, and the only surprise was exactly when), was how flaccid the Soviet response was. The USSR indeed sent an envoy, Dr. Yevgeni Primakov, an academic, an Arabist, and a senior Communist Party figure, to Beirut in late spring 1982, essentially to convince PLO officials that the USSR had quite limited capabilities and was only able to extend a defensive shield to the territory of Syria itself. He made it absolutely clear to his Palestinian interlocutors that the Soviets did not have the capacity to protect the PLO, Syrian forces in Lebanon, or Lebanon itself when Israel launched its expected attack.[65] Soviet actions once the war started in June 1982 bore out Primakov's words: the Israeli military was able to operate freely against Syrian forces and the PLO in Lebanon, and in all areas of Lebanon. It did so with the full, unstinting support of the United States,[66] ultimately expelling the PLO, occupying much of Lebanon, and helping to install a friendly regime in Beirut under Bashir Gemayel, commander of the LF, all of this without the Soviet Union lifting a finger. This was all portrayed as a great victory over Soviet influence by the Reagan administration, which immediately after the war floated an initiative to resolve the Arab-Israeli conflict on American-Israeli terms, the so-called Shultz initiative (named for the new secretary of state, George P. Shultz), now that the PLO had apparently been crushed, Syria had been defeated, and the Soviet Union had been shown to be a paper tiger. The mood of euphoria and Cold War triumphalism in Washington did not last long, however.

In very short order, Israel's apparent victory in Lebanon and its attempt, together with the Reagan administration, to exploit it to create a permanent structure of power favorable to Western interests in that country and the region both collapsed like a house of cards. Public opinion in the United States was deeply alienated first as Israel bombarded the besieged city of Beirut for weeks on end. The reaction in both Israel and the United States was even more negative after the capture of the city and the departure of the PLO, when Israeli forces in control of the region introduced into refugee camps at Sabra and Shatila members of right-wing Lebanese militias allied with them, who massacred over two thousand unarmed Palestinian and Lebanese civilians. These camps were under Israeli military control, in a city occupied by the Israeli army, and were lit overnight by Israeli army flares as the butchers went about their work.[67] The architect of the Lebanese invasion, Ariel Sharon, lost his post as defense minister in the wake of the conclusions of an official Israeli commission of inquiry, which held him and senior Israeli officers indirectly responsible for the massacre.

Moreover, having driven out the PLO, which had carried out military operations against Israel relatively ineffectually from South Lebanon, Israel soon found itself facing sustained Lebanese armed resistance to its occupation of the Lebanese South. This proved far more tenacious than that of the Palestinians to Israel's occupation of the West Bank and Gaza Strip. For unlike the Palestinians, the Lebanese groups resisting the Israeli occupation had the advantage of open borders with friendly allies, mainly Syria and Iran, which were able to supply copious supplies of weapons and other forms of support. After eighteen years of a bloody and futile rearguard action, Israel was ultimately obliged to withdraw its occupation forces unconditionally from Lebanon in 2000, leaving the south of the country in the hands of a far more formidable military foe than the PLO had ever been. This was Hizballah, an entirely new enemy dedicated to militant armed resistance, an enemy that Israel itself had called into being by its occupation. In the words of Ehud Barak, chief of Israeli Military Intelligence from 1983 to 1985, deputy chief of staff from 1987 to 1991, and chief of staff from then until 1995, who knew well whereof he spoke: "We entered into Lebanon ... [and] Hizbullah was created as a result of our stay there."[68]

Even more quickly, things turned sour for the American and French forces that had landed in Lebanon in August 1982, originally to supervise the withdrawal of the PLO, immediately after which they were precipitously withdrawn. They then returned to cope with the consequences of the massacres at Sabra and Shatila, which the United States had faithlessly promised the PLO to prevent.[69] There they rapidly found themselves confronting the armed hostility of forces representing a large majority of Lebanese. American forces could not prevail, in spite of the full might of the United States, including the American battleship *New Jersey*, which bombarded the Lebanese mountains with its sixteen-inch guns. Ferocious subsequent attacks on these troops (hundreds of U.S. Marines and French paratroopers were killed in simultaneous suicide attacks on their barracks) and on American interests in Lebanon soon broke the political will of the Reagan administration. American and allied troops withdrew ignominiously, bringing an end to the ill-advised attempt to create an American-Israeli client regime in Lebanon, and to tie that country to Israel by a peace treaty imposed on it while it was under Israeli occupation. An American policy driven by Cold War imperatives and based on ignorance of the real forces on the ground had proven utterly bankrupt. It was undermined not by the increasingly enfeebled Soviets, but rather by the savage realities of a Lebanon that had been turned into a battlefield in large measure by the callous machinations of the superpowers and their clients, ruthlessly seeking advantage over one another at the expense of the hapless Lebanese people and Palestinian refugees on their soil.

The PLO, too, suffered from this situation, and from its reliance on its waning superpower patron. In the last years of the Cold War, the Soviet Union had gravely exacerbated strained relations with the United States by its doomed invasion of Afghanistan, thereby helping to bring into office a ferociously anti-Soviet American president, Ronald Reagan. When the United States reacted vigorously in a variety of realms, among them via support for Israel's 1982 invasion of Lebanon to destroy the PLO, the USSR thereupon showed itself so feeble that it could not even extend serious support to one of its few remaining Middle Eastern clients in a moment of its greatest need. It once again let down the PLO, as it had in 1976 when the Palestinians confronted Syria.

Although the Cold War was winding down, and the Soviet Union was on its last legs, to the uninitiated it may still have appeared like a serious rival to the United States. No one who experienced the ten-week Israeli siege of Beirut in 1982, as I did, would ever have made that mistake. Thus, only for those who could not see the Soviet weakness revealed in Beirut in 1982, and in many other Middle Eastern contexts—in other words, only for those blinded by preconceptions and ideology—was the collapse of the USSR in 1989–90 a surprise. This collapse took place at a particularly crucial moment in the evolution of another Middle Eastern arena where the Soviet Union's Cold War policies and those of its American rival had gravely exacerbated events, the conflict between Iran and Iraq.

THE IRAN-IRAQ CONFLICT

As I showed in earlier chapters, the involvement of the Soviet Union and the United States in Iran go back to the beginnings of the Cold War and before. After the American-British-initiated coup that brought down the elected Mosaddeq government and reinstalled the autocratic Mohammad Reza Shah in 1953, American influence predominated in Iran for the next quarter century, as part of a policy driven largely by Cold War considerations. This deep and long-lasting American intervention in Iran's internal affairs, the close relations between Washington and Tehran under the last shah, and the latter's dependence on the United States in a number of spheres became constants of Middle Eastern politics, and determined alignments and political dispositions throughout the region. The importance of this alignment can be deduced from the fact that the 1979 collapse of the American policy constructed on the foundation of the shah's precarious regime has continued to produce regional and global reverberations over the decades until the present day. A whole generation of American policymakers was traumatized by it, as was American public opinion, with the 444-day crisis involving American diplomats being held hostage in Tehran an ongoing sore point. Iranians were at least as severely affected, if not more so, by the close U.S. relationship with the hated shah, and the hostility from Washington that followed his disappearance.

Iraq was an entirely different matter. A state created on Ottoman foundations but in its modern form by British colonialism in the 1920s, it had been a pillar of British regional power for decades. After the 1958 revolution overthrew the monarchy and ended paramount British influence in Iraq, however, both the Soviet Union and the United States became much more deeply involved there. The Soviets at this point had a major ally in Iraq in the powerful Iraqi Communist Party, one of the biggest and most active in the Arab world.[70] This party had played a central role in the popular opposition to the hated British-supported monarchy, and came to exercise strong influence in the regime of Brig. Gen. Abdul Karim Kassem, which emerged from the 1958 coup.

Given the Cold War environment prevailing in Washington, the strength of the Iraqi Communist Party was inevitably a source of abiding concern to American policymakers. As elsewhere, they developed ties to forces that were seen as capable of opposing local Communists, in the case of Iraq most notably the Iraqi Ba'th Party. In the internecine conflict between the two parties that reached a peak of intensity during the Kassem regime from 1958 until 1963, and that continued without respite thereafter, the CIA provided information to the Ba'thists that helped them to arrest and kill thousands of Iraqi Communists during a brief period when the Ba'th Party was precariously in power, from February until August 1963.[71] The ferocious competition between the Iraqi Ba'th Party and the Iraqi Communist Party continued for decades, and although whenever the Ba'thists were in power they were occasionally obliged to allow the Communists to operate under tight constraints, they denied them any access to real decision-making.

Once the Ba'th Party took firm control in Baghdad in July 1968, dominating the country for the next thirty-five years with a fist of iron, Iraq's relations with Washington tended to be a function of the competition between the superpowers, and of the balance of power between Iraq and its traditional regional rival, Iran. Following the 1958 revolution, Iraq was generally aligned with Moscow against Iran, which as we have seen was closely linked to Washington until the 1979 Islamic Revolution. Under Ba'th rule from 1968 onward, this pattern generally continued. In the on again, off again confrontations between Iran and Iraq, therefore, there eventually developed the same kind of Cold War polarization that characterized the Arab-Israeli conflict from the 1960s onward, with Iran firmly aligned with the United States, and Iraq with the Soviets.

In supporting their clients against one another, both superpowers used all available means, as they did elsewhere. Thus, in the mid-1970s, the shah of Iran cynically exploited and covertly supported a rebellion against the Baghdad government by the Iraqi Kurds as a means of exerting pressure on his Iraqi rivals. As we saw in chapter 1, the United States supported this approach with its own covert assets (as did Israel[72]), and then looked on coldly as the shah dropped the Kurds once he had achieved his aims with the 1975 Algiers agreement. Needless to say, this allowed the Ba'thist regime to extract its brutal revenge completely unhindered against Iraqi Kurdish civilians, whose leaders had mistakenly come to rely on their Iranian, American, and Israeli patrons. It is important to recognize that there was no particular animus toward the Kurds in Kissinger's dismissal of an aide's shocked reaction at this betrayal with the words quoted in chapter 1: "Covert action should not be confused with missionary work."[73] This was just part of the Cold War game, as a major client dropped its minor client and the superpower patron looked on impassively. Kurdish civilians paid most of the price for their people's being dragged into this great-power game, as they did again and again in subsequent years, for example in the savage gassings at Halabja and elsewhere during the Iran-Iraq War and in the brutal suppression of the Kurdish revolt against the Ba'th regime after the 1991 Gulf War. The fact that this price was in some measure inflicted as a result of the cold instrumentalism of American and Soviet Cold War policies, and those of the clients they armed and supported, is rarely acknowledged in the sanctimonious cant about the sufferings of the Kurdish people that has been heard in Washington in recent years.

In a similarly callous fashion, the USSR never at any stage allowed the Iraqi Ba'th regime's deep anticommunism, or its almost unremittingly brutal treatment of Iraqi Communists, to interfere with Moscow's generally good relations with the Ba'th regime. Strategic Cold War imperatives that involved countering the United States were clearly far more important to the Soviet leaders than protecting their Iraqi comrades from Saddam Hussein's murderous henchmen. Such Soviet behavior was not, of course, restricted to Iraq. One can follow the contortions of Soviet ideologists who attempted in a whole body of ostensibly academic literature to demonstrate the "progressive" nature of regimes such as the Iraqi, the Egyptian, and the Syrian—in spite of these regimes' often anticommunist domestic policies and sometimes savage repression of their respective communist parties—in order to justify the USSR's Cold War–driven alignment with them.[74] It is not a pretty picture. The wonder is that so many Communists in these countries were able to maintain their faith in Marxist-Leninist ideology and their loyalty to the USSR in spite of the cold, unideological, realpolitik nature of Soviet policy.[75]

Even more cynical behavior by both superpowers followed the Iranian Revolution. This upheaval, which took place under the slogan "neither East nor West," and marked a serious attempt by the new Iranian Islamic regime to follow a nonaligned path between the superpowers, deeply discomfited both Washington and Moscow. As we have seen, American policy under the Nixon-Kissinger strategy of "Vietnamization" had counted on building up powerful regional allies that could play the role of proxies after direct American intervention in different parts of the world became more difficult in the wake of the Vietnam debacle. I have already pointed out that Iran under the shah was a key Middle Eastern pillar of this strategy, and that the collapse of his regime was an extraordinarily telling blow to American policy in that region and to American prestige worldwide.

The virulence of the anti-Americanism that had been building up in Iran as a reaction to over a quarter century of unceasing American interference in Iranian domestic affairs was
symbolized by the humiliating treatment of American diplomats who were held hostage in Tehran for over a year after
the Islamic Revolution. Understandably, this cruel behavior
shocked and angered Americans, who knew little of their country's unpopular history of systematic meddling in Iran. The
hostage crisis set in train a popular hostility against Iran and Islam in American public opinion that, far from abating in the intervening decades, has only been exacerbated by subsequent
events. At the level of American policymakers, there were fears
that Iran would spread its Islamic revolution to neighboring
countries, including key American clients with Shi'a populations on the southern shores of the Gulf, notably Saudi Arabia,
Kuwait, and Bahrain. Finally, revolutionary Iran, as a major oil
producer, played a militant role in pushing prices upward in the
oil-producing cartel, the Organization of Petroleum Exporting
Countries (OPEC). All of this caused Washington to look with
serious dismay on the new regime in Tehran, and to display con-
sistent hostility toward it after the 1979 Islamic Revolution.

The Soviet Union was no less concerned and no less hostile.
Iran under the shah had been a major American client, but the
monarch's relations with the Soviet Union had generally been
correct. The shah indeed had purchased military equipment
from the USSR, benefiting from favorable prices and the sim-
plicity and reliability of some Soviet weapons systems. At the
same time, he intentionally provoked the concern of Washington and prodded it to be more forthcoming in meeting Iranian
arms requests. Moscow now found, to its consternation, that
in place of a conservative regime that rigorously suppressed the
Iranian Communist Party, the Tudeh, but was not aggressive toward the Soviet Union, Iran was now dominated by a fiercely

ideological religious regime that was viscerally hostile to communism and the USSR, and even more savagely repressed the Tudeh party than had the shah. Even worse, and most ominously, the new Islamic regime threatened to proselytize Muslims in the southern republics of the USSR with its fervent anticommunist religious radicalism. Soviet policymakers were also concerned that revolutionary Iran would complicate the USSR's already difficult situation in neighboring Afghanistan to the east, where Soviet troops faced an uphill struggle, and that the regime of Ayatollah Ruhollah Khomeini might destabilize the USSR's ally in Ba'thist Iraq to the west. For the Soviets, the Islamic revolutionary regime projected threatening instability in all directions.

The two status-quo-oriented superpowers, essentially conservative in many respects, were thus both horrified by the radical anti-American and anti-Soviet revolutionary zeal of the new regime. Both acted decisively to rein it in. In the absence of unimpeachable evidence, we can only guess at the covert activities they may have engaged in, together with their allies, to sabotage the new Islamic regime in Tehran.[76] In the more public realm, however, it was common knowledge that American policymakers and their client regimes in the Arab world strongly encouraged Iraqi leader Saddam Hussein in his ill-advised 1980 attack on Iran, which sparked an eight-year war that proved catastrophic for both countries.[77]

The United States and its European allies extended various forms of support to the Iraqi war effort, including the United States removing Iraq from the list of state sponsors of terrorism in March 1982. This made Iraq eligible to purchase a wide range of high-tech "dual-use" items, including weapons, and thereafter with its allies West Germany and France provided some of the technology necessary for Iraq to produce internationally banned weapons, notably poison gas. Equally important, the

United States and its Western allies protected Iraq from suffering any international sanctions when it used these illegal weapons against both Iranian forces and its own Kurdish population. This is clear from official U.S. government documents that detail American support for Iraq in this period, notably acquiescence in its use of chemical weapons, obtained by the National Security Archive. These documents include accounts of the support extended personally to Saddam Hussein during two visits to Baghdad in December 1983 and March 1984 by American presidential envoy Donald Rumsfeld.[78] Additionally, during the war the CIA "provided intelligence for Iraq to use against Iran," most likely in the form of satellite photographs of Iranian military dispositions.[79]

The Soviet Union at the same time was offering absolutely essential military support to the Iraqi war effort. The Soviets provided the bulk of the vast supply of imported weapons and munitions that Iraq used in its eight-year war with Iran. These weapons purchases led to Iraq running up a nearly $13-billion debt to Moscow.[80] Iraq itself manufactured some Soviet-designed weapons in factories provided by the USSR, mainly light arms, as well as much of the ammunition it expended. Importantly, Moscow also carefully refrained from condemning Iraq's massive employment of poison gas on the battlefield, the first time any state had employed it since fascist Italy did so in Ethiopia in 1936. Iran soon responded in kind, and with the use by both powers of these appalling weapons, a major barrier to the utilization of so-called weapons of mass destruction had fallen.[81] The collusion of the superpowers and their allies was essential to preventing the United Nations from acting to halt Iraq's initial employment of poison gas in violation of this important international restraint on barbarism in warfare, or to prevent Iran's later use of similar means.

Even as it was massively arming Iraq, the USSR also supplied arms to Iran, notably replacements for those purchased under the shah, as well as some new weapons systems. Equally cynically, and perhaps even more surprising, the Reagan administration secretly supplied Iran with American weapons and spare parts, including TOW antitank missiles, Hawk antiaircraft missiles, and spare parts, both directly and via America's ally Israel. This harebrained scheme was part of the amateurish arms-for-hostages diplomacy run out of the White House basement by Lt. Col. Oliver North and his coconspirators. The entire sordid and illegal scheme was later exposed and developed into the Iran-Contra scandal, when it was revealed that the proceeds from these sales were used to finance covert operations in Nicaragua against the express intent of legislation passed by Congress.[82] At the same time as the CIA was providing similar information to the Iraqis, it also offered Iran "battlefield intelligence for the war against Iraq" as part of the Iran-Contra deal.[83]

In the case of both the USSR and the United States, a similar hostility toward what they saw as the destabilizing radicalism of the new Islamic regime in Tehran drove their policies, in particular the basic support of both for Iraq. At the same time, the contradictory policies that led both to extend some support to Iran were also driven by their obsessive rivalry with each other, and by the fear of each that the other might secure a decisive advantage with either of the two combatant powers. In fact, a reported remark of Henry Kissinger's, that the ideal outcome for the United States would have been for both powers to lose, may best have reflected the true basis of the tortuous policies of Washington and Moscow.[84]

The duplicitous support of both superpowers for both sides in this savage eight-year war was a particularly sordid result of the uncompromising rivalry that finally ended with the demise of both the USSR and the Cold War, only a couple of years after the Iran-Iraq War came to an end. In the Middle East, the

superpower rivalry had significant direct and indirect consequences, exacerbating, sharpening, and intensifying regional
conflicts, and fueling them with massive amounts of sophisticated and deadly armaments. Most of the estimated 1 million
casualties suffered by both sides in the Iran-Iraq War were inflicted by weapons delivered by the two superpowers, in sales
from which both profited handsomely. The same was undoubtedly the case for the weapons used to inflict most of the casualties in the other two Middle Eastern conflicts I have surveyed (in
which the total number of casualties on all sides was considerably smaller than in the Iran-Iraq War).

The harm inflicted by the weapons they manufactured and
sold was only one indication of the cost of the superpower rivalry, a cost that is rarely weighed when either the Cold War or
these conflicts are analyzed. This chapter has shown part of the
price paid by the peoples of the Middle East when their region
became a premier battlefield of the Cold War. But this price was
not only paid in the form of the worsening and prolongation of
conflicts in the Middle East. Just as peace in different parts of
this highly penetrated region was probably measurably retarded
by the superpowers' adoption of local conflicts as proxy wars in
their duel with each other, so was the political evolution of the
countries of the region. These countries paid a high price in this
realm as well, in the form of the distortion of their political systems, the sabotaging of democracy, and the curtailment of human rights.

V

THE COLD WAR AND THE
UNDERMINING OF DEMOCRACY

Since World War II, there has been halting but nonetheless significant progress toward establishing democratic, constitutional regimes in many areas of the globe. One region, however, stands out as a glaring exception to the general picture of the gradual spread of democratic systems worldwide. This region is the Middle East, which for nearly half a century has been an almost universally bleak desert as far as the development of vibrant, full-fledged democratic systems is concerned. The very few exceptions to this rule are themselves hedged around with conditions.[1] All that has seemed to thrive in recent years in this vast zone of undemocratic governance stretching from the Atlantic to the Caucasus and the frontiers of Pakistan and Afghanistan have been autocracies, kleptocracies, absolute monarchies, and other forms of despotic and authoritarian rule, some covered with a transparent fig-leaf of sham "democratic" forms.

Indeed, in some respects the situation is palpably worse today in many Middle Eastern countries than it was in the 1940s and 1950s, when various forms of parliamentary democracy, albeit marred by significant flaws in each case, obtained in Egypt, Syria, Lebanon, Iraq, and Iran, as well as in Turkey and Israel. At that time, it appeared as if countries in the Middle East might have the possibility of continuing to evolve toward more democratic forms of governance. That has certainly not been the case in the intervening decades down to the present. By contrast, many areas of Latin America, East Asia, Southeast Asia, and even some parts of Africa, all of which were bywords for arbitrary, or autocratic, or otherwise undemocratic governance for the first decades of the postindependence period after 1945, are today characterized by new and often thriving democracies, reinforced by economic growth, the expansion of new middle classes, and the growing maturity of constitutional institutions.

With little or no serious historical or other scholarly underpinning, a plethora of commentaries purport to ascribe the undemocratic nature of most current Middle Eastern regimes to something inherent in Islam, the predominant religion in the region. These ahistorical, essentialist, and occasionally borderline-racist theories (of the genre "Muslims are incapable of...") are belied by the growth of democracy, albeit often in a troubled fashion, in large majority-Muslim countries like Indonesia, Malaysia, and Nigeria. They are belied as well by the lengthy history of struggles for democracy and constitutionalism in Middle Eastern countries between the latter part of the nineteenth century and the middle of the twentieth. These go back to the Ottoman constitutional periods from 1876 to 1878 and 1908 to 1918; the struggle between the autocratic Egyptian khedive and an assembly that insisted on more power in the 1870s and until 1882; and the first Iranian constitutional period from 1905 to 1911. While none of these efforts were ultimately successful, they reveal the attraction of democratic and constitutional ideals for the elites and many of the people of this region. These struggles to achieve more democratic governance continued under the sometimes unstable parliamentary regimes that lasted in more than a half-dozen Middle Eastern countries for many decades during the twentieth century. Very rarely, if ever, over the years down to World War II did the European great powers use their influence in favor of democracy or constitutionalism in these countries. They often did quite the opposite, subverting democracy, aligning with autocrats, and preventing free expression of public opinion.[2] Notwithstanding all of this evidence for the compatibility of democracy with Islamic societies, and the establishment, albeit sometimes temporary and sometimes checkered, of democratic systems in the Middle East over several generations since the 1870s, there clearly is a serious problem today where democracy is concerned in most of that region.

In some measure, that problem has to do with some of the well-known obstacles to democratic governance: much of the Middle East is certainly affected by having powerful states with a tradition of strong rulers; elites loath to give up their privileges or their control of the political system; high levels of poverty and illiteracy in some sectors in certain countries; and weak political parties, unions, and professional associations. In an earlier era, the Middle East also suffered from the constant interference of European powers, some of which, like absolutist tsarist Russia, were ideologically opposed to democracy in any form, and all of which tended to undermine democratic regimes whenever these obstructed their economic or strategic interests. In the case of the Middle East, a region that was subject to a very high degree of such external intervention, this was a particular problem for the Ottoman and Persian constitutional experiments and for democratic governance in Egypt, Syria, Iraq, Iran, and a number of Middle Eastern countries thereafter. These and other specific obstacles certainly prevented greater progress toward democracy before World War II, and have done so again over the past sixty-five years.

Like most historians, I hesitate to offer a single explanation for a multidimensional problem like the retarded growth of democracy in a region as vast and varied as the Middle East over so long a period. Nevertheless, it is worth considering whether the Cold War, which I have tried to show in preceding chapters played a particularly important role in the Middle East, may have been a factor that contributed to this bleak situation. For the Cold War was only another episode in this region's recent history of being a target for external intervention, which rendered it, to use L. Carl Brown's term once again, a highly "penetrated" system for more than two hundred years.[3] And as I showed in the previous chapter, the Cold War seriously exacerbated the conflicts that erupted in that region between 1945 and 1990. This in turn intensified the wars that scarred the Middle East during most of this period, and that still persist there.

Often these conflicts and the wars they engendered have been described as if they were sui generis, as if they were all age-old, particularly complex, and particularly resistant to analysis in terms of standard categories. Even cursory examination shows that this is simply not the case: the Iran-Iraq and Arab-Israeli conflicts, to take the two most prominent examples, far from having been ongoing since time immemorial, are essentially products of the twentieth century. The fact that the current protagonists (for complex reasons having to do with the obsessive need of modern nationalisms to manufacture ancient roots) quite arbitrarily choose to look back to Abraham and Moses, the Jebusites and the Israelites, the Sassanians and the Umayyads, and the Safavids and the Ottomans in framing their disputes does not make this any less the case, or these far-fetched parallels any more correct. For all their undoubted complexity, these and most other conflicts in the region, like that over the western Sahara, or between Libya and Chad, or in Sudan or the Horn of Africa, or those involving the Kurds or Lebanon, are essentially common, garden-variety outcomes of colonization, the arbitrary drawing of boundaries by the colonial powers, the decolonization process, and the rise of nation-state nationalism. Similar conflicts, with similar roots, can be found in every region of the formerly colonized world.

Moreover, Middle Eastern countries have witnessed precisely the same processes whereby war has led to the strengthening of the executive authority at the expense of other branches of government and at the expense of the citizenry and its rights, which is well known to have operated in countries in other regions. For examples, one need only think of the governments of Woodrow Wilson, David Lloyd George, and Georges Clemenceau in World War I, or of Franklin Delano Roosevelt and Winston Churchill during World War II, or of George W. Bush after September 11, 2001. Of the Middle East, as of any other region of the world, one can say with James Madison that "war is in fact the true nurse of executive aggrandizement."[4] If this is true in countries with old and well-established constitutional systems like Britain, the United States, and France, it is all the more the case in the Middle East, where there is such a strong tradition of powerful executive authority, a tradition that stretches back to the very first states and empires in human history, established there well over six millennia ago. So in the wars and nagging conflicts that have afflicted this region since World War II, wars whose flames I have shown in the preceding chapter were often fanned by the superpowers in their heated competition with each other, and that reinforced an already strong tradition of executive monopolization of power, we have one possible cause of the retardation of the spread of democracy in the Middle East over the past sixty years or so. There were other causes.

In his perceptive analysis of the Cold War in the third world, historian Odd Arne Westad describes the core motivations that drove the efforts of the United States and the Soviet Union in their global endeavors and in their competition with each other as the quests for "liberty" and "justice," respectively.[5] Thus, Westad argues, the United States saw itself as leading an "Empire of Liberty," self-described as the "free world," while the USSR claimed that it led an "Empire of Justice," self-described as the "socialist camp." By this he meant that each proclaimed that in its global policies it was seeking to represent and spread these core ideals. For Americans, according to Westad, spreading liberty meant above all things fostering private enterprise and individual freedom, and the conditions for maximizing these freedoms. For Soviet ideologists, the extension of justice meant essentially progress toward social justice and freedom from economic exploitation. For each, other ideals and rights were entirely secondary to these core goals.

In their competition in the third world, the two superpowers were in some measure faithful to their core ideals, as they understood them. The United States saw as its primary task keeping developing countries from succumbing to the blandishments of communism and thus being excluded from the free-market system, which it saw as the sine qua non of true liberty. "Freedom" in the American lexicon thus meant primarily a free-market economic system, freedom to choose, freedom to consume, markets that were freely accessible to American manufactured goods, the free production of primary products that the advanced industrial economies needed, and American freedom to invest the world over, and to repatriate the profits of such investment. In general, American policymakers had concluded, such policy goals were best achieved by alignment with the wealthy local elites in these developing countries.

The Cold War was not the first time American decision-makers had recited such a free-market mantra abroad. The same principles had earlier been espoused by the United States in its relations with the countries of the Caribbean and Latin America, and they found an echo in the "open door" policy of the United States toward China. The antecedent of these American ideas, of course, was the espousal of free trade by Great Britain over the centuries when its global dominance in the fields of finance capital, trade, and industry meant that "free trade" necessarily translated into considerable advantage for British economic interests, and was a pillar of the hegemony of the liberal British Empire.[6] Even before the United States achieved comparable ascendance in these fields, American business elites perceived the advantage this form of freedom would give their interests, especially in small or weak countries.

In the period antecedent to World War II, in spite of occasional lip service to the need to promote democracy in the world, neither Great Britain nor the United States had interpreted this doctrine to mean that they were necessarily obliged to make strenuous efforts where democracy in Asia, the Middle East, Africa, and Latin America was concerned. Unspoken, but just beneath the surface, was the belief that the world's darker peoples were not "fit" for democracy, at least not without lengthy supervision by their richer, whiter, and more powerful big brethren. Such thinking lay behind the Mandate system for former colonies of the defeated powers championed by Woodrow Wilson after World War I and incorporated into Article 22 of the Covenant of the League of Nations, which stated that the "tutelage of such peoples should be entrusted to the advanced nations."[7]

By contrast, the Soviet Union worked diligently to encourage socialism and other redistributive approaches to the economy in the developing countries under its influence as a means of reducing social inequalities. "Justice" for the Soviets meant the end of European colonialism and economic exploitation by the Western capitalist economies, the end of exploitation by the local upper classes in the poor countries of the third world, and a just distribution of resources. All of this, Soviet doctrine taught, could best be achieved through the leadership of the working classes, themselves led by communist parties obedient to the wishes of the first socialist state, the Soviet Union.[8] In the absence of such parties, or where they were suppressed, the USSR eventually tried to align itself with forces or regimes at least nominally committed to these goals. This abandonment of a strict reliance on disciplined, obedient Communists to advance this "justice" agenda was begun reluctantly and hesitantly at first, and with many tergiversations, under Stalin.[9] Soviet support of the Chinese Nationalists in the late 1920s was one of the first examples of this shift. It was later continued with somewhat fewer inhibitions under Stalin's successors, as with the exception of East and Southeast Asia it became apparent that there were very few regions in the developing world where communist parties had any chance of coming to power.[10]

Whatever else one might say about the superpowers, and whatever else they may have claimed, both of them did strive to uphold their core values of liberty and justice, as they understood them, as long as this did not interfere with their other goals. It is important to recognize, however, that throughout the Cold War neither the goal of "liberty" nor that of "justice," as American and Soviet policymakers interpreted these terms, included a core commitment to the promotion in the third world of democracy per se, or of human and other rights. This was the case although both claimed to be paragons of democracy at home and in their alliances in Europe (with the "free world" on one side of the iron curtain, and "people's democracies" on the other), and although both occasionally used the language of rights, which in the American case came to be heard more frequently toward the end of the Cold War. Whatever their record elsewhere—and in advanced capitalist states like those of Western Europe and Japan after World War II, the United States certainly did promote democracy, even as it advanced the core free-market components of its "liberty" agenda—there is little if any evidence that at any stage during the Cold War either superpower made the promotion of democracy a central tenet of its third world policies. They certainly did not do so in the Middle East, where superpower meddling in the internal affairs of the countries of the region often served exactly the opposite purpose.

THE SUBVERSION OF
IRANIAN DEMOCRACY

Iran is perhaps the quintessential case of both superpowers not only failing to promote, but actually undermining, Middle Eastern democracy in their headlong pursuit of their strategic and economic objectives. Throughout its modern history, Iran had suffered from the heavy-handed interference of external powers in its internal affairs, including repeated episodes of being occupied in whole or in part by tsarist Russian, imperial British, and American and Soviet troops. These foreign interventions included the notorious efforts of Russia and the British to sabotage the constitutional regime and the elected Majlis, or Assembly, in the years after the 1905–6 Constitutional Revolution. These efforts were finally crowned with success, ending in the closing of the Majlis and the suspension of the Constitution in favor of the renewed absolutism of a puppet shah during the 1911 Russian occupation of Tehran and northern Iran and the British occupation of the south of the country. In another episode already discussed, a later ruler, Reza Shah Pahlavi, was dethroned by the British and Soviets in 1941 for having pro-Axis sympathies and replaced by his son Mohammad Reza Shah. This occurred when their two countries jointly occupied Iran once again after the Soviet entry into World War II had been precipitated by Hitler's invasion of Russia. The bitter experience of repeated, often concerted, intervention in Iranian internal affairs by the great powers to their north and south was deeply imprinted on Iranians in general, and in particular on the generation of democratic and nationalist politicians like Mohammad Mosaddeq who led the Majlis that came to dominate Iranian politics in the later stages of World War II and in the immediate postwar years.

I have shown in chapter 2 that Iran was the site where the

forces of the United States and the Soviet Union first came into direct contact during World War II, as by 1942 both countries, together with Britain, had troops in joint occupation of Iran. Moreover, as I have also shown, the nascent superpowers very quickly entered into a rivalry in and over Iran because of the country's vital strategic position and its valuable oil resources. This rivalry drove most of what both sides did in the Middle East in the years that followed and until the end of the Cold War. The impact on Iranian domestic politics, and ultimately for the fate of the precarious democratic experiment in Iran, was disastrous.

In the initial stage of the postwar superpower competition over Iranian resources and over strategic position in the country, however, Great Britain maintained its traditional influence in Tehran, and its paramountcy in the vital south of the country, where Iran's oil fields were located. The Soviet attempt to obtain oil concessions or, failing that, surreptitiously explore for oil in the north, as well as the USSR's reluctance to withdraw its wartime occupation forces when the war was over, all described in chapter 2, were probably driven largely by Stalin's long-standing obsession with the British. This obsession went back to the Russian Civil War that erupted just after the Bolshevik Revolution. At that time, Stalin was in charge of Soviet forces in the southern parts of the former tsarist domains in their struggle against the British and the counterrevolutionary White Army, which Britain was supporting in an effort to strangle the revolution in its cradle. The fact that his old antagonist of more than twenty years earlier, Winston Churchill, that inveterate anti-Soviet Cold Warrior before his time, was back in control of British Near East policy from 1940 onward, could only have reinforced Stalin's already intense paranoia about the British.

Crucially, there was now a new situation in Tehran that neither the Soviets, nor the British and Americans, fully took into account in the years that followed. This situation was created by the Allied powers' 1941 removal of Reza Shah, formerly an officer in the Cossack Brigade who had been the founder of the modern Iranian state, and of the short-lived Pahlavi dynasty. In the 1920s Reza Shah had taken advantage of the preoccupation elsewhere of both the British and the Soviets to expel the feeble Qajar dynasty and establish a new autocratic order at the expense of a tame and weakened Majlis. The disappearance of the overbearing Reza Shah and his replacement by his weak-willed young son Mohammad Reza Shah in 1941 had given free rein to the Majlis to exercise the power that since 1906 had frequently been denied to it by the autocratic bent of the rulers of the Qajar and Pahlavi dynasties, and by the incessant interference of foreign powers. During World War II, the Majlis had shown its new power by rejecting an oil concession to the USSR, and again, after Soviet occupation forces had withdrawn, by supporting the Iranian prime minister's effort to crush the autonomous regions that had been established in Iranian Azerbaijan and Kurdistan with the support of Soviet troops. In 1946 the Majlis again rejected a Soviet request for an oil concession in the north of the country.

Even before the war ended, the Majlis was thus exercising its power, which Iranian leaders felt was constrained in particular at this stage by the blackmail of the Soviets. As we have seen, the latter had demanded an oil concession in an area controlled by their troops, troops that at the same time were preventing central government forces from putting down the insurrections in the north and bringing under control the Azeri and Kurdish autonomous regions that the Soviets had fostered. Iran, together with other southern neighbors of the Romanov Empire, had frequently been pressured by Moscow in this way before 1917. However, we have seen that the 1921 treaty with the new Soviet

state, which was extremely weak at this early stage of its existence, had for two decades relieved Iran from most forms of
pressure from the north. Now, after two decades of relative
quiet on its northern borders, and after the Allies had deposed
the shah—his departure had not displeased democratically inclined Iranians, who had suffered under his autocratic rule—
Iranians found themselves facing the same kind of pressure and
bullying from the newly powerful Soviet Union as they once had
faced from tsarist Russia.

With the withdrawal of all foreign troops from Iran by 1946,
internal conditions in the country evolved further. In this fluid
situation, the new shah proved completely unable to impose his
authority as his autocratic father had once done, and the representative Majlis rapidly filled the vacuum. The Majlis and the
Iranian prime ministers who answered to it now had free rein to
stand up not only to the Soviets, but also to the other great
power that had traditionally dominated Iran, Great Britain.
This proved to be a more daunting task than facing down the
Soviets had been, particularly since in 1945–46 the other two
concerned powers, the United Kingdom and the United States,
had strongly backed Iran in its resistance to Stalin's bullying.
There was no great power backing it this time. The showdown
came, not surprisingly, over oil once again. It developed in 1951
after the Majlis, now led by Mohammad Mosaddeq, a popular
nationalist prime minister whose government enjoyed a large
parliamentary majority, was stymied in its attempt to extract a
better profit-sharing deal from the British, who still maintained
their virtually absolute control over the production of Iranian
oil. At Mosaddeq's urging, the Iranian assembly responded by
voting to nationalize Iran's oil resources. It thereby undid the
effect of the unequal ninety-nine-year concession obtained by
William Knox D'Arcy in 1901, which had thereafter been purchased and controlled by the British government in the form of
the Anglo-Iranian Oil Company (AIOC).[11]

During the interwar period, Reza Shah had tried and failed to obtain a better deal for Iran's oil, and the postwar nationalization of the AIOC was initially seen as a great coup for the constitutional regime, which appeared to have succeeded where the autocratic shah had failed. Thereupon Britain, unwilling to contemplate losing the oil resources its empire had depended on for over forty years, began a concerted campaign to undo Iran's action. This involved persuading world oil companies not to buy nationalized Iranian oil (the major American oil companies, having recently suffered from the Mexican oil nationalization, abhorred the idea of producing countries nationalizing "their" assets, and so needed little persuasion to join the boycott). It also involved using Britain's considerable influence inside Iran, built up over many decades of cultivating clients, supporters, agents, and spies, to covertly undermine Mosaddeq's government and the constitutional regime. The Iranian government argued in vain to world public opinion that a British Labour government had only a few years earlier nationalized its *own* coal and steel industries and its railways from private owners. Why could Iran not do the same with its own resources? It was clear from the frosty response from London that what was sauce for the British goose was not sauce for the Iranian gander.[12]

As often happens to countries dealing with the United States during an electoral cycle, the Iranians proved to be unlucky when administrations changed in Washington, D.C., in January 1953. Although the Truman administration had been generally sympathetic to the concerns of its British ally, like that of Roosevelt it was also motivated by residual anticolonial impulses and by a vague sympathy with anticolonial nationalism in the third world. Moreover, at home Truman had had his own problems with big business, and in particular with the big oil companies, and he was not overly inclined to favor them abroad.[13] All of this changed when the Republicans took over the American executive branch for the first time in twenty years, after Truman's defeat in the 1952 elections. The new Eisenhower administration was highly favorable to business interests, and to the oil companies in particular. Moreover, Eisenhower's secretary of state, John Foster Dulles, had been an international banker who had worked closely with the oil industry. Dulles and his brother Allen, the director of central intelligence, were profoundly anticommunist in outlook, and looked moralistically on any nationalization of private property as natural steps toward the horrors of socialism and communism.

During the Truman administration, the British had repeatedly importuned the United States to join in a sharp rejoinder to the intolerable "insolence" of Mosaddeq. This, the British argued, should take the form of a pro-shah coup d'état, which they were already preparing. Harry Truman and his secretary of state, Dean Acheson, had resisted the idea. But with Eisenhower in office, the Dulles brothers very soon fell in with the plan, and convinced President Eisenhower of the necessity of this drastic step. The pretext that the British used to convince John Foster and Allen Dulles, and that they in turn used to convince the president, was the alleged danger of Iran falling into communist hands. A Communist Iran was in fact quite a far-fetched prospect, given the relative weakness of the pro-Soviet Iranian Communist Party (the Tudeh) the breadth of the nationalist coalition that supported Mossadeq, and the fear with which Iranian nationalists across the political spectrum regarded Russia, tsarist or Soviet. Nevertheless, the specter of Iranian reds under the bed was enough to scare Washington, which finally went along with British urgings. The result was Operation Ajax, the joint CIA/M16 overthrow of Iran's elected, constitutional, parliamentary regime in 1953 by the two great democratic Western powers. It was replaced with the despotism of Mohammad Reza Shah, directly behind which stood both of these powers, although the Americans, with their far more extensive re-sources, quickly won the upper hand in Tehran.

The Iranian coup was a crucial turning point for the United States in the Middle East, as had been Stalin's unprecedented bullying of Turkey and Iran in 1945–46 for Soviet policy in the region. In a certain peculiar sense, both superpowers had been loyal to their core ideals (if not necessarily their proclaimed ones) even as they intervened in their different ways in Iran's internal affairs. The Soviets claimed they were acting in the name of the "working masses" and of the oppressed nationali-ties of Iranian Azerbaijan and Kurdistan, while the Americans were only upholding the sanctity of private property and the paramountcy of free enterprise. The results were nevertheless traumatic for Iranians and others in the region, and highly dele-terious to one of the oldest and most closely watched exper-iments in democratic and constitutional government in the Middle East. Deep and abiding Iranian fears of Russia and Britain were rekindled, to be joined by what proved to be a last-ing resentment toward the United States.

Even more serious, the leaky ship of evolution toward democracy in Iran had been driven firmly aground, blown there by Stalin's brutal pressure tactics, the cynical cupidity of British policymakers, and the shortsightedness and alarmist gullibility of American decision-makers. The bitter legacy left by these ar-bitrary interventions in Iranian politics, and the subsequent in-tensive American patronage for the hated regime of the shah, would fester for over a quarter of a century. Eventually, with the Iranian Revolution of 1978–79, the inevitable happened, pro-ducing an incandescent eruption of anger at the United States that has continued for many years, and that helped to produce the grim, theocratic regime in power today in Tehran. As might have been expected, the undermining of a shaky but potentially viable liberal, democratic system, first by the USSR and then by the United States and the United Kingdom, two states that were great apostles of liberal and democratic values, naturally produced an authoritarian and illiberal reaction in Iran, just as did similar actions elsewhere in the Middle East, both before and after the Iranian Revolution.

If author Tim Weiner's 2007 chronicle of the CIA's covert actions is to be believed, the 1953 coup was the first major post–World War II American effort at "regime change." It was to be followed in short order by the removal of another democratically elected leader who was no more a communist than had been the hapless Mohammad Mosaddeq: Jacobo Árbenz in Guatemala.[14] This was not to be the last such American effort at government overthrow, but what is most important for our story is that the regime the CIA and MI6 were changing in Tehran was a democratic, constitutional one. Its replacement by an autocratic and repressive regime, pliable and obedient to the wishes of its powerful American backers, became the first element in a pattern where democracy was rarely if ever a consideration for American policymakers in the Middle East, any more than it was for their Soviet opposite numbers, or than it had been for their British predecessors as regional hegemons.

The Iranian coup announced to the entire Middle East that receptiveness to Western economic demands and rigid, knee-jerk anticommunism were the main criteria for those who wanted American support. Regional economic elites quickly got the message and learned to tell the Americans what they wanted to hear. American approval was what these elites themselves generally wanted, in any case: for the other side of this coin was the opportunity to get a share of the profits of the free-market system, and to get American support for repression of their domestic rivals. These rivals could easily be painted as communists or communist sympathizers to a receptive audience in

Washington in situations where an insufficiently threatening number of genuine communists existed, guaranteeing the supportive Western response that local elites desired.

ABORTIVE MIDDLE EASTERN ALLIANCES

While Iran was the first and most important site of superpower interference that undermined the possibility of progress toward stable, democratic governance in the Middle East, it was far from being the last. In the immediate aftermath of World War II, however, most of the external meddling in the Middle East did not come from the superpowers, but rather from the old colonial powers, Britain and France, both of which still retained great residual influence in much of the region. They continued to intervene systematically in the internal affairs of nominally independent countries like Iraq, Jordan, Egypt, Lebanon, and Syria, while they maintained their direct and indirect colonial rule over the other countries of North Africa, the Gulf, and southern Arabia: Morocco, Algeria, Tunisia, Sudan, Libya, Aden, Oman, the Trucial States (now the United Arab Emirates), Bahrain, Qatar, and Kuwait.

We have seen that in addition to Iran, the exceptions to this situation of the lingering predominance of British or French influence included three cases where the superpowers rapidly became involved: these were the 1947–48 great-power maneuvering over the establishment of Israel, the crises in postwar Turkey (and Greece), and Saudi Arabia. In all three cases, one or both of the superpowers became implicated at a very early phase of their rivalry with each other in the Middle East. Indeed in Saudi Arabia this took place even earlier than the inception of the Cold War, with the granting of an oil concession to American companies in 1933. Meanwhile, Saudi Arabia had established diplomatic relations with the Soviet Union in 1926, another example of Ibn Sa'ud's efforts to reduce his kingdom's lingering dependence on Britain.[15] Once they had established their predominant position in all these arenas, the superpowers rapidly elbowed out the old colonial powers. This was true of Iran, Turkey (and Greece), and Saudi Arabia. The only exception was Israel, where after 1948 France and to a lesser degree Britain became the main arms suppliers, and the former retained strong residual influence until the mid-1960s.

As we have seen, Israel owed its existence in large measure to American and Soviet support for the 1947 UN General Assembly resolution for the partition of Palestine and the creation of a Jewish state, and to the superpowers' diplomatic and military support for the new state after it was established in May 1948. Both the United States and the USSR hoped to win Israel to its side, albeit for different reasons. The Soviets were rudely disillusioned when Israel aligned itself with the United States over the Korean War in 1950. Stalin, moreover, had been dismayed at the enthusiastic reception that Golda Meir, the first Israeli ambassador to the USSR, received from Soviet Jews, which awakened the latent anti-Semitic tendencies of the aging and suspicious Soviet leader and his entourage.[16] Israel thereafter drifted into the orbit of France, and later Britain, although U.S. economic and diplomatic support continued, albeit at a relatively low level. As I showed in the preceding chapter, this situation only changed fully after the 1967 war, by which time Israel had become completely aligned with the United States on Cold War and other issues.

Turkey, meanwhile, after the 1945–46 crisis over Stalin's imperious territorial demands, became one of the focal points of the Truman Doctrine, and was incorporated into the North Atlantic Treaty Organization (NATO) soon after the alliance's formation in 1949. Both Israel and Turkey had democratic systems, although in the latter the country's governmental institutions were in the last analysis in the grip of the military and other elements of the state apparatus. Members of this secular elite saw themselves as the true heirs of the founder of the Turkish Republic, Kemal Atatürk, and acted as if they knew better than the electorate, the parliament, or the prime minister what was good for the people and the republic. Acting on these sentiments, the Turkish military was to depose and execute the country's first freely elected prime minister, Adnan Menderes, in 1961, severely setting back the cause of democracy in Turkey. Thus began a series of overt and barely covert interventions by the military and its civilian allies in the government bureaucracy and the judiciary in that country's politics that continues in some measure until the present day. The coup elicited no serious protest from Washington, which appeared to care far more about Turkey's continued international alignment with the United States than about how the country was governed. This lack of interest in democracy on the part of the two superpowers became a common Cold War pattern, and could be seen early on in Saudi Arabia, the first American foothold in the Middle East.

Saudi Arabia, as I described in chapter 2, was the scene of a stroke of good fortune by what eventually became a consortium of the biggest American oil companies when they outbid their British rivals and obtained an exclusive concession to explore for and exploit Saudi oil reserves. We have seen that President Roosevelt and later American presidents highly appreciated the value of this privileged position. As I have already noted in chapter 1, the United States was thereafter careful to ensure that it maintained its paramountcy in Saudi Arabia, establishing an air base at Dhahran in 1945. To this day American policymakers have carefully treated Saudi Arabia and its regime as the major strategic asset that they were and are to the global position of the United States. In spite of the xenophobia of some of the Saudi monarchy's Wahhabi supporters, Saudi Arabia remained untroubled for many years by nationalist agitation against the American connection, which was largely screened off from the view of most of the Saudi public.[17] By the mid-1950s, however, with the spread of modern education and the greater openness of Saudi Arabia to the strong nationalist currents in the rest of the Arab world, the situation began to change. These developments did not impel the ruling family to loosen its absolute grip on political power. Far from encouraging it to do so, the United States fully supported this absolute monarchy in resisting pressures from external sources as well as pressures to liberalize from within Saudi society, particularly after the highly competent King Faisal succeeded his profligate brother Sa'ud in 1962.

As the Cold War developed, the United States and the Soviet Union inexorably became more deeply embroiled in the affairs of other Middle Eastern countries beyond Iran, Israel, Turkey, and Saudi Arabia. The Soviet Union, which had been shut out of the region in the interwar years in part because of its own weakness and that of most regional communist parties, attempted to make up for lost time after World War II and establish itself there. It initially did so by such diverse stratagems as supporting Kurdish and Azeri autonomy inside Iran, support of the establishment of Israel, and asking to be granted a UN trusteeship over the former Italian colony of Libya. None of these efforts was successful in producing a foothold for Soviet power. Nor was the USSR initially able to exploit another potential avenue for Soviet influence, the local communist parties in the Arab world. These parties became highly unpopular with Arab nationalist public opinion in 1947–48 after the USSR suddenly changed its previous position of opposition to Zionism and voted for the creation of a Jewish state in Palestine. Immediately thereafter, all the Arab communist parties had obediently changed their stands and supported the creation of Israel. The turnaround made them appear to be what they in some

measure were: stooges of a foreign power rather than independent political parties.

Thanks to their highly trumpeted anticolonial stance, however, the Soviets had one major asset in the region: the deep
and lingering resentment of nationalists all over the Middle East
against British and French colonialism. Although the United
States had also enjoyed an anticolonial reputation in the Middle
East since the era of Woodrow Wilson, the USSR was often able
to align itself with anticolonial sentiment more effectively than
the Americans, since the latter had to show some deference to
the interests of their British and French allies. These old colonial
powers were eager in particular to retain their influence in the
region, and to continue to maintain military bases there, which
often made them, and by extension the United States, anathema
to nationalist public opinion in the Middle East.

The United States labored under another related disadvantage by comparison with the USSR: its drive to obtain Middle
Eastern bases of its own in order to complete the encirclement
of the USSR from the south. This pursuit at times led the United
States to fall in with the British, in particular in their desire
to maintain their unpopular Middle Eastern military bases. The
idea of the "containment" of the Soviet Union's perceived aggressive behavior found its origins in George Kennan's 1946
"Long Telegram" from Moscow, later transformed into the well-
known anonymous 1947 *Foreign Affairs* article, "The Sources of
Soviet Conduct."[18] By the end of the decade, Kennan's thesis, or
at least a popularized understanding of it, had grown inexorably
into an American idée fixe: the constitution of a chain of military alliances around the entire Soviet periphery. The first and
the most important of these alliances was NATO, established
in 1949 to confront the massive Red Army in Eastern Europe.
In the Middle East, plans for such alliances were floated under a number of rubrics, including the Middle East Command,

the Middle East Defense Organization (MEDO), and the one that was eventually established, the Central Treaty Organization (CENTO), commonly known as the Baghdad Pact.[19] Although the United States in the end did not join CENTO (Great Britain, also a prime mover in all these alliance schemes, did become a member), this grouping constituted another link in the notional chain Washington was building, and was thus a crucial element in the global American strategy of military containment of the Soviet Union.

The problem for the United States when it tried to preach the virtues of such Middle Eastern alliances against the Soviet Union, which involved host countries providing bases for Western troops while receiving American weapons and support, was that in light of their history, most people in this region had come over many years to see foreign military bases of any kind as outposts of colonialism. In Egypt, for example, the nationalist struggle against Britain's much-hated military bases had been going on since the British occupation of 1882. Only a few years earlier, in 1936, Britain had finally removed its garrison from the heart of the Egyptian capital to the Canal Zone, whence successive Egyptian governments had thereafter tried in vain to evict them. These proposed alliances boiled down to Western powers, including Britain and France, as well as the United States, maintaining bases in countries that had just gotten rid of British and French troops or were still trying to do so. It did little good for American envoys to raise the alarm about the danger of the Soviet Union's looming presence. Outside of Iran and Turkey, where Soviet power was close by and historical memories of continuous earlier Russian encroachments and of Stalin's recent bullying was fresh, American warnings of the menace of Soviet expansionism aroused little fear in the Middle East. To public opinion in Cairo, Damascus, Beirut, Amman, and Baghdad, such arguments were unconvincing, and the idea of the British and the French coming back through the rear window (now together with their American friends) after being shown the front door was thoroughly unacceptable. If some of the Arab countries felt danger from another power, it was from Israel, which by 1956 had decisively defeated several of them in two wars in the space of eight years. The Soviet Union, needless to say, had a field day painting the United States with the colors of the old European colonialist powers, and in depicting all the Western powers as the neocolonialist patrons and backers of Israel in its confrontation with the Arabs.

The pressure to join American-sponsored alliance systems continued nonetheless, and played a large role in the polarization in the Arab world that, as we saw earlier, developed into what Malcolm Kerr called the "Arab Cold War,"[20] between a camp headed by Nasser's Egypt and another headed by King Faisal and Saudi Arabia. The same East-West polarization later affected the Arab-Israeli conflict, and, again as we have seen, both this conflict and the regional conflicts of the Arab cold war eventually came to track closely with the Cold War itself, with the superpowers aligned with one or another side in each of these confrontations. Arab states, including Egypt and Syria, that resisted pressures to join superpower-dominated alliance systems and tried to remain nonaligned were stigmatized by John Foster Dulles's moralistic foreign policy as little better than communist dupes. Earlier, under the influence of chief communist ideologist Andrei Zhdanov's 1947 "two camps" theory,[21] which appeared to presage a division of the world as rigid as that described by Kennan's famous *Foreign Affairs* article two months earlier, the Soviet Union initially seemed to take an equally dim view of nonalignment as between the communist and capitalist camps.[22] However, even before the death of Stalin in 1953, the USSR had begun to take a more flexible view of nonalignment. It thus was able to benefit in an opportunistic fashion from the Eisenhower administration's relative rigidity on this score. It benefited as well from the global resistance on the part of many countries to joining great-power-dominated alliance groupings, which led to the formation of the Non-Aligned Movement at the Bandung summit in 1955, at which Indonesian leader Sukarno hosted other leading third world figures like Jawaharlal Nehru of India, Josip Broz Tito of Yugoslavia, Kwame Nkrumah of Ghana, and Egypt's Gamal Abdel Nasser.

For Egyptian president Nasser, the pressure from Washington to take sides eventually proved intolerable.[23] He rapidly found himself cut off from the United States, which in 1955 abruptly withdrew a World Bank offer to help fund the Aswan High Dam. This led to the nationalization of the Suez Canal, and thereafter to the 1956 Suez War. Willingly or unwillingly, Egypt, Syria, and later Iraq and other Arab countries eventually found themselves drawn into the orbit of the Soviet Union, partly because the United States, with its "with us or against us" approach, left them little choice, and partly to obtain arms made necessary by the regional conflicts described in chapter 4. On the other side of this divide, Iraq before the 1958 revolution, Jordan, Saudi Arabia, and other countries ended up aligning themselves with the United States and Britain. In the end, only Iraq and the non-Arab states Iran and Pakistan, as well as Great Britain, joined CENTO: as mentioned, the United States, ironically, never joined the alliance, and Iraq left it after the 1958 revolution. Thus an alliance system meant originally to encompass both Arab states and the "Northern Tier" of Turkey and Iran ended up including only the latter. The agitation and polarization precipitated by the formation of Western alliance systems nevertheless roiled the politics of the Arab world for nearly a decade. Among the countries that were the most destabilized by Western pressure to join these Cold War alliances during the

1950s were Lebanon and Jordan, to whose complicated internal politics, and troubled attempts to establish democratic governance, I now turn.

RIDING ROUGHSHOD OVER DEMOCRACY: LEBANON AND JORDAN

Under the pressure of the growing regional polarization just described, smaller, weaker Middle Eastern countries like Lebanon and Jordan were subjected to the greatest stresses, and it was here that some of the greatest damage to the region's halting and uncertain progress toward democracy was done. As I pointed out in the previous chapter, in a highly penetrated system such as that of the Middle East, it is often hard to disentangle the intertwined roles of international, regional, and local actors. Jordan and Lebanon provide perfect examples of this phenomenon: in the midst of a succession of grave internal crises, they were subject to strong external pressures from the superpowers, from other great powers, and from a plethora of regional actors, ranging from bigger Middle Eastern states to transnational parties like the Ba'th.

Contemporary observers differed widely as to the nature and the identity of the main source of such pressures. In official Washington and London, most saw the intervention of "international communism," and what they at times perceived as its pawn, Arab nationalism under Egyptian president Gamal Abdel Nasser, as the guiding force behind the turbulent events destabilizing both countries. In Moscow as well as in some quarters in the Arab world, it was the intervention of the United States, Britain, and local clients acting entirely at their behest that was perceived to be the main factor at work. Both views failed to give sufficient credit to the agency of indigenous political forces within the two countries, but in such penetrated systems it was (and often still is) at times truly difficult to be sure precisely who was doing what and to whom. In any case, these events led up to the climactic crisis year of 1958, when a bloody revolution in Iraq in July resulted in the overthrow of the Hashemite monarchy and the pro-Western prime minister, Nuri al-Said. Fearing that the Iraqi example would cause the toppling of a series of regional dominos starting with Jordan and Lebanon, the Western powers panicked, and four thousand British paratroopers landed in Amman and nearly twenty thousand U.S. Marines and soldiers landed in Beirut.[24] Although these forces' presence was not long-lasting, it was indicative of how gravely the situation was viewed by American and British policymakers.

While we may not be able to determine fully the balance between internal and external factors in these crises, there is enough evidence for us to assess the results of some external pressures, and of these Western interventions in particular, for the fate of democracy in Lebanon and Jordan. Each was a divided polity in some fashion, and each had a precarious political system. Each had also been created as a national entity partly in response to the needs and requirements of an imperial power, France in the case of Lebanon, and Great Britain in the case of Jordan, although important internal elements were also at work in the formation of both of these states, and came to play important roles within them.

The League of Nations Mandate system had bequeathed each of these countries a nominally functional representative body in the early 1920s, within the context of a constitutional republic in the case of Lebanon and a constitutional monarchy in the case of Jordan. Both of these political systems had been consistently subjected to extraordinary pressure, manipulation, and intervention by the Mandatory powers in order to assure these powers' continued ultimate control. In a variety of ways, these constant interventions over a period of decades by the democratic Western powers discredited the forms of democracy and constitutionalism, as similar interventions did in Syria, Iraq, Iran, and Egypt.[25] Upon their achieving nominal independence (in 1943 for Lebanon and 1946 for Jordan) there was some question whether such external interference would cease, and also whether the Lebanese and Jordanian parliaments and the two countries' respective constitutions would be able to stand up to their powerful chief executives, the first president of independent Lebanon, Beshara al-Khoury, and Amir—later King—Abdullah of Jordan.

In the case of Lebanon, at the end of World War I, France, which since 1861 had been the traditional great-power patron of the autonomous Ottoman administrative Governorate of Mount Lebanon, inhabited mainly by Maronite Catholics, had desired to expand the area dominated by its Maronite allies. Seeing the opportunity to kill two birds with one stone, France sought to further its "divide and rule" strategy in Syria by adding to the area of the Mount Lebanon Governorate those regions it desired to separate from the rest of Syria, thereby at the same time turning the governorate into a Greater Lebanon, or Grand Liban. The Syrian regions to be added to Mount Lebanon were inhabited mainly by Sunnis, Greek Orthodox, and Druze, who were strongly influenced by Arab nationalism and generally hostile to French colonial designs. France was also responding to the aspirations of pro-French Maronite leaders who desired to see their domain expanded, now that their patron had won World War I and was in a position to fulfill both its ambitions and theirs.

France therefore in 1920 had created this Grand Liban, which eventually became today's Republic of Lebanon. It did so by attaching to the relatively homogenous Governorate of Mount Lebanon, with its large Maronite majority, districts on the coast (including the cities of Beirut, Tripoli, Sidon, and

Tyre) and in the south (Jabal 'Amil), east (the al-Biqa' Valley) and north (the Koura, 'Akkar, and Hirmil regions). These areas contained primarily large Sunni and Shi'a Muslim and Greek Orthodox populations, and some Druze. None of these groups had the slightest reason to desire being brought as minorities into a Maronite-dominated Greater Lebanon, or to become "Lebanese." Needless to say, they were not consulted by French colonial planners, who were no more accommodating of the voices of inconvenient natives than had been Lord Balfour, cited at length in chapter 3.[26]

France's ambitious and acquisitive policies in the wake of World War I thus set the stage for some of the divisions that have bedeviled Lebanon down to the present day, creating some of them *ab initio* and exacerbating others. Thereafter, the French Mandatory authorities systematically manipulated the political system within the new Lebanese state they had created. They did so by creating a confessional democracy, one in which members of parliament are chosen by their religious or ethnic (but not geographic) origin, and which favored their clients and allies. Other manipulations included the 1932 census, the reliability of which has since been questioned, as it inflated the number of Christians and deflated those of Muslims,[27] sophisticated gerrymandering of electoral districts, and a collection of other stratagems and tricks that ensured the outcomes their policies required.[28]

However, when French power was crippled by the defeat of Vichy forces in Syria by the British in 1941, the weight of heavy-handed French intervention was lifted for the first time since 1920. With the French thumb lifted from the scales, a major re-equilibration of the Lebanese political system rapidly took place. This occurred in the context of the 1943 National Pact between Sunni and Maronite leaders without, however, changing the confessional nature of the Lebanese political system or its domination by selected elites. Under the 1943 pact's new dispensation, the president would remain a Maronite, more power would be granted to the Sunni prime minister, the Sunnis would accept the legitimacy of Lebanon's separation from Syria and its existence as a separate nation-state, which many Sunnis had previously contested, and the country would remain open to both the West and the Arab world, rather than tilting exclusively toward France. Other sects, notably the large underprivileged and underrepresented Shiʻa community, were ignored in this deal, although few protests were heard at the time. There was nevertheless a serious question as to whether this fragile system could endure the internal and external strains it faced. It was to be severely tested in the mid-1950s.

Jordan was also a peculiar case, albeit for different reasons.[29] Unlike Lebanon, where the new state was built around the nucleus of the previously existing Mount Lebanon Governorate established by the Ottomans, which in turn had its origins in the well-established Ottoman-era Emirate of Mount Lebanon, never in the history of the previous centuries had the region today known as Jordan had any sort of separate existence. The sparsely populated area had traditionally been governed from Damascus, where it had its main trade and administrative connections, and it also had long-standing commercial and family links with Palestine, especially with Nablus, Jerusalem, and Hebron.[30] After the French had extinguished King Faisal's Syrian kingdom in 1920, Faisal's older brother Abdullah in early 1921 had ridden northward from the Hijaz with a military force, ostensibly to avenge this defeat, and halted in what is now Jordan, the only part of the short-lived Syrian kingdom that the French had not occupied after their defeat of Faisal's army, as they did not want their forces to enter an area that had been allocated to the British under the World War I Sykes-Picot partition of the region between the two powers. Meanwhile, British forces in

Palestine had never extended their control eastward across the Jordan, since this area had previously been under the control of Faisal's government in Damascus.

At this moment, in March 1921, British policymakers and experts from all over the region happened to be gathered in Cairo for a conference with the new colonial secretary, Winston Churchill.[31] They were there to decide how to continue to maintain control over the Middle East in the wake of the shocks to Britain's regional position from the Egyptian revolution of 1919, the Iraqi revolt of 1920, and the disappointment with Britain of Arab nationalists after the destruction of the first modern independent Arab state in Syria by the French in the same year. The inclination of these British mandarins, in the face of the failure of previous attempts at direct rule in Egypt and Iraq, was to grant the appearance of self-government while as much as possible withholding the substance of real power. This formula was adopted in several areas of the Arab world. It led both to the prolongation of British dominance of the region, which for a brief moment had seemed in jeopardy, and also to long-lived Arab resentment against Britain, as the limits of the nominal independence that the British were granting rapidly became apparent.

Churchill and his advisors in Cairo found themselves confronted in Jordan with the delicate problem of a client preparing to attack an ally from an area that constituted something of a vacuum between French power in Syria, that of Britain in Palestine, and the Arab kingdom to the south in the Hijaz. They decided to make a virtue of necessity by creating an Emirate of Transjordan and installing Abdullah as its ruler.[32] This was the genesis of the peculiarly shaped entity (although the shape also owed much to other, earlier British decisions and deals)[33] that eventually became the Hashemite Kingdom of Jordan. The main institution thereafter created by the British in Jordan was the British-commanded, British-officered, British-armed, and British-financed and controlled army, called "the Arab Legion."[34] The name of this force constituted a fine piece of irony, of the sort perhaps only the British colonial mentality was capable of. However, Jordan eventually also came to have a government, a parliament, and all the trappings called for by the Mandate system, although the entire state apparatus was at all times thoroughly dominated by the overbearing Abdullah, behind whom stood his imperious British patrons.

By the 1950s, however, things in Jordan had begun to change, notably after the formal annexation by Abdullah of the West Bank in 1950, and after the old king's assassination in 1951 by Palestinian nationalists, and his subsequent replacement first by his son Talal and then almost immediately by his extremely youthful grandson, Hussein.[35] Deprived of the experienced and wily Abdullah as their local ally, British influence diminished in Jordan, as the palace and the British embassy slowly lost their previously nearly complete control. Nationalist Jordanian politicians of various stripes and growing nationalist and radical political parties for a time partially filled the resulting vacuum, politics moved into the street and became more unruly and less predictable, and the country veered away from American- and British-backed alliance systems and swung toward nonalignment.

In the mid-1950s, powerful new external pressures would be brought to bear on the vulnerable political systems of both Lebanon and Jordan.

THE LEAD-UP TO THE "REVOLUTIONARY YEAR" IN JORDAN

The events leading up to the "revolutionary year" of 1958 in the Middle East have been extremely well detailed elsewhere.[36]

They came to a head in Lebanon and Jordan, as well as in Iraq, where the British-installed and -dominated monarchy was overthrown that year in a tumultuous revolution. This upheaval provoked fears in Washington and London that a wave of radicalism would wash over Amman and Beirut as well, bringing to power there nationalist regimes aligned with Egyptian leader Gamal Abdel Nasser, which would be under Soviet influence. Cold War reflexes were at work here, and only this can explain the panicked response of American and British policymakers in sending troops to Lebanon and Jordan.[37] In what follows, I will focus on how what transpired in the years leading up to the climactic events of 1958 affected democracy in the two small and unstable countries we are looking at. However, it is essential to keep in mind that events in Lebanon and Jordan took place as part of a broad, radical, nationalist current that was sweeping the entire Arab Middle East, the precipitate decline of British and French power and prestige in the region in the wake of the Suez fiasco, and the growth in the regional influence of the two superpowers, which in some measure was taking place at the expense of the shrinking profiles of the two old colonial ruling powers.

We have already seen that in Jordan, British influence was waning in the early 1950s after the assassination of King Abdullah and the accession to the throne first of his son Talal, and then a year later of the young Hussein. Although surrounded by the same cast of obliging palace politicians as had ably served his grandfather, like Tawfiq Abu al-Huda and Samir al-Rifaʻi, and strongly supported by most senior army officers, by his formidable mother, Queen Zein, and by the British, King Hussein faced a totally different situation than had Abdullah for most of his reign. This was partially the result of the natural growth of the Jordanian population and increases in literacy and urbanization, and partially the consequence of Abdullah's ambitions, which had led to the annexation of the West Bank in 1950. The young king was thus facing an increasingly urbanized, politicized, and nationalist body politic, the volatility of which had been significantly augmented by the addition of the largely anti-Hashemite and anti-British Palestinians of the West Bank. Many of these were embittered refugees driven in 1948 from their homes in Palestine, who blamed the British and the Hashemite monarchy in Jordan in part for their predicament. But it was Jordanian politicians, the political parties, and the swelling population of Amman and other East Bank cities that posed the biggest problem for the king and his British allies.

To this considerable internal problem of a radicalized and politicized citizenry were added external regional influences. The most powerful of them was that of Egypt. Jordanians were susceptible to the appeal of the nationalist Egyptian military regime that had come to power in 1952, as were others in the Mashriq, the Arab East running from Syria to Lebanon to Iraq, the Arab principalities of the Gulf, the Arabian Peninsula, and Yemen. In 1954 this regime, led by the charismatic Col. Gamal Abdel Nasser, had finally ended seventy-two years of British occupation, in 1955 had helped pioneer the Non-Aligned Movement and had nationalized the Suez Canal, and in 1956 had survived the tripartite aggression of Britain, France, and Israel (largely due, as we have seen, to both superpowers' opposition to the attack). The Egyptian regime capitalized on these perceived successes, actively propagating its influence through multiple means, including its powerful radio station Sawt al-Arab, the "Voice of the Arabs." Large numbers of Jordanians (and other Arabs) responded to Egyptian calls to Arab states to boycott Western alliances by opposing the Baghdad Pact (CENTO) and increasingly criticizing what was perceived as the Hashemite kingdom's excessive reliance on the British.[38]

Bombarded by this Egyptian propaganda, and under intense popular and increasing parliamentary pressure, King Hussein attempted to appease his critics by dismissing the British commander of the Arab Legion, Sir John Bagot Glubb, known as Glubb Pasha, and most other senior British officers in March 1956. The swing of Jordan toward Arab nationalism continued, however, with the parliamentary elections of October 1956. These were the first and possibly the last fully free and fair elections in Jordanian history, and returned a parliament dominated by nationalists and a few leftists, leading to the formation of the government of Suleiman Nabulsi, the first Jordanian prime minister chosen truly as a result of elections rather than by the palace and the British. Indeed, the British ambassador, Charles Johnston, admitted privately that these elections were "the first approximately free ones in the history of Jordan."[39] For the six months of its existence, the Nabulsi government struggled to establish a new relationship with the monarchy, the army, and the British. Complicating this process was the fact that Jordan had never before been allowed this degree of freedom by its royal and British masters, and the new government was thus finding its way in entirely unfamiliar territory. Meanwhile, the external pressures on the country did not diminish. Events came to a head in April 1957, when the king, fully backed by the British, used the pretext of an alleged military plot against the monarchy to dismiss the government. After a very brief interlude when another government, this one less overtly nationalist but independent and including some ministers from Nabulsi's cabinet, was brought in, the king installed a government made up entirely of trusted palace retainers (described by the British ambassador as "frankly authoritarian"[40]).

Thus ended Jordan's brief democratic experiment, but only after a farcical meeting at the royal palace, when the young king and the British ambassador initially failed to browbeat the Jordanian politicians who had been selected to adorn the new cabinet into taking their portfolios. It was left to the queen mother, the formidable Zein, to openly threaten the reluctant would-be ministers, finally bringing them around and persuading them to join the new government, which they knew would serve as no more than window dressing for what would amount to martial law. The British ambassador's description of this incongruous scene is worth quoting: "Finally Her Majesty told the Ministers designate that they would not be allowed to leave the Palace until they had taken the oath of office, and it was on this not altogether encouraging basis that the new Government was eventually formed."[41] Although this episode may seem like a scene from the days of gunboat diplomacy (combined with Ruritanian comic opera), it was in fact driven not just by the reflexes of an autocratic monarchy or by Britain's neocolonial relations with Jordan and its elite, but by an obsessive underlying fear of communism on the part of both the British and the Americans. This fear is what animated British and American opposition to Jordanian nationalists, who were luridly (and incorrectly) pictured as communists or under Soviet influence in the dispatches of Western diplomats in Amman.[42] Among the casualties here, and the following year, when British paratroopers arrived in Jordan to prop up the still shaky monarchy and the "frankly authoritarian" regime that the British and the Jordanian king and queen mother had imposed, was the evolution of Jordanian democracy: the victim of its own enforced immaturity, of the unrestrained autocratic impulses of the Hashemites, of old British habits of neocolonial rule, and of the Cold War.

THE TURN OF LEBANON

Lebanon during the 1958 crisis was described in Washington as suffering primarily from the meddling of Egypt and Syria, which had just joined together in the United Arab Republic

(UAR), a unitary state run from Cairo that was seen as strongly backed by the Soviet Union. Lebanon's legitimate government, headed by the pro-Western president Camille Chamoun, was seen from the same perspective as suffering this fate largely because it was inclined to join in Western defense schemes and was willing to align itself with the West. While this analysis was true in some measure, in the eyes of most Lebanese and Arab observers, and nearly all historians since, the country was also going through a serious constitutional crisis: Chamoun was making an effort to amend the Lebanese constitution to allow him to serve a second six-year term. In order to do so, the Lebanese president needed an overwhelming parliamentary majority, which he just happened to have secured in 1957 in one of the most notoriously rigged elections in Lebanese history. Incumbents all over the country went down to defeat, all of them ferocious opponents of the president's unpopular plan to amend the constitution in order to prolong his stay in office, and all of whom should have been secure in safe parliamentary seats located in their traditional fiefdoms. Beyond rigging the elections for this purpose, in his excessive pro-Western orientation and hostility to the UAR, and in his disdainful diminution of the role of the Sunni prime minister, Chamoun was seen by many of his opponents as ignoring the balance between the West and the Arab world and between the Maronite office of president and the Sunni office of prime minister, which were both prescribed by the confessional provisions of the 1943 National Pact.

This was the crucial background to the Lebanese civil war, and to the upheavals of 1958, which ended with the landing of U.S. Marines in Beirut. To this background should be added two elements. The first is that a similar constitutional crisis had arisen when Lebanon's first president, Beshara al-Khoury, had attempted to do the same thing Chamoun was trying to do, to prolong his term unconstitutionally. Khoury had been forced out of office by massive opposition after only three years of a second term, and was replaced, ironically, by Chamoun. The second is that we know that Chamoun was able to rig the 1957 elections through the distribution of massive bribes, which were made possible by large sums delivered to him by the United States. We know this because the American intelligence agent who served as the bagman in this operation, Wilbur Crane Eveland, describes personally performing this service in his memoirs in some detail. Thus, Eveland tells of driving up to the presidential palace in Baabda in his Cadillac, and of handing Chamoun briefcases full of cash for him to use in order to rig the election.[43]

Given that American policymakers perceived that Soviet and Egyptian money and influence were guiding the actions of the Lebanese opposition to Chamoun, which they saw as Muslim-dominated and Arab nationalist and radical, even communist, in orientation, the Cold War reasoning behind this sort of policy can be understood. In fact, Chamoun and his foreign minister, Dr. Charles Malik, were telling the Americans things that they knew would alarm them about the opposition (things they may themselves have believed[44]), which in fact was neither Muslim dominated, nor entirely Arab nationalist, and certainly not communist influenced. It was made up mainly of traditional, conservative politicians, who were enraged at having been unfairly unseated from Parliament in rigged elections. The opposition was led among many others by the Maronite patriarch, Cardinal Meouchi, and the leading Maronite politician of the north of Lebanon, Hamid Franjieh. Neither of them was a Muslim, or exactly an Arab nationalist or a radical, and certainly none of the most prominent opposition leaders was a communist by any stretch of the imagination, although many were supporters of Gamal Abdel Nasser, and the Druze leader, Kamal Junblatt, proclaimed himself a socialist. The opposition was in fact in essence no more than a new iteration of the very same coalition of Lebanese politicians that had opposed Beshara al-Khoury's similar unconstitutional shenanigans only a few years earlier.

The damage done by American meddling in service of Cold War objectives based on a complete misreading of the Lebanese situation was not restricted to the rigging of the 1957 elections. This blatant undermining of the legitimacy of the parliamentary system was a major precipitant of the 1958 civil war, perhaps the most important one, combined with the unsettling impact on Lebanon of the union of Egypt and Syria into the UAR in early 1958. Perceived in Washington as yet another dangerous shift of Arab nationalism toward the Soviet orbit, this union in fact did not end up giving any advantage to Moscow; quite the contrary. Indeed, the small but active Syrian Communist Party was obliged to dissolve against its will in March 1958, a few months after the union between Egypt and Syria went into effect and as one of the conditions of its formation. This showed that communist influence was in fact shrinking rather than growing as a result of the union of Egypt and Syria, and gave those American policymakers capable of reading these events correctly another in a series of recurring indications of how useful Arab nationalism might be as a bar to communist influence.

The Lebanese crisis found rapid resolution after the landing of American forces in Beirut, by means of a diplomatic deal struck between the Egyptians and U.S. presidential envoy Robert Murphy to replace Chamoun with the commander of the Lebanese Army, Gen. Fuad Chehab. This solution showed that earlier perceptions of many in Washington about both Lebanon and Egypt had been highly flawed, not to say utterly detached from reality. The crisis in essence revolved around the constitutional question of the presidential succession and the related question of the prerogatives of the Maronite president, and not around Egyptian (or Soviet!) "interference in Lebanon's internal affairs." As soon as the succession question was resolved by refusing Chamoun another, unconstitutional, term, which he had originally sought with the support of Washington (ironically, this could only be done with the aid of Cairo), the crisis ended immediately.

The American-Egyptian deal nevertheless had a negative long-term impact on Lebanon. While it resolved the constitutional crisis, preserved the confessional system by providing for somewhat broader prerogatives for the Sunni prime minister, and eased tensions within the country, it also taught the lesson that Lebanese crises could not be resolved by the country's political system. It taught the further lesson that Lebanese crises could only be dealt with by external powers, which held the keys to Lebanon's stability, reinforcing beliefs among many Lebanese that had persisted since the nineteenth century.[45] The deal established a dangerous precedent that was to be repeated in 1969, when a crisis over the Palestinian military presence in Lebanon was resolved in Cairo by the Egyptian president. The same precedent was repeatedly invoked during the much more bloody Lebanese war of 1975–90, which was finally brought to an end via accords negotiated at Taif in Saudi Arabia. It was repeated once again with the resolution of a grave governmental crisis in May 2008 by the amir of Qatar and the Arab League meeting in Doha, discussed in the next chapter. Long after the Cold War has ended, many Lebanese today still await a resolution from without to their internal problems, because of this precedent set in large part as a result of misguided Cold War considerations and great-power blindness to the realities of a small country which, like Jordan, has the misfortune of being part of a highly penetrated system.

FURTHER SACRIFICES ON THE
ALTAR OF THE COLD WAR

The fate of democracy in Iran in the early 1950s, and in Lebanon and Jordan, two small Arab countries, in the mid- to late 1950s, may seem unimportant. The example of how and why democracy was undermined by, among other things, the Cold War, may not seem sufficient to prove that the superpowers cared far more for their interests and their rivalry with each other than they did about anything else in the Middle East, notably the evolution of democratic governance. But to see how true this was, one need only consider how in the years that followed, events in this region hewed rigidly to this pattern. Again and again, Middle Eastern regimes (many of whose roots were entirely indigenous, like those in Turkey, Iran, Iraq, Syria, and Egypt) were enthusiastically encouraged in their authoritarian bent by their superpower patrons—indeed, sometimes, as in the cases of Egypt and Iraq, they were encouraged to move in this direction by both superpowers, serially of course.

In Iraq, for example, a liberal parliamentary regime that had been thoroughly corrupted and profoundly undermined by the naked manipulations of the British and the rulers they had imposed on the country[46] collapsed in 1958. It was replaced for nearly five years by a dictatorship headed by Brig. Abdul Karim Kassem that relied partly on the large and powerful Iraqi Communist Party for mass support. Needless to say, as we saw in the last chapter, where real Communists in serious numbers and with considerable influence were concerned (a situation quite unlike the Jordanian and Lebanese cases), both the Soviet Union and the United States immediately became deeply involved. In support of their Communist comrades in Iraq, Soviet leaders initially went to the point of jeopardizing the USSR's close relations with Egypt, the biggest, strongest, and most influential country in the Arab world, and its first client in the

region. The new Iraqi regime did "progressive" things in this period, such as initiating land reform, spreading literacy, extending electrification, and expanding education, but so did the
UAR, which was also building a big dam, which to the Soviets
was a sine qua non of progressive modernity.[47] Eventually, after
the bloody 1963 coup that ousted Kassem, the Soviets reconciled
themselves to the loss of his regime, and maintained their good
relations with its successor and with the Egyptian government.
The point is that for the Soviets, in the end what was truly vital
was the extension of their influence and the curtailment of that
of the United States, not their "progressive" ideals about justice,
or the fate of their Iraqi comrades. The Soviets showed that this
was the case later on by retaining close ties to Iraq under the
Ba'th Party, notwithstanding the Ba'thist regime's repeated, ferocious anticommunist purges.

Similarly, the United States quickly made up to its former
archenemy in Cairo in 1958 and 1959 when it was perceived in
Washington (after the departure of the inflexible John Foster
Dulles from the State Department) how useful the Egyptians
and their Ba'thist allies could be in undermining the Kassem
regime and in confronting the power of the Iraqi Communist
Party. This lesson was not forgotten, and as we saw in the last
chapter, the CIA was to make use of it in cooperating with the
Ba'thists when they came to power in Baghdad briefly in 1963
and again much more permanently in 1968, assisting them with
their bloody eradication of Iraqi Communists. It is easy to see
what all of this might have had to do with the Cold War. It is
harder to see what Communists killing Nasserists and Ba'thists
in Iraq before the Kassem regime was overthrown in 1963, or
Ba'thists killing Communists later on, had to do with the ideals
of the USSR and the United States, notably the promotion of
democracy as regards the United States. Undoubtedly, however,
both sides could relate their support for such actions in some
contorted way to their stated ideals of liberty and justice.

There may well not have been any chance to revive some type of democratic governance in Egypt, Syria, and Iraq after the forms of parliamentary democracy and constitutionalism were so thoroughly discredited by their manipulations by local rulers, the old colonial powers, and later the superpowers, from the 1920s through the 1950s. However, what is certain is that the covert and occasional overt interventions of the superpowers from World War II onward, besides exacerbating regional conflict, as we saw in the previous chapter, profoundly undermined whatever limited possibility there might have been of establishing any kind of democratic governance in a range of Middle Eastern countries from the late 1950s and through the 1970s and 1980s.

Speaking at a public event at the Woodrow Wilson International Center for Scholars in Washington, D.C., toward the end of the Cold War, a retired senior Central Intelligence Agency analyst who had served as national intelligence officer for the Middle East and vice chair of the National Intelligence Council stated retrospectively that throughout the Cold War, policymakers and analysts in the U.S. government paid attention to only one thing in the Middle East: the Soviets and their local allies. Once the USSR ceased to be a factor in a Middle Eastern country, he noted, that country almost ceased to be of interest in Washington.[48] While these remarks provoke several reflections about the Middle East since the end of the Cold War—a period that has seen a massive upsurge in U.S. interest in the region keyed to terrorism rather than communism—one reflection is pertinent to this chapter: how much harm to the internal political development of this region, and in particular to its peoples' aspirations for democracy, was done by the two superpowers' obsessive focus on each other, sometimes to the exclusion of all else, and their constant, insidious jockeying for Cold War advantage? The evidence of Iran, of Lebanon and Jordan, and also of Iraq and other countries in the region is that it was grave.

VI

VICTORY IN THE COLD WAR, AND THE GLOBAL WAR ON TERROR

For at least four millennia, the region we today call the Middle East, including the southern and eastern shores of the Mediterranean basin and adjacent areas, has been a focus of the ambitions of the Eurasian, African, European, and global empires that have competed for dominance over the central region of the great European-Asian-African landmass.[1] For some of them, this broader Middle East was crucial to their expansion. For others it was the key to their domination of adjacent regions. For the British Empire, with its determination to control "the route to India," it was the vital hinge of Britain's global hegemony for nearly a century and a half. For yet other would-be empire builders, it was the graveyard of their aspirations for dominance. In addition, many of the most powerful of world empires arose in this region, which was the cradle of human civilization. It was the site of the first agriculture, the first cities, the first writing, the first states, and the first great empires known to date.

I have already touched on, at various points in this book, the strategic significance of the Middle East. The strategic nature of the region is largely related to the fact that the different components of the vast tricontinental body of land that dominates the Eastern Hemisphere are physically connected around the eastern Mediterranean basin. Moreover, even the region's waterways do not usually present major obstacles to movement, as there is easy passage across the Red Sea, the Persian/Arabian Gulf, and other adjacent narrow bodies of water. For this reason, the Middle East is the location of a number of historic trade routes and land passageways that have been utilized for millennia. The coastal plains of Palestine and Lebanon, the passes through the Caucasus Mountains, Bab al-Mandab at the entrance to the Red Sea, the Strait of Hormuz at the entrance to the Gulf, the Dardanelles, and the Bosphorus are among the region's many ancient crossing points for culture, trade, and conquering armies.[2]

This same region, with its easily navigable seas, is also the nexus of a number of important seaways, easy-to-navigate straits, and ancient ports. Starting nearly three and a half millennia ago, the ancient seafaring Phoenicians, followed by the Greeks and their nautical counterparts in Eritrea, Sudan, Egypt, Yemen, Oman, and the Gulf, created vast networks of trade, colonization, and sometimes conquest that spanned much of the Eastern Hemisphere, starting from ports in the eastern Mediterranean, the Red Sea, the Indian Ocean, and the Persian/Arabian Gulf.[3] The Romans, the Byzantines, the Arabs, the Ottomans, the Genoese, the Venetians, and other seafaring peoples followed their example over the succeeding centuries.

Thanks to these unique benefits provided by its location, and because of many other factors, including its rich agriculture, its early industries, its importance as a trade entrepôt, and its fabled ancient cities, the eastern Mediterranean and the Middle East were seen as being of great economic and strategic importance in a variety of different ways from the time of the pharaohs until the Napoleonic Wars. As often as not, those assets were capitalized on by states based mainly or partly within the Middle East, from the Egyptian and the Assyrian empires to those of the Arabs and the Ottomans. This abruptly ceased to be the case once the region became prey to European powers as their might grew and their rivalries intensified from the late eighteenth century through World War I and World

War II. In several cases, European great powers vigorously opposed, sometimes with force, the rise or the revival of powerful states in the region during this period. These included the potent Egyptian state refashioned by Muhammad Ali in the early nineteenth century, the reformed Ottoman Empire in the early twentieth century, and Gamal Abdel Nasser's Egypt in the mid-twentieth century. As we saw in chapter 2, the significance of the Middle East grew even further during the twentieth century, when the extraordinary wealth of its oil resources became known, and especially during the Cold War, when this oil became vital to both superpowers, albeit in different ways.

From the French Revolution until 1945, the eastern Mediterranean was a regular theater of rivalry and confrontation between the great powers, and was the site of important battlefields where the armies, navies, and later air forces of these powers and the major competing alliance systems warred with one another. The region saw some of the world's most important battles over that century and a half. The first was Aboukir in 1798, when Napoleon's fleet was sunk by that of Admiral Nelson, ending the Corsican general's hopes of conquering the land route to India and the East and thereby obtaining for revolutionary France a decisive advantage over imperial Great Britain. The last was at El Alamein in 1942, when the eastward advance of Field Marshal Rommel's panzers across North Africa toward strategic military and naval bases and oil fields under British control farther east, as well as toward the shortest route to India, was finally stopped.

However, the Cold War between the United States and the Soviet Union marked a significant change in this age-old pattern whereby the Middle East was often the decisive scene of great-power rivalry. It can be argued that the Cold War was the first international conflict that was truly *global* in its scope, in every sense of that word. This was so because during the Cold

War the main protagonists were in some measure extra-European states, and the stage of their rivalry was the entire world. In this, it was unlike the century of wars between Britain and France from the early eighteenth through the early nineteenth centuries, and the seventy-five years of wars from 1870 until 1945 that grew out of conflicts between Germany and France and Britain. All of these previous rivalries, and the wars that resulted from them, took place in some measure on a world stage, but they were between European powers and were in essence directed at achieving hegemony over Europe. While, for example, important battles in the sequence of Anglo-French conflicts from the time of Louis XIV until that of Napoleon were fought in the Indian Ocean, in India, and in North America,[4] at heart these were essentially European wars, between European powers, to determine who would dominate the European continent.

The two greatest wars of the twentieth century were undoubtedly truly world wars in many respects, since they involved major extra-European powers like the United States and Japan and were fought on a world stage. Nevertheless, they, too, were at least in their inception basically European continental wars between European powers that were competing for world dominance. Thus World Wars I and II both started in Europe, and at the outset at least were fought between European powers over issues of traditional concern to the European balance of power. The fact that they started in the Balkans in 1914 and Poland in 1939, respectively, is the best evidence of this. The development and the global extensions of World War II marked the beginning of a new era that only came to maturity during the Cold War, and represented the shift in world hegemony away from the traditional Western and central European powers. Because of their essentially European nature, in all of these wars before the Cold War, including World Wars I and II, the Middle East could and often did play a central role, due to its vital strategic position where Europe adjoins the African and Asian continents to which it is linked.

All of this changed with the Cold War. The eastern Mediterranean and the Middle East of course continued to be important to both superpowers, for they abutted on the southern frontiers of the Soviet Union and contained vast reserves of energy. As we have seen, this region witnessed major confrontations between the United States and the Soviet Union, from the crisis over the Turkish Straits in 1945 through the Greek civil war of 1946–49, the covert and overt involvement of both powers in Iran, the naval rivalries of the 1960s, and four major Arab-Israeli wars. Nevertheless, these events were part of a different pattern than that which characterized previous rivalries and conflicts involving the region. For the Cold War, unlike the previous two and a half centuries of international conflicts involving the Middle East, which were essentially centered on western Europe, took place simultaneously on several continents (even if Europe, the Mediterranean, and the Middle East remained central to the concerns of both sides throughout the Cold War). This was obvious in a number of ways. Neither of the Cold War's two main protagonists, the United States and the Soviet Union, was a western European power: one was located in North America and the other lay astride the Eurasian landmass, inside and outside Europe at the same time. The only three major hot wars directly involving either of the superpowers were fought in Asia: in Korea in the early 1950s, in Vietnam in the 1960s and 1970s, and in the 1980s in Afghanistan, which is beyond the eastern edge of the Middle East as traditionally defined. Finally, although we have seen that the Middle East was at times a base for American strategic weapons systems, the nuclear weapons competition between the United States and the USSR was always truly intercontinental in its dimensions, whether it involved strategic intercontinental bombers, intercontinental ballistic missiles (ICBMs), or submarine-launched ballistic missiles (SLBMs).

I have argued that during the entire Cold War period, after the confrontations over Iran, Turkey, and Greece in the immediate post–World War II years, perhaps the most important crises involving the superpowers in the eastern Mediterranean region were those relating to the Arab-Israeli wars. Six of these wars involved the superpowers, sometimes in quite different alignments. The first two were the 1948 war and the 1956 Suez conflict. As I showed in chapter 4, in both of these conflicts, in spite of the rivalry between them, the United States and Soviet Union incongruously found themselves on the same side, both aligned with Israel against the Arab states in 1948, and with Egypt and against Britain, France, and Israel in 1956. These anomalous instances were followed by four major Arab-Israeli wars—the June 1967 war, the War of Attrition of 1968–70, the October 1973 war, and the 1982 Israeli invasion of Lebanon. During these conflicts the superpowers took opposite sides, in a familiar pattern, with the USSR supporting the Arabs, and the United States, Israel. There were also many less severe Arab-Israeli confrontations that at times involved the superpowers, some of them related to the war of 1975–90 in Lebanon. In addition to being a civil war, as we have seen, this prolonged and lethal conflict attracted the intervention of a broad range of regional and international actors, notably major protégés of the superpowers, like Israel, Syria, and the PLO.[5]

In the four major Arab-Israeli wars starting with that of 1967, the superpowers became ever more deeply involved in their support of the warring sides, with the United States increasingly supporting Israel, and the Soviet Union increasing its backing for the Arabs. The first three of these conflicts erupted in the envenomed international atmosphere of a major East-West confrontation over the wars that were raging in Indochina.

They therefore developed into major crises between the United States and the Soviet Union, causing the Middle East once again to become an important strategic arena for the rivalry between the two superpowers. But after the Cold War, a fundamental change regarding conflicts in the Middle East and its peripheries appears to have occurred.

INTERCONNECTED CONFLICTS IN THE WAKE OF THE COLD WAR

For all their severity and their potential for provoking a wider conflagration, it is important to note that each of the four Middle Eastern crises growing out of an Arab-Israeli war was in some measure *self-contained,* at least in regional terms. This may have had to do with the fact that the international confrontations that developed around the Arab-Israeli wars took place within the context of what had by the 1960s become a fixed and defined Cold War system, characterized by American containment of the USSR, and a precarious nuclear balance involving mutual assured destruction. Conflicts involving superpower proxies in the Middle East were seen as having to be rigorously curtailed, because of the danger that an unlimited local conflict might drag in the superpower patrons and lead to escalation, with the ultimate fear of a potential nuclear holocaust.

The self-containment of these Arab-Israeli wars may also have been a function of the fact that they took place in the context of a regional system that was generally relatively stable, whereby a certain degree of balance had developed between differing Arab states, and between Arab and non-Arab states. Finally, self-containment may have resulted from the fact that the Arab-Israeli conflict—at least insofar as serious warfare was concerned—was essentially restricted to a small number of states (Israel, Egypt, and Syria, and occasionally Jordan and

Iraq), and to one narrow, clearly defined region (the territory of these states, as well as Lebanon and the occupied Palestinian territories). Whether for these reasons or others, the Arab-Israeli confrontations did not lead to a wider regional conflagration. This was true even of the 1982 Israeli invasion of Lebanon, which was the longest of these wars since 1948, and witnessed nearly ten weeks of siege and bombardment of an Arab capital, the first and only time such a thing had happened in all six Arab-Israeli wars.[6]

Whatever the explanation (and in 1982 the growing strategic weakness of the USSR vis-à-vis the United States may have been a factor in limiting the spread of this conflict), the grave international crises that developed around the periodic Arab-Israeli wars rarely threatened to spill over into broader region-wide conflagrations, although these crises were often influenced by region-wide contexts. The fierce Egyptian-Saudi rivalry of the mid-1960s, which I have already discussed in terms of what Malcolm Kerr called the "Arab cold war,"[7] for example, contributed measurably to the slide into the June 1967 war. The intense rivalry between the two Arab powers, and in particular the constant outbidding of Saudi Arabia and its conservative allies, pushed the Egyptian leadership, whose military forces were already deeply entangled in the Yemeni civil war, to take risky escalatory steps against Israel during the April–May phase that led to the 1967 war. These were steps that the Egyptian leaders perhaps otherwise would not have taken but for the taunting of the Saudis and their allies about Egyptian troops "hiding behind" the United Nations Emergency Force in Sinai. Gamal Abdel Nasser and his colleagues saw themselves as obliged to shore up their threatened position as paramount leaders of the Arab world, and to act in support of their prickly allies in the radical Syrian regime when it appeared seriously threatened by Israel in the spring of 1967.[8] Inter-Arab politics thus played a crucial role in precipitating one of the most important of the Arab-Israeli wars, and exacerbated an already critical situation.

The only possible exception to this general rule of the self-contained nature of the Arab-Israeli wars was the 1968–70 War of Attrition, which, in addition to Egypt and Israel, in time came to involve Syria, the PLO, Jordan, and Iraq in a direct way, as well as the United States and the Soviet Union indirectly. I have already argued that this was an underappreciated phase of the Arab-Israeli wars, which was crucially important in a number of ways. Among other things, the tactical military results of the War of Attrition made it possible for Egyptian forces to cross the Suez Canal three years later, during the October 1973 war.[9] And we have seen that both superpowers committed significant military resources to their protégés. In the case of the Soviets these included many pilots and thousands of air defense personnel and others serving covertly in combat roles.[10] Moreover, in large part because of the region-wide radical appeal of the Palestinian cause, it appeared for a time as if the War of Attrition might provoke extensive regional ramifications, including possible revolutionary upheavals in a number of Arab states.

Thus, the reasons the stakes were perceived as so high during the War of Attrition did not only have to do with the strategic importance of the ferocious battles that raged for over two years along the Suez Canal, or with the full superpower backing of both sides and the concomitant danger of superpower confrontation. Beyond this, a truly radical regime was in power in Damascus from 1966 onward which strongly supported the most militant elements among the Palestinians.[11] At the same time, important elements of the PLO like the Popular Front for the Liberation of Palestine and the Democratic Front for the Liberation of Palestine at this stage were strongly influenced by Marxist and other radical and revolutionary ideas. These and other Palestinian factions were avidly preaching the virtues of armed struggle and Arab revolution (as were the radical neo-Ba'thists in power in Damascus). Practicing what they preached, various Palestinian factions were carrying out attacks in Israel and inside the Israeli-occupied territories via Jordan and Lebanon, where they had established bases at the expense of the sovereignty of the host states. They took heart from the fighting along the Suez Canal and argued that it justified their thesis that only armed struggle could liberate occupied Arab land. Much of Arab public opinion was apparently dissatisfied with the status quo and was attracted by radical theses like those put forward by the Palestinians, while fragile regimes were tottering in both Lebanon and Jordan. In view of this explosive situation, at the time there seemed every possibility that the continuation of the War of Attrition, which by 1968 had extended to include sporadic fighting along Israel's eastern military fronts opposite Syria, Lebanon, and Jordan, might produce widespread regional upheavals, and a change in the composition of many regimes.[12]

In the end, the prospect of such a dangerous turn of events provoked the reaction of the status quo powers in the region, which preeminently included the superpowers, and none of this happened. As we have seen, in August 1970 a cease-fire was achieved along the Suez Canal on the basis of the American Rogers Plan and Soviet mediation, and was accepted by both Egypt and Jordan with the support of Saudi Arabia. Clearly, both the superpowers and the governments of many major states in the region were horrified by the prospect of unlimited region-wide instability growing out of continued Arab-Israeli fighting. Thereafter, the PLO was crushed in Jordan during the Black September 1970 confrontation with the Jordanian army, and in 1971 was completely driven out of the country, Iraqi and Syrian troops left Jordan, and the putative revolutionary moment in the Arab world passed.[13] A dangerous extension of the Arab-Israeli conflict into other potentially highly destabilizing developments was thereby avoided and this conflict remained contained.

Throughout the Cold War, and indeed until its final stages, it ultimately proved possible to localize and insulate crises and conflicts involving the superpowers growing out of the Arab-Israeli wars, and to limit their connections to other Middle Eastern hot spots. This was true even if these wars had a broader regional dimension, and even though this region was an important arena of the Cold War. Thus from the 1960s until the 1990s, Arab-Israeli wars were, as it were, largely compartmentalized and separate from other crises involving the superpowers and their proxies. These included the civil war in Yemen, the conflicts between Libya and Chad and Morocco and Algeria, and the series of major wars and confrontations in the Gulf region, including the Iraq-Iran War and the first round of conflict in Afghanistan provoked by the Soviet invasion. This was true even though the United States and the Soviet Union (and occasionally other lesser powers like France, Britain, and China) were major protagonists in all these conflicts, and often saw these hot spots as linked to one another and as part of a larger global struggle for influence.

My major argument here, and my reason for recapitulating all this history, some of which was covered in detail in earlier chapters, is that while this situation obtained for some years after the end of the Cold War, something important has changed in what, since the end of World War II, had been a relatively fixed pattern. In this pattern, as we have seen, crises in the eastern and southern Mediterranean and the rest of the Middle East, notably those involving Israel and the Arabs, and others involving Iran, Iraq, and the Gulf, remained relatively isolated from one another and from broader regional ramifications. Since the collapse of the Soviet Union, it has been quite striking that crises in the entire Middle East region and adjacent ones have appeared harder to isolate and more and more closely entwined with one another. This change unquestionably had something to do with the collapse of the Soviet Union and the consequent end of the Cold War in 1989–90, and with it the demise of a generally stable, if dangerous, system of international relations that had prevailed for forty-five years. This system certainly restrained the Soviet Union, indeed it "contained" it in some measure, but it also restrained the United States in certain ways. In the two decades since the disappearance of the Soviet Union and the demise of the Cold War system, these restraints on American action have been removed, and nothing has taken their place.

This change was also triggered by indigenous Middle Eastern factors. These included notably developments growing out of the Iranian Revolution of 1979, which it is already clear was one of the major events of the latter part of the twentieth century, but whose full impact it is still too early to assess. Other factors emerged from the ongoing wars inside Afghanistan that began with the Soviet invasion of that country in the same year, and have continued to be fought almost without interruption in some fashion ever since. Finally, this change also appears to be related to the connection that developed at the very end of the Cold War between the American response to Iraq's disastrous 1990 invasion of Kuwait, and the launching in the following year of the Madrid peace process. Since then, the Gulf and Arab-Israeli regional subsystems have been intertwined in ways that they were not before. It is of course true that Iraq was involved in the Arab states' conflict with Israel from its beginnings in 1948, and that Iraqi public opinion has been moved by the Palestine issue since the 1930s. However, Iraq always had relatively little if any impact on this conflict, whether during the 1948 war, when its forces' played an entirely secondary role, or during the War of Attrition and the 1973 war, when their role was even more minor. Even Iraq's firing of Scud missiles at Israel during the 1991 Gulf War had little strategic importance. Before the post–Cold War era, disputes in the Gulf had never been so intimately connected with the Arab-Israeli conflict, let alone with an attempted resolution of it. There may well be other linkages that go farther back and deeper than any of these.

What appears to have happened over the past couple of decades is that driven by all of these and other events, lasting and close connections have been developing between long-standing unsolved problems in the eastern Mediterranean, and others farther away. These include notably unsettled issues related to the Palestine question and the final definition of Israel's borders with Syria and Lebanon; the conflict within and over Lebanon; and other problem areas farther afield, some as far from the Mediterranean as Iraq, Iran, and the Gulf, and others outside the Middle East entirely, like Afghanistan and Pakistan.

Perhaps the most striking recent example of how these connections operated could be seen during the conflict in Lebanon over the summer of 2006.[14] The Israeli war on Lebanon was not itself in any way an isolated bilateral phenomenon. It developed directly out of the ongoing Israeli siege of the Gaza Strip, which in turn was part of the joint American-European-Israeli effort to boycott, isolate, and bring down the Hamas-dominated Palestinian government that emerged from the Palestinian Legislative Council elections of January 2006. Over time, this effort developed into a form of collective punishment, which operated essentially by imposing extreme deprivation on the 1.5 million people inside the hermetically sealed Gaza Strip, through Israel limiting or halting shipments of fuel, construction materials, commercial goods, and food and water. The idea, presumably, ridiculous on the face of it and an utter failure in the event, was that a totally impoverished populace would prevail on their rulers, who had both won the 2006 election and then seized power in the Gaza Strip in an armed coup in June 2007, and somehow persuade or force them to step down. There was little apparent concern in Jerusalem or Washington about whether targeting a large civilian population in this way violated international humanitarian law.

After the capture by Palestinian factions, including the Islamist Hamas movement, of the Israeli soldier Gilad Shalit and the killing of two other soldiers on June 25, 2006, Israel escalated considerably its pressure on the Gaza Strip, with the benevolent approval of the Bush administration. There followed many weeks of air and artillery bombardments of the towns, refugee camps, and cities of the Strip, the death of large numbers of Palestinian civilians,[15] and Israel's blockade of entry into and egress from Gaza for people and goods. This campaign was combined and coordinated with an intensification of the international financial blockade that had been instituted by the United States and the European Union in order to punish the Palestinian people collectively after they committed the egregious sin—in Israeli, American, and European eyes—of giving Hamas a majority in the January 2006 elections to the Palestine Legislative Council.

The leader of the Lebanese Shi'a Islamist group Hizballah, Shaykh Hassan Nasrallah, described (whether sincerely or not is irrelevant) his organization's capture of two more Israeli soldiers on July 12 along the Israeli-Lebanese border, which was the proximate cause of the subsequent Israeli summer offensive against Lebanon, as a response to this intense Israeli-American-European siege of Gaza. This testifies not only to the increasing linkage between crises in Palestine and Lebanon, but also to the close connections that Hizballah and Hamas have developed with each other. These connections went back to Israel's shortsighted decision in December 1992 to exile over four hundred senior Hamas militants to Marj al-Zuhour on the

Israeli-Lebanese border, where Hizballah cadres took them under their wing, beginning a close relationship between the two movements.

More important, Israel and its prime backer, the United States, increasingly came to see Hamas and Hizballah as inextricably connected in terms of the support they both received from Syria, and especially from Iran. Indeed, in the eyes of the Bush administration, both groups were no more than nearly identical terrorist pawns of Iran and Syria. They were seen as proxies of these powers in a situation where U.S. policymakers had made clear their belief that Iran and Syria, as "state sponsors of terrorism," were the root cause of the region's problems, and therefore became the main targets of U.S. hostility. Thus, the Arab-Israeli conflict, the internal Lebanese crisis, American efforts to exert pressure on Syria, and, most important, the intensifying American-Iranian standoff were all closely connected during the July–August 2006 Israeli war on Lebanon. In some sense, this war was a product of all these factors. It was also a clear instance of the way in which previously separate issues and problems have become intertwined in the Middle East since the end of the Cold War.

There is nothing particularly unusual about a connection between the Arab-Israeli conflict and crises involving Lebanon. As we saw in chapter 4, this linkage goes back at least to the first Israeli attack on Lebanon in the immediate aftermath of the 1967 war, when Beirut airport was devastated in 1968 by Israeli air strikes on airport installations and civilian airliners on the ground.[16] Soon thereafter, Israeli raids on Lebanon and the presence of armed Palestinian factions in Lebanon provoked the first of many governmental crises, eventually leading up to the Lebanese war of 1975–90. What was unusual in the summer 2006 war was that this was not just a further phase of the Arab-Israeli conflict, and not just another crisis involving Israel and

Lebanon. Rather, it appeared in important respects to be a proxy war between the United States and Iran, via the intermediary of their respective local allies, Israel and Hizballah.

It is irrelevant whether in fact the latter are proxies of the former, or if the key decisions in unleashing this conflict were taken in Beirut, Jerusalem, and Tel Aviv, or in Washington, Tehran, and Damascus. Whatever the case, there was a definite and justifiable perception on the part of leaders of the local, regional, and international actors that this was in some measure a war by proxy, and part of a much larger confrontation, one that transcended Lebanon, Israel, and the entire Arab-Israeli conflict. This is only one striking example among many of the linkages that appear to be developing in the post–Cold War era between conflicts in sometimes widely separated parts of the Middle East and its vicinity. Another equally striking example would be the growing organizational and other linkages between the original Afghanistan/Pakistan-based al-Qa'ida organization, on the one hand, and what appear to be largely homegrown militant Islamist groups in North Africa, Somalia, Yemen, Iraq, Afghanistan, Pakistan, and elsewhere, on the other. Although it is not clear what the precise connections between them are, there can be little question that in many cases inspiration, training, recruits, and probably other resources move from one to another. This, too, is a new phenomenon, albeit one not entirely without precedent.[17]

If the above analysis is broadly correct, what happened in the summer of 2006 in Lebanon, and subsequent developments, represents a new element in the Middle Eastern strategic equation. Now, we are not only witnessing extensions of the Arab-Israeli conflict into the domestic politics of neighboring countries, which is a very old pattern, aspects of which I examined in chapter 5. And we are not only witnessing external great-power involvement in this and other local conflicts, also an old pattern, which was explored in chapter 4. What we are now also seeing is a close connection, indeed an increasingly tight linkage, between conflicts in the eastern Mediterranean involving Israel, Palestine, Lebanon, Syria, Egypt, and other local actors, on the one hand, and other conflicts in the Gulf region, notably involving Iraq and Iran, as well as various other arenas far afield, like Afghanistan, Pakistan, Yemen, and North Africa, on the other.

GEORGE W. BUSH'S WAR ON TERROR

Disparate arenas, quite distinct conflicts, and a range of dissimilar organizations were explicitly grouped together under the Bush administration's rubric of the "global war on terror." This war is in fact not truly global, although it certainly has some global aspects, much hyped by its American partisans. It is rather being fought by the United States and its allies predominantly within lands inhabited predominantly by Muslims. Its battlefields range from Iraq to Afghanistan, from Palestine to Lebanon, and from central Asia to Morocco and Algeria, the Horn of Africa, and Darfur. Moreover, the terrorist "enemy" is in fact quite different in each place: in Afghanistan, in addition to the global terrorist/nihilist al-Qa'ida organization (which may in fact no longer mainly be based there), there is the Taliban, a Pushtun Afghani fundamentalist group whose aims and actions are entirely restricted to Afghanistan. They have little or nothing in common with, for example, Hamas, a Sunni Islamist Palestinian nationalist group whose aims and actions are entirely restricted to Palestine/Israel, or with the motley collection of Sunni and Shi'ite factions often savagely opposed to one another but whose main objective is fighting the United States' occupation in Iraq, or with Hizballah, a Lebanese Shi'ite Islamist group that grew up as a result of and in direct reaction to the Is-

raeli occupation of southern Lebanon in 1982 (in the words of
Israeli defense minister Ehud Barak, already quoted, "We entered into Lebanon . . . [and] Hizbullah was created as a result of
our stay there"[18]).

The only thing all of these movements and forces share in
common is a relationship to political Islam, and a dependence
on violence, often directed indiscriminately against civilians,
as the main means of achieving their political goals. Nevertheless, only a subset of the many groups—and states—that use
violence against civilians in ways that are similarly indiscriminate have been chosen as targets in this war. Among them all,
solely al-Qaʻida is an international terrorist organization that
specifically targets the United States. Moreover, in the words of
journalist Robert Scheer: "Terrorism is a social pathology that
needs to be excised with the surgical precision of detective
work, inspired by a high level of international cooperation, the
very opposite of the unilateral war metaphor that recruits new
generations of terrorists in the wake of the massive armies we
dispatch."[19]

It might be argued—I think wrongly—that the Bush administration's war on terror was no more than an illusion, an
artifact created as a projection of the powerful, deep-seated ideological drive that animated President George W. Bush, Vice
President Dick Cheney, and their closest advisors.[20] In fact, for
all the oversimplifications and all the falsehoods that are embodied in the concept, there can be little doubt that for these
and other Republican (and some Democratic) politicians who
have made it the centerpiece of their early-twenty-first-century
foreign and domestic policy, this conflict is very real. For many
of them it has a quasi-religious significance, much as had the
crusade against "international communism" fifty years ago.
In certain senses, driven by this partisan agenda, Americans
have simply exchanged communism for terrorism as an all-
encompassing, terrifying threat to their well-being.[21]

Whatever the degree of sincerity of its proponents, waging this war was absolutely necessary in American domestic terms for several quite prosaic reasons. The first was to show that the Bush administration was doing something in the face of the threat to the security of American citizens revealed by the attacks of 9/11. As it happens, in the assessment of most competent observers, the clumsy, inept, and poorly planned campaigns the Bush administration unleashed, whether in Afghanistan and Iraq or against al-Qa'ida or groups described as linked to it elsewhere, may have increased the actual risk to American citizens at home and abroad, creating terrorists where none previously existed. By the same assessments, these campaigns have most probably multiplied the number of enemies American forces are fighting abroad, notably in Iraq, which of course had nothing whatsoever to do with terrorism directed against the United States.[22] This outcome provided all the more reason for its partisans to proclaim the necessity of such a war, in a remarkably self-fulfilling cycle, whereby the failure of the Bush administration's policies to combat terrorism, indeed their success in expanding the ranks of America's enemies, was successfully exploited to justify the continuation of these same failed policies.

The "global war on terror" was necessary as well in order to maintain an atmosphere of fear in the American public at large. American citizens might otherwise have objected far more vigorously to the Bush administration's expansion of the powers of the presidency and of executive privilege generally, including its manifold expansion of presidential power at the expense of Congress, using a highly expanded definition of the president's war-making powers as the fulcrum, keyed on a tendentious interpretation of the 2002 congressional resolution authorizing the use of force in Iraq.[23] Specifically, were it not for this government-generated cloud of fear (and the impugning of the patriotism of critics by the administration and its right-wing media chorus, facilitated by this atmosphere), Americans might

have objected in particular to detention and surveillance policies that ignored constitutional protections and infringed on
citizens' rights at home, and to illegal practices including the use
of torture, whether at Guantánamo or Abu Ghraib or elsewhere,
that have tarnished the image of the United States around the
world.[24] The raising of terrorism alert levels at politically op-
portune moments, and the dramatic announcement of arrests
of would-be terrorists engaged in horrifying plots (which later
are downplayed or prove to be illusory) played a crucial part
in this manipulation of American public fears.[25] Only a war depicted in apocalyptic and existential terms as potentially affect-
ing all Americans, much as the struggle with communism was
depicted, would have been sufficient to justify the Bush administration's massive inroads on personal freedoms and its viola-
tions of the Constitution and the Bill of Rights.[26] As the eminent
legal scholar Geoffrey Stone has pointed out, citing cases going
back to the eighteenth century, the exploitation of war abroad
to justify the curtailment of freedoms at home is by no means a
new phenomenon in American history.[27] By these means, the
Bush administration took this shabby American tradition several steps further.

Third, the war on terror was necessary in order to justify and
explain the manifold expansion of America's invasive military
posture in the Middle East, Afghanistan, and elsewhere since
2001. This expansion was clearly intended to be the basis for a
massive, long-term American military presence throughout the
region. The fact that in and of itself this presence is a striking in-
novation is something that is almost totally ignored in American public discourse. The depth and novelty of the engagement
of United States military forces in various countries in the Middle East and adjacent states, whether in combat operations or in
other ways, has been little appreciated or understood by public
opinion, the press, and Congress. Nor has the public appreci-

ated that this new and massive military presence constitutes a radical departure from past practice. Few people realize that from the 1960s through the 1980s, at the height of the Cold War, when the United States faced a formidable Soviet rival and its regional allies and proxies, it somehow managed to protect its vital interests in the Gulf region and most of the Middle East successfully, essentially through an "over the horizon" military presence combined with the tiniest regional military footprint. During these decades, there were few American military bases (all of them small and unobtrusive), no occupations, and no high-profile U.S. military presence anywhere in the Middle East. The broad rubric of the "global war on terror," with the concomitant exploitation of fear to cow citizens and prevent them from asking pertinent questions, conveniently obviates explaining why, long after the demise of such a formidable rival as the USSR, it is today necessary to have a much more extensive American military presence in this region than at any time since World War II. It also makes it possible to obscure the fact that this presence involves deployments and bases that go far beyond those directly related to the ongoing wars in Iraq and Afghanistan.

Finally, the war on terror has become an indispensable new justification for the mammoth annual U.S. defense budget. This justification became all the more urgent in the wake of the Cold War and the demise of the former Soviet bogeyman, which nominally justified such prodigious and disproportionate expenditures: the U.S. defense budget was $483 billion in 1988 and $546 billion in 2007. USSR/Russia, Britain, and France *together* spent $336 billion and $147 billion in the same years: down from 69 percent to 26 percent of the expanded U.S. total in less than two decades.[28] For a short time, at the outset of the George W. Bush administration, it appeared as if a resurgent China would be recruited to play the essential role of justifying such bloated spending.[29] Then 9/11 intervened, providing a much more urgent and slightly more plausible pretext for inflated defense budgets.

We should never forget, however, that while the global war on terror may serve the base ulterior purposes shared by some American politicians, the Pentagon, and the military-industrial complex, it is also a real war. As of July 2008, more than forty-one hundred American service personnel had been killed and thirty thousand wounded in Iraq, with over five hundred American troops killed and nearly twenty-two hundred wounded in Afghanistan. Meanwhile, untold and uncounted tens of thousands of Iraqis, Afghans, and others have died.[30] This war constitutes a monumental global military-intelligence-political effort, to which is devoted much of a current annual United States defense budget of nearly $550 billion, including a requested "emergency" supplementary appropriation for 2007 of over $100 billion to fight the Iraqi and Afghan wars,[31] and a large proportion of the huge confidential budgets for the many components of the U.S. intelligence community, as well as other large sums hidden within other parts of the U.S. federal budget.

In the end it is irrelevant whether these hundreds of billions of dollars have been spent on the wars in Iraq or Afghanistan, or in Israel or Somalia or Pakistan, or at home on unnecessary weapons systems. In any case, this was all part of a larger effort by a United States administration that for eight years was led by individuals who appeared to believe seriously, or at least pretended to believe, that all of the entirely discrete and separate wars, conflicts, and forces that the United States has been engaged with from the Middle East through central Asia, with manifold extensions elsewhere, were integrally linked. In their view, the United States is fighting a single enemy in all of these disparate arenas, which some of them, including Senator John McCain before and during the 2008 presidential campaign, have termed "Islamofascist." This neat Madison Avenue conflation of two stock bogeymen was a typically cynical concoction of the Bush administration's neoconservative fellow travelers and spinmeisters. These individuals showed no compunction and absolutely no shame in arbitrarily invoking Munich, appeasement, a nuclear holocaust (or the Nazi Holocaust),[32] or any other ahistorical precedent to justify their extreme twenty-first-century policies. In the rhetoric of the Bush administration, this single hydra-headed enemy that it proclaimed the United States must fight the world over was the same one that attacked the United States on 9/11, and was responsible for numerous other terrorist outrages against Americans and others.

Is this a correct view, or a well-informed and objective one? It is certainly not correct: I have already discussed the extreme diversity, in some cases the complete dissimilarity, among the disparate targets of this "war." I have also pointed out that most of them clearly have no intention of harming the United States or its citizens. Moreover, it is not a well-informed and objective view. We know this from many sources. One is the devastating account of Paul Pillar, the experienced professional intelligence official who from 2002 until 2005 was national intelligence officer for the Middle East, in effect the American intelligence community's most senior analyst. He damningly describes how his and other expert advice was systematically overruled on the basis of spurious "evidence" trumped up by political appointees like Lewis Libby, David Addington, Stephen Cambone, and Douglas Feith, doing the bidding of their ill-informed political superiors, notably Vice President Cheney and Defense Secretary Donald Rumsfeld, in order to justify the rush to war with Iraq.[33]

Another damning piece of evidence is an article by an editor of the *Congressional Quarterly* showing that many top members of the Bush administration (and of the congressional leadership as well) did not know some of the most elementary things about Islam and Middle East politics, like the difference between Sunnis and Shi'a, or between Hamas and Hizballah.[34] Given this abysmal degree of ignorance regarding basic facts about Islam and the Islamic world today, it is inconceivable that these senior officials could have had any clear idea about the true nature of the links—if any—that existed between the elements of the international concatenation of "rogue states" and Islamist "terrorist organizations" which they described as the monolithic "Islamofascist" enemy of the United States. There was clearly much else such senior figures inside and outside government did not know and did not want to learn about the Middle East and the Islamic world, as their superficial, Manichaean depiction of this struggle and their fumbling conduct of the wars in Iraq and Afghanistan have amply demonstrated. This grievous lack of basic knowledge, and a stubborn unwillingness to listen to experts or to hear contrary views, was in fact broadly characteristic of the Bush administration. Given these realities, one must ask how these individuals could have had any serious understanding of the enemy against which they claimed the United States must wage an unending struggle.

It is not coincidentally an article of blind faith among those of the neoconservative ideological persuasion that dominated the Bush administration (and an enduring staple of Israeli government rhetoric as well) that such "rogue states" are the driving engines of terrorism, even in the absence of any concrete evidence for this assertion. The obsession with fighting "state sponsors of terrorism," which the Bush administration and earlier administrations have firmly embedded in United States law, helped justify the invasion of Iraq, and has been used as a justification for a future war with Iran. The pursuit of this white whale is central to the worldview of these policymakers and their ideological soul-mates in the plethora of generously funded right-wing "think tanks" that have played such a prominent role in Washington in recent decades.[35] It is almost invariably wedded to a lack of any in-depth historical, linguistic, cultural, or other expertise about the countries in this category, or indeed about the broader Middle East.[36]

Nevertheless, however misguided, simplistic, and ill-informed these views may have been, they constituted the fundamental basis for the policies and actions in the Middle East of the Bush administration from its inception. These initiatives escaped virtually without public scrutiny inside the United States for several years because of the powerful aftereffects on the American national psyche of the terrorist attacks on New York and Washington, D.C., of September 11, 2001. At least where Iraq is concerned, some of these policies were finally called into question by American public opinion, and provoked the skepticism of a growing segment of the higher ranks of the U.S. officer corps, as well as many experienced intelligence professionals and diplomats. However, these public attitudes and the private doubts of those in government service hardly affected the course of the war in Iraq, which would enter its seventh year in March 2009. Nor did they have much impact on the policy of the Bush administration in its last years in a variety of other areas in the Middle East.

Throughout George W. Bush's second term, expressing the slightest doubt about the near-sacred construct of the "global war on terror" was perceived as being lethally dangerous to American politicians, particularly Democrats. Casting doubt on central aspects of this concept seemed nearly as toxic then as was the accusation of being "soft on communism" at the height of the Cold War. This blanket dispensation in turn covered a multitude of sins. Thus, since al-Qa'ida was based in Afghanistan and was allied to the Taliban, it is virtually impossible to question whether it makes sense for the United States to continue to fight a war in Afghanistan against the Taliban. One looks in vain for American politicians or policy "experts" who will ask whether the United States and it allies should continue to occupy and try to pacify Afghanistan after eight years of trying, without success, to prevail over the Taliban. Even less likely is public questioning of whether there might be some means of achieving the universally-agreed-upon end of defeating the global terrorists of al-Qaʻida other than an unending war in exceedingly difficult terrain against what is, and for nearly a decade has been, the strongest force among the Pushtun population of Afghanistan (who constitute the country's largest single ethnic group and whose fellow Pushtuns dominate Pakistan's adjacent northwest provinces). Not entirely surprisingly, therefore, during the summer–fall 2008 election campaign, both presidential candidates dutifully made it clear that in spite of their differences over Iraq, they would expand the war in Afghanistan with the dispatch of further units of American troops.

The stubbornness with which its proponents put forward the basic idea that in order to deal with terrorism, the United States must make war all over the Middle East and in its environs, and that full-fledged war is the only means to deal with this scourge, should give us a clear sense of how deadly serious is the "global war on terror" and its concomitant, the cold war the Bush administration has waged with Iran and what are described as its proxies, notably Hizballah and Hamas. Those who disseminate these ideas affect this seriousness in spite of the fact that rational assessment would reveal that both global Islamist terrorism directed against the United States and the threat posed by Iran and all its minions are in fact far less formidable and lethal in their potential than were the Soviet Union and the "international communist movement" in their heyday. And yet the levels of hysteria, hyperbole, and hyperventilation among the Chicken Littles who propagate such ideas are at least as high as at the apogee of the Cold War. What makes this situation particularly dangerous is not the connections they have imagined between elements of a shadowy and sinister Islamic "terrorist international," but the interaction of this vivid fantasy world with the dangerous actual linkages that have emerged between a number of real-world hot spots.

I have argued that the years since the end of the Cold War have witnessed the growth of closer linkages between the Gulf, the eastern Mediterranean, and global terrorism. Most notable among these linkages have been the connections between the Arab-Israeli conflict and issues related to the conflicted American-Iranian relationship since the fall of the shah. This has meant that the ongoing crises, conflicts, and friction involving Palestine, Lebanon, Syria, Iraq, Iran, Afghanistan, and Pakistan are now ever more closely related. This process has been enhanced significantly in consequence of the impact over the past few years of a number of important, novel phenomena:

1. *The destruction of the Iraqi state.* Iraq, while barely over eighty years old in 2003 and nominally created by the British, was firmly rooted in governmental processes and institutions left behind by the Ottoman state, which ruled this region for four hundred years. The most important of these institutions was Iraq's military establishment, which was created in its entirety by former Ottoman officers.[37] The dissolution of these hard-won state structures began with the suicidally misguided decision of Saddam Hussein's Ba'th regime to attack Iran in 1980. This decision, it is worth recalling again, was strongly encouraged and supported at the time by the United States and its European allies and Arab clients. There followed nearly nine devastating years of war with Iran, and then the Ba'th regime's equally foolhardy decision to invade Kuwait in 1990. The resulting slow disintegration of Iraqi society and economy, and

with them of the power of the Iraqi state, was then com-
pounded by Iraq's defeat and expulsion from Kuwait in 1991,
and the ravaging of the country through the U.S./UN sanctions regime for the next twelve years. This process of disintegration was finally completed and may have been made
irreversible by the Bush administration's decision to invade
and occupy Iraq and dismantle its state structures and army,
without putting anything in their place but an overstretched
and underprepared army of occupation. The result was, for a
time at least, the virtually complete dissolution of one of the
most powerful Arab states and the potential disappearance of
Iraq as a unified country; the sparking of acute sectarian civil
strife, which at one point reached the level of an Iraqi civil war;
grave possible ramifications for sectarian conflict in various
parts of the Islamic world; and the creation of a lasting power
vacuum in a critical part of the Middle East. Even if the Iraqis
can succeed in reconstructing the Iraqi state themselves (once
the American occupation of their country has finally ended),
hopefully on a more equitable and democratic basis than that
of the pre-2003 state, the process will be painful and will take
many years. Moreover, until this process is completed, a power
vacuum will remain at the heart of the region.

2. *The growth in power of an independent Iran completely outside
    the orbit of any other state.* The Iranian Revolution of 1978–
    79 was followed by the radicalization and entrenchment in
    power of an authoritarian Islamist clerical regime that was
    hostile to both communism and the West and that has domi-
    nated Iran ever since. This regime further consolidated its
    power—and its turn toward radical isolationism was acceler-
    ated—as a result of a Pyrrhic victory in the war launched
    against it by Iraq, with the support of most Arab countries,
    Russia, and the West. The regime grew in strength with the
    gradual decline of Iraq under the crushing international sanc-

tions regime after the 1991 Gulf War. The regional rise of Iran was capped by the defeat and destruction of Iraq's Ba'th regime in 2003, and earlier, that of the Taliban in Afghanistan, as well as the postoccupation dismantling of the remaining state structures in Iraq. Much of this took place courtesy of the wars of the George W. Bush administration, which thereby eliminated two of the Iranian regime's most deadly enemies. Relieved of these two neighboring predators, Iran has been free to pursue nuclear power, whether it turns out to be for civilian or military ends, and to extend aggressive support to its allies and proxies like Hizballah throughout the region. These actions have been signs of the clerical regime's growing power, confidence, and reach, even as they were a response to the fierce overt and covert campaign waged against it by the Bush administration and its allies.[38] It is worth noting that the past three decades mark the first extended period in over a century that Iran has not been dominated by external powers or subject to their direct interference. It remains to be seen whether Iran's actions and the provocative and bellicose rhetoric of leading regime figures like President Mahmoud Ahmadinejad will play into the hands of powers like the United States, Israel, and Saudi Arabia, which have seemed determined to limit its influence, if not, at times, to destroy its current regime.

3. *The destruction of the Afghan state, and the creation of a power vacuum in that country.* This process began with the ill-fated 1979 Soviet invasion, and the decision by the United States and its clients to intervene covertly in Afghanistan to defeat the USSR. It was accelerated by the equally ill-fated U.S. decision to support the most radical and extreme Islamic factions inside Afghanistan against the Soviets, including fanatical volunteers recruited by the intelligence services of the United States, Saudi Arabia, Egypt, Pakistan, Israel, and other coun-

tries from all over the Arab and Islamic worlds. In the course of the war, the Red Army, its allies, its opponents, and other forces devastated the country, leading to the near-destruction of the Afghan central government and making Afghanistan nearly ungovernable. The defeat there of the Soviet Union and the latter's subsequent collapse was followed by the callous abandonment of the country by the United States and eventually by the rise to power of the Taliban, sponsored by Pakistani military intelligence, and by the emergence of al-Qai'da. Following 9/11, Afghanistan was the scene of overt U.S. military intervention. This provoked the descent of the country once again into a low-grade civil-*cum*-regional war involving the United States, NATO, Pakistan, Iran, and other actors which has been ongoing for nearly eight years. As I write in late 2008, it does not appear that this war is close to an end, that an Afghan state which can exert control over the entire country is going to be rapidly reconstructed (it is questionable whether such an entity ever existed in the entire history of Afghanistan), or that the power vacuum there is about to be filled. Nor does it appear that the current external intervention in Afghanistan will be any more lasting or successful than was that of Alexander the Great or others who followed him, from the Russian and British to the Soviet empires.

4. *The Gulf-Palestine connection.* In 1990 and 1991 U.S. secretary of state James Baker offered this linkage in exchange for the support of Arab governments for the American-led counteroffensive against the Iraqi occupation of Kuwait. As a sort of quid pro quo, Baker held out the willingness of the first Bush administration to launch a comprehensive negotiation for a resolution of the conflict between Israel and the Arab parties, including the Palestinians. This linkage resulted in the convening of the 1991 Madrid peace conference and later in the negotiation of the 1993 Oslo Accords and the Israeli-Jordanian

peace treaty. The inconclusive—indeed in most respects negative—outcome of the Oslo process had become apparent to
most observers less than a decade after the Oslo Accords were
signed in Washington, D.C., in 1993.[39] This in turn has called
into question the wisdom of those Arab governments and the
PLO leadership, which accepted the sincerity of the commitment of successive U.S. administrations to a serious effort to
end Israel's occupation of Arab territories and to achieve a just
peace between Israel and the Palestinians in particular. The attempt by Secretary of State Condoleezza Rice in late 2007 and
in 2008 to launch a new round of Palestinian-Israeli negotiations was linked to the Bush administration's ongoing region-
wide campaign against Iran in ways reminiscent of the linkage
with the war with Iraq that was promoted by Secretary Baker
seventeen years earlier. It appeared, however, highly unlikely
that history would judge that it achieved even the limited success of her predecessor's initiatives. What is clear in any case is
that Palestine-Israel and Gulf issues are more closely linked
than they ever had been in the past.

5. *The invocation by the Bush administration, discussed in this
chapter, of a "global war on terror" as a rubric covering intensive
direct and indirect American military intervention and covert
operations ranging from the wars in Afghanistan and Iraq to
less visible instances in Iran, Somalia, Sudan, and elsewhere.*
Among the indicators of the broad extent of the war on terror
are the expanded American military presence throughout the
Middle East and central Asia, including the development of
many large, new "enduring" bases in Iraq and elsewhere,[40] and
the creation of a new military command, the United States
Africa Command.[41] This effort ties together an entirely new
level of American activities across a vast range of the Islamic
world, from Northwest Africa to central Asia, Pakistan, and
perhaps farther afield. It was certainly meant by the Bush ad-

ministration to put in place a long-term American military presence, at least insofar as Iraq was concerned. The term "enduring bases" was employed by Bush administration officials early on during the occupation of Iraq, and it then faded from their rhetoric, although the major bases there have grown relentlessly larger and more permanent in the six years since the occupation began. The term was reprised in President Bush's speech of September 13, 2007, in which he spoke of an "enduring relationship" with Iraq, and a U.S. military presence there that "extends beyond my presidency." By contrast, in July 2008, Democratic presidential candidate Barack Obama wrote, "I would not hold our military, our resources and our foreign policy hostage to a misguided desire to maintain permanent bases in Iraq. . . . we seek no presence in Iraq similar to our permanent bases in South Korea."[42] It remains to be seen how an increasingly assertive Iraqi government will deal with this issue under a new administration, given that Iraqi public opinion is overwhelmingly opposed to the long-term presence of U.S. bases in Iraq.[43]

6. *The precipitate decline in the influence and standing of the United States in the Middle East, the Islamic countries, and elsewhere.* This decline in American stature has in large part been a consequence of the various phenomena just described, the cumulative impact of which has been to lead the United States in a few short years from a position of unparalleled worldwide power, influence, and popularity at the end of the Cold War, to one of nearly universal opprobrium with public opinion in the Middle East and the Islamic world, and also in many other parts of the globe.[44] The degree of self-inflicted damage done by the disastrous American occupation of Iraq in particular both to American deterrent capabilities and to perceptions of American capabilities is also clearly great, but hard to quantify. This decline in the influence of the United States, and in

other major powers' perceptions of its capabilities, which may or may not have reached its nadir, has not yet led these powers to attempt to step in to fill the resulting power vacuum. However, other powers may eventually be impelled to do just that if after the departure of George W. Bush from the White House in January 2009 there is a continuation of the trend established in U.S. policy over the years of the Bush administration of ill-considered decisions based on extreme ideological readings of the Middle East, combined with aggressive resistance to relying on real expertise about that region or to considering the interests and views of allies. The Middle East is simply too important to the vital interests of too many people the world over to be left much longer to the sometimes brutal ministrations of a reckless, stumbling, delusional giant.

There have been many consequences of the interaction of these phenomena. Among the most important of them was a steady decline over several years in American public support for President Bush and especially for his administration's Iraq policy, a policy that CNN polls showed was steadily opposed over more than a year from mid-2007 to late 2008 by about two-thirds of Americans.[45] This precipitate decline in popular support for the president's signature issue, the Iraq War, marked a rapid comedown for a man who won two presidential elections and enjoyed high poll ratings as recently as 2004. Popular rejection of the Iraq War is an indication that American citizens, notoriously insulated from news about the real situation in many parts of the world by the mainstream media's meretricious and shallow coverage of global events (if serious international coverage is provided at all), nevertheless managed to figure out that things were not going at all well in the Middle East, all the spin notwithstanding, and that the Bush administration's policies were at least partly to blame.

AFTER THE COLD WAR

What more can be said about this new post–Cold War situation centered on the Middle East, where one crisis spills over into another, and where dangerous flashpoints, from central Africa to central Asia, are increasingly linked? It is clear that this new regional configuration poses different and more unpredictable dangers than did the more controlled and localized Middle East crises of the Cold War period. However adventurous or dangerous were the occasional actions of the superpowers in the eastern Mediterranean, however volatile were the Middle Eastern conflicts they became involved in, there were always clear rules of the game. Moreover, these crises were largely compartmentalized, and there generally was the sense at the end of the day that responsible, sober adults were in charge (even if this may well have been an illusion at times[46]). For one thing, most of the major protagonists during the Cold War—the PLO in its early years being the major exception—were states rather than non-state actors, unlike the situation today, where shadowy terrorist groups and nebulous proxies for various states appear to play a key role.

At the same time, it is important to note that the potential price of a misstep during the Cold War was far greater than it is today: this price included the very real, if remote, possibility of collective annihilation of the entire human race in a nuclear war. For all the concrete dangers posed by al-Qaʻida and other Islamist terrorists—as opposed to illusory dangers emanating from them that have been imagined and inflated by professional panic-mongers in Washington since the end of the Cold War —these groups do not pose an existential threat to Western societies and states. Quite unlike the situation during the Cold War, the United States and its allies in Europe and Japan are at no risk whatsoever of annihilation by al-Qaʻida and similar organizations, even if such groups have proven that they have the certain capacity to launch cruel acts of mass terrorism that pose a serious threat to the safety and security of American citizens and those of its allies. This crucial difference—between a true existential peril and the grave potential danger to innocent citizens from random, heinous acts of terrorism like those directed against the World Trade Center, the Atocha train station in Madrid, and the Underground in London—has been cynically elided by those in Washington who after 9/11 made it their business to try to keep the American public in a permanent state of fear.

Today the United States, as the globe's sole superpower, is operating in a world without rules. Most of the rules fashioned during the Cold War disappeared with the collapse of the Soviet Union, while the framework of international law and institutions painstakingly devised at the end of World War II has been systematically disdained and degraded in part by the arrogant unilateralists who were in power in Washington for eight years, at times openly expressing their contempt for the United Nations, international law, and human rights. Moreover, as had already been established in Afghanistan, in the fight against al-Qa'ida, and in the war in Iraq, it became painfully apparent once again during the summer 2006 war in Lebanon and in subsequent events in that country and in Palestine that the most senior U.S. policymakers, from Vice President Cheney and the president on down, were little more than fumbling amateurs where the Middle East was concerned. They were revealed once again as willfully ill-informed, and as driven by a thoroughly mistaken set of idées fixes. To the extent that they had a policy, it was radically misguided and largely unsuccessful. They were operating in the Middle East without a compass, in a post–Cold War international system in a state of flux.

For all the terrors of Cold War doctrines like "mutual assured destruction," for all the cynical manipulation by the superpowers of their clients and allies, for all the Cold War's many other negative effects, once the U.S. government decided on a policy of containment, and once it was clear that the Soviet Union could and would only challenge this policy at the margins, the Cold War system provided a relatively stable international environment. This was certainly true as far as the Mediterranean and the Middle East were concerned, even if the danger of a nuclear confrontation always hovered in the background. Today, in a unipolar world, there are no agreed-upon rules, there is no clear system that governs international relations, and there appears to be little impetus toward a better arrangement of global governance. This is particularly the case since, following the achievement of uncontested U.S. hegemony as a result of the sudden and unexpected disappearance of the Soviet Union, three successive American administrations failed to contribute to a vision for a world order to help organize the new post–Cold War configuration. Indeed, the George W. Bush administration played the central role in creating a new world of disorder by aggressively denouncing or undermining many of the existing pillars of the international system, from strategic arms limitations agreements with Russia to crucial aspects of international humanitarian law. It is the terrible misfortune of the Middle East to be at the epicenter of this new galaxy of disorder, and of intertwined wars, crises, flashpoints, and failed, failing, or precarious states, ranging from Afghanistan and Iraq to the east, to Palestine and Lebanon in the center, to Sudan and Somalia in the south and west.

This new situation is not just a function of the failure of Presidents George H. W. Bush, Bill Clinton, and George W. Bush and their principal advisors to define clearly a new role for the United States in the post–Cold War world, or to try to work multilaterally toward a new international synthesis to replace that erected during World War II, although all three achieved relatively little in this regard. Nor is it solely a function of the growing conflict between the United States and certain forces in the Arab and Islamic worlds, including those that target the United States and are nihilistic, murderous, and ruthless. It also represents the egregious failure of other international actors to shoulder international responsibilities commensurate with their size and power. This failure ranges from that of a European Union that barely has an organized, unified international presence (outside of the economic sphere, where it is a formidable giant), to that of a Russia that exercises its power fitfully, selfishly, clumsily, and often brutally, to that of India and China, great world powers of the future that still do not behave with confidence outside their narrow immediate neighborhoods. None of these actors has succeeded in defining a new and more constructive role for itself in the post–Cold War world, and in the vital Mediterranean–Middle Eastern region in particular. Two of these powers, Europe and Russia, border directly on that region, and have historically been deeply concerned with its strategic importance, and more recently with its importance in terms of world energy supplies. India and China, while located farther away, are also increasingly affected by both strategic and energy considerations relating to the Middle East. Nevertheless, none of them has yet acted decisively in the region, whether positively or negatively, in a fashion commensurate with their important interests in it. Were they to do so in a cooperative, collective way, one that might channel and curb the unbridled exercise of U.S. power there, it might indeed have a positive effect.

There is one final factor that defines the situation in the Mediterranean–Middle East region. This is the inability of the Arab states, or of any single Arab state, to assert themselves successfully in events taking place largely within the confines of the

Arab world and its peripheries. With the partial exception of the initiatives taken by nonstate actors like Hizballah and other parties and militias (and a very few rare exceptions like the May 2008 Qatari mediation of the Lebanese crisis), the Arab states, thanks to the manifold incapacities of their leaders, are no longer an actor or a force, and are no longer subjects of their own history. After millennia when it was the home to great world powers, the Middle East has in recent decades been turned in large measure into the object of the actions of others. The Arab world in particular has become an arena where other actors—whether external powers, substate actors, or the few powerful non-Arab Middle Eastern states with significant ability to act independently, like Israel, Turkey, and Iran—take all the initiatives, and where the Arab states respond passively. The contrast between the Arab states and these three major non-Arab states in the region is striking: for all the disadvantages and problems each of the latter has to confront, all three have become powerful and feared independent actors on the regional stage, are subjects rather than objects of the actions of others, and have to be taken very seriously by the United States and other world powers.

This situation in the Middle East looks as if it may continue for some time. If it is to change, that change could come from several directions:

1. *When stronger, reformed democratic Arab states begin to address seriously the pressing demands of their own peoples, and at the same time begin to act with a minimum of cohesion and solidarity as a group.* This end would require common interests and a commitment to collective action being placed above the selfish, greedy, narrow interests of the unrepresentative cliques of autocrats and kleptocrats that cling to power in most of these states, against the wishes of their people. Given

the glaring and growing inequalities and disparities within and between Arab states, such action would probably involve, at the very least, intensive, targeted regional investment in the most populous states (most of which have limited or no oil resources) by the small Arab states of the Gulf (the United Arab Emirates, Oman, Kuwait, Qatar, and Bahrain), which along with Libya are very sparsely populated—together all six have only 14 million people—and have huge reserves of petrochemicals, and a total GDP of $513 billion. By contrast, Egypt in 2007 had over 80 million people and a GDP of $404 billion. The Saudi GDP, at $564 billion, was larger than that of Egypt or of the other six states put together.[47] The Arab states have witnessed stagnation and an absence of regime change in most cases for decades, and suffer from a definite democratic deficit, a situation that I argued in chapter 5 was exacerbated by the Cold War. It has continued since then. A move to democratic governance and a change for the better in the current dysfunctional relations between the Arab states may occur. If not, it is likely that some weak Arab regimes, including perhaps that of Egypt, will be drawn further into a spiral of regional destabilization, and may even fall victim to revolution and regime collapse as a result of their weaknesses and their clinging dependence on an American giant, which has stumbled repeatedly over the decades in its policies toward them.

2. *When other major powers, like Europe, Russia, China, and India, finally begin to develop a coherent world role for themselves, and recognize the vital importance to their long-term interests of an active and enlightened policy in the Mediterranean–Middle East region.* This objective need not require directly confronting the actions of the United States. It could consist simply of these states asserting their vital interests in the stability of this region—stability that has been endangered over the past few years by, among other things, shortsighted American

policies—and affirming the consequent need for rational, collective action to remedy the dangerous situation created by the interlocking crises from Palestine to Pakistan that the Bush administration aggravated and exacerbated. This course might involve the following: a) active participation in defusing the dangerous American-Iranian confrontation; b) addressing forthrightly the problem of nuclear proliferation in the Middle East, including by Israel, rather than just the question of Iran's potential acquisition of nuclear weapons; c) helping to end the American occupation of Iraq and Afghanistan and helping the peoples of those countries to achieve peace and stability free of foreign interference; and d) aiding in brokering an Arab-Israeli peace settlement and securing a rapid end to Israel's military occupation and colonization of Palestinian land. Failing such robust action, the interests of all these major powers will continue to be ignored by the United States, and harmed by the ongoing crises that rack this region, as they have been harmed in the past in part as a consequence of American policy there.

3.   *When the American people wake fully from the nightmare illusions fostered by the George W. Bush administration, and begin to deal pragmatically with real-world problems instead of responding to the exaggerated phantasms and false images that the U.S. government and its allies in the media have projected onto the region, from Afghanistan to Darfur, most of them keyed to terrorism.* This last change cannot begin in earnest until after the Bush administration has left office in January 2009. It may not begin for some time after that, if then: shallow, uninformed, hackneyed thinking about the Middle East is certainly not restricted to the Republican Party; it is indeed alive and well among many politicians and would-be policymakers in the orbit of the Democratic Party. There is, moreover, the possibility that the policies of the Bush administration will

leave behind time bombs that might worsen an already bad situation, by encouraging regional Sunni-Shi'a sectarian strife and Arab-Iranian and Israeli-Iranian tensions, if not by provoking a war with Iran, leaving a poisoned legacy that any new administration in Washington will have to struggle with for many years.

Change of a negative kind could also come from a particularly provocative action by the Iranian regime, from a major terrorist outrage, from the sudden collapse of a major Middle Eastern regime, from an unexpected and rapid worsening of the internal situation in Iraq, Afghanistan, Pakistan, Lebanon, Yemen, Israel/Palestine, or one of the region's other potential flashpoints.

Until the futility and fecklessness of the policies the United States has pursued in the Middle East for many years is finally brought home to the American people, forcing a radical change for the better in these policies, it is up to a variety of actors, whether the hitherto absent Arab states on the southern and eastern shores of the Mediterranean, or the feeble European Union on the Mediterranean's northern shores, or nearby Russia, or other powers, to attempt to fill the vacuum left by the decline of American influence and the irresponsibility and destructiveness of the actions of the United States in this region over at least eight years. This decline was attested to by a host of regional initiatives taken by local and middle-sized powers in mid- and late 2008 against the wishes and without the participation of the United States. Among them were the Qatari mediation of the Lebanese conflict, the Israeli-Syrian negotiations mediated by Turkey, arrangements reached indirectly between Israel and Hizballah and Israel and Hamas for a prisoner exchange and a cease-fire, respectively, and France's brokering of the establishment of diplomatic relations between Lebanon and Syria. If such major initiatives could be taken by regional and middle-sized actors, major outside powers like the EU, Russia, China, and India have the capability to attempt to become active and responsible players in this volatile region. The alternative is to continue to allow the lead to be taken by the United States, after the Bush administration's behavior rightly forfeited the confidence of people around the world and lost it the support of an overwhelming majority of the American people. We must await evidence that a succeeding administration can free itself from the delusions and fantasies that have entrapped American policymakers in their engagement with the Middle East.

THE FUTURE OF AMERICAN
POWER IN THE MIDDLE EAST

Let me conclude by returning to the questions about the future of American power in the Middle East with which I ended the first chapter of this book. As a historian, I am naturally reluctant to make predictions. But I would suggest, on the one hand, that there are both institutional factors and a powerful element of inertia at work here, which together would militate in favor of a much larger long-term American military presence in the Middle East than was either possible or likely before George W. Bush became president, or than is in the interest of the United States or the Middle East.

The illogic, indeed the absurdity, of destroying regimes and occupying countries in order to deal with amorphous transnational terrorist networks, and of using a military machine that currently costs over $550 billion annually to chase after a few thousand clandestine terrorist operatives, has forcibly struck many sensible observers in the United States and around the world. It has even occurred to many of the American politicians who cravenly vote for these bloated military budgets, which produce weapons systems unusable against terrorists, and in some cases weapons that were originally designed to be used against enemies that no longer exist.[48] But the far-fetched connection between launching wars in the Middle East and protecting the American public against terrorism was successfully made by the Bush administration, and has been faithfully repeated by its sounding board in the right-wing "think tank" world and in much of the media. In spite of the evident bankruptcy of this argument, it continues to dominate public discourse.[49]

The seductive siren song of the "global war on terror" has mesmerized many Americans. Opposing it, and with it the concentrated power of what President Dwight D. Eisenhower warned against in his Farewell Address as the "military-industrial complex," terrifies most American politicians. Eisenhower explicitly cautioned the American people: "In the councils of government we must guard against the acquisition of unwarranted influence, whether sought or unsought, by the military-industrial complex. The potential for the disastrous rise of misplaced power exists and will persist. We must never let the weight of this combination endanger our liberties or democratic processes."[50] Eisenhower's speech here echoes George Washington's Farewell Address of September 19, 1796, in which the first American president warned against "overgrown military establishments, which, under any form of government, are inauspicious to liberty, and which are to be regarded as particularly hostile to Republican Liberty."[51] It is certainly worth recalling that these were the two American presidents with the broadest experience of high military command, and perhaps the deepest understanding of how war and alarms of war can cloud the understanding of rational men and women. The lethal combination of the fear of appearing "soft on terrorism" (which has almost imperceptibly replaced communism as an American bogeyman) with the unparalleled clout of the American military establishment and arms industry may therefore well help to prolong the agony brought on by the current heavy American footprint in the Middle East.

On the other hand, against these factors, it can be argued that lost wars have a leaden political logic of their own, as we saw in Vietnam with both France in the 1950s and the United States in the 1960s and 1970s. We may well see that the Iraq War will eventually have the same effect, turning American public opinion not only against the war, which solid majorities of Americans have opposed for over four years, since mid-2004, but forcefully against any and all foolish and ill-conceived military adventures abroad.[52] If public opinion goes beyond its basic opposition to the Iraq War and turns broadly anti-interventionist, as it did after the Vietnam War, Congress may finally be forced to do the constitutional duty it has neglected to do: act to check and balance the imperial executive that has arisen in what Daniel Yergin called the national security state bred by the Cold War.[53]

This has happened before. The prerogatives of the bloated imperial post–World War II executive were cut back slightly in the wake of the Vietnam debacle through the 1973 War Powers Act, the mid-1970s work of the Pike Committee in the House and the Church Committee in the Senate on intelligence oversight, the Foreign Intelligence Surveillance Act of 1978, the Boland Amendment of 1982 banning aid to the Contras, and other acts of true legislative courage. Nevertheless, the specter of the imperial war-making executive answerable to nobody and nothing was not banished and arose again. It was first revived in the Reagan era, with the vast expansion of the military budget and with the Iran-Contra scheme and other illegal attempts to subvert the intent of Congress. It rose again during the administration of George W. Bush, in a far more dangerous shape. This time it took the form of unceasing efforts to expand without limit the authority of the executive branch domestically and internationally on the basis of the most expansive possible reading of the president's war-making prerogatives. This effort was made by President Bush and his closest advisors, especially Vice President Cheney and his former colleague Donald Rumsfeld. Neither of the latter was ever reconciled to the post-Vietnam downsizing of these executive prerogatives in the mid-1970s, when they both served in senior positions in the Ford administration. They and George W. Bush were able to remedy this situation after the 2000 election.

This is part of a decades-old struggle for a constitutional balance between the executive and the legislature over foreign policy and war-making, the latter backed by citizens who would restrain the executive and its actions in the world. Its outcome will perhaps determine not only whether the United States will continue to play the kind of overweening military role in the Middle East that it has played since the end of the Cold War, and especially during the presidency of George W. Bush. It may also determine whether the United States will revert in some measure to being a republic, responsive to the wishes of its citizens and, because of its enormous economic, technological, and military power, necessarily first among equals among the nations of the globe, but no more than that. The alternative is that the United States will become even more of an empire, with its leaders imperiously ignoring the wishes of its own citizens and those of other peoples in the world.

I have argued that the global war on terror is in practice an American war in the Middle East against a largely imaginary set of enemies, or at least against enemies quite different from those imagined by the Bush administration. This war, in its many theaters, will be the scene where this epochal American constitutional struggle, with implications for the entire world, will be decided. Resistance to exaggerated American hegemony in various parts of the world, and the decisions made by America's citizens and by future administrations, will determine whether or not the United States will go forward on the course of folly in the Middle East that it embarked on during the first years of the twenty-first century. It is vital to recall that this "war on terror" was always seen by its proponents as a permanent war, as a war without limits or end, akin to the Cold War but hotter and longer. If it is continued after January 2009 in the form in which it was initiated in the wake of the attacks of 9/11, through primarily military means, and through the use of overwhelming force in areas that have little or nothing to do with actual terrorism directed against the United States, the United States may be facing a series of campaigns even longer, and certainly bloodier, than the Cold War.

The open-endedness of the war that George W. Bush and his administration launched and have called on the American people to wage into the indefinite future thus has profound implications not only for the Middle East and the world but for our entire form of government at home. This state of affairs should bring to mind the prescient words of James Madison quoted in part in chapter 5:

> Of all the enemies of true liberty, war is, perhaps, the most to be dreaded.... In war...the discretionary power of the executive is extended; its influence in dealing out offices, honors and emoluments is multiplied; and all the means of seducing the minds are added to those of subduing the force of the people.... No nation can preserve its freedom in the midst of continual warfare.... War is in fact the true nurse of executive aggrandizement.[54]

ACKNOWLEDGMENTS

The genesis of this book owes a great deal to the many people who read parts of it, contributed to the research for it, provided materials or resources, or otherwise helped me as I worked on it. It owes much as well to those who invited me to present my work in its initial stages.

Foremost among the institutions that helped in the shaping of this book is Bryn Mawr College, where I was honored to deliver the Mary Flexner Lectures on this topic in the fall of 2007. I owe a special debt of gratitude to Suzanne Spain, the associate provost of Bryn Mawr, and to its president, Nancy J. Vickers, both of whom were hospitable and gracious, far beyond the call of duty, to an itinerant visitor. Bryn Mawr provided me not only with a pleasant, collegial environment in which to lay out my main themes, but also with attentive, questioning audiences for all three lectures. This book would not have the form it does but for the generous welcome I received at Bryn Mawr in the context of the Mary Flexner Lectures, which I am happy to acknowledge with deep gratitude.

Among other venues where I delivered lectures based on the research for this book are the Alexandria Library in Alexandria, Egypt, the Middle East Center at the University of Illinois at Urbana-Champaign, the Heyman Center for the Humanities at Columbia University, Virginia Tech University, the Graduate Institute of International Studies in Geneva, Switzerland, the University of Connecticut at Storrs, the Gallatin School at New York University, the Fares Center at Tufts University, and the Center for Middle Eastern Studies at the University of Chicago.

As any scholar who gives lectures about a book they are working on will attest, the effort is more than recompensed by the chance to have one's ideas and evidence tested, and to try out different formulations in a supportive but critical environment. For this reason, I am grateful to all these institutions, and to the many individuals who invited me and organized my visits there.

Other institutions have been instrumental in making it possible for me to do the research and writing of this book. Columbia University provided generous research funding over the past five years, for which I am grateful to the School of Arts and Sciences, and its libraries were an invaluable resource, as were the online documents in the *Foreign Relations of the United States* series, published online by the Office of the Historian at the Department of State. The Institute for Palestine Studies library in Beirut was helpful as always, and the Maison Mediterranéene des Sciences de l'Homme in Aix-en-Provence repeatedly offered me use of its library and other assistance, as well as a collegial environment.

I also owe a special debt of gratitude to two extraordinary scholarly endeavors, both of which are "virtual realities" at the same time that they are real institutions, the Cold War International History Project at the Woodrow Wilson International Center for Scholars, and the National Security Archive at George Washington University. Both were originally funded by the John D. and Catherine T. MacArthur Foundation under its far-sighted then-president Adele Simmons. I have benefited more than I can express from the remarkable array of previously classified and inaccessible American and Soviet documentary materials for the period I have dealt with, which these two projects have obtained and provide easy access to online. They have made readily available to me and others historical resources that were absolutely invaluable, and without which I could not have written this book, as is apparent from the notes. Both offer the scholar and the citizen an insight into processes that governments tend to try to keep secret, but that are crucial to understanding the past and the present and determining what the future may have in store. Both are to be highly commended for their enlightened and public-spirited work.

Among those who played a role in shaping this book through discussions of its ideas and in sundry other ways were my colleagues at Columbia, Akeel Bilgrami, John Coatsworth, Partha Chatterji, Victoria de Grazia, Nick Dirks, Eric Foner, Carole Gluck, Mahmoud Mamdani, Mark Mazower, Brinkley Messick, Shelly Pollock, and Anders Stephanson. My old friend Jim Chandler once again did me the favor of reading parts of the manuscript, and brought his sharp eye to bear on some of its flaws. Others have helped to influence my thinking on the relationship between the United States and the Soviet Union in the Middle East over the more than thirty years I have been thinking about this topic, and also researching and writing about it on and off over that time. They include, among others, Haydar 'Abd al-Shafi, Hussein Agha, Sami' al-Banna, Faruk Birtek, Musa Budeiri, the late Marwan Buheiry, the late Hanna Batatu, L. Carl Brown, Naomi Chazan, Alvaro de Soto, Thierry Fabre, Sheila Fitzpatrick, Graham Fuller, Michael Geyer, Galia Golan, Muhammad Hasanain Heikal, Shafiq al-Hout, the late Yusuf Ibish, Noha Khalaf, Ahmad Khalidi, the late Idriss Khalidi, Raja Khalidi, Walid Khalidi, Roger Louis, Camille Mansour, Fouad Moughrabi, Ghassan Salameh, Peter Sluglett, Salim Tamari, and Fawwaz Trabulsi. Many students, probably more than I can in fact remember, have also helped me develop some of the conclusions presented in this book, by their critiques and their questions, especially those who were in courses I taught on the subject, whether in Beirut in the 1970s and early 1980s, or at Chicago and Columbia from 1985 onward.

Rosie Bsheer helped me greatly with research assistance in

her customary rapid, efficient fashion, while my colleagues at the Middle East Institute, Astrid Benedek and Mirlyne Pauljajoute, in addition to carrying out their appointed tasks flawlessly, responded repeatedly to my urgent requests for assistance from all over the world, and did much else to make this book possible. Linda Butler, Laurie King-Irani, and Michelle Esposito at the Institute for Palestine Studies' Washington, D.C., office also provided invaluable expert advice and assistance, as did other members of the staff of the institute, in Washington, Beirut, and Ramallah. Professor Roger Louis provided me with copies of a number of unpublished documents used in chapter 5.

To my dedicated and efficient friends at Beacon Press, I once more owe sincere thanks. Helene Atwan was yet again much more than an editor as she helped to shape the ideas for this book as it was in gestation, was again indefatigable in providing advice and help, and uncomplainingly cleaned up my tangled prose and clarified my muddled thinking one more time. Tom Hallock, Pam MacColl, and P.J. Tierney were all supremely competent, while Melissa Dobson did much to make the book read more smoothly with her rapid, precise copyediting, and made some extremely helpful suggestions.

Needless to say, none of those mentioned above is responsible for the views expressed here or bears any fault for the flaws of this book.

No man is an island, although anyone who writes a book must perforce work at least partly in isolation. Producing this book while I was engaged full-time in teaching and carrying out administrative and departmental duties at Columbia over the past few years, not to speak of other tasks that fell my way, necessitated a certain measure of solitude, for which the patient and forbearing members of my family had to pay a price. Lamya, Dima, and Ismail, and especially Mona, had to put up with my absences, physical and otherwise, as they have every previous time I have gone into occultation to work on a book. For their generous tolerance and indulgence, and their sustenance, material and spiritual, I am especially grateful. I hope they will feel that the product is worth the effort it has once again required of them.

NOTES

PREFACE

1. For eight articles and short monographs I published on Soviet policy in the Middle East between 1977 and 1985, see the bibliography.
2. "Vice President's Remarks at the Ambrosetti Forum," Cernobbio, Italy, September 6, 2008, Office of the Vice President: www.whitehouse.gov/news/releases/2008/09/20080906-1.html.
3. Daniel Vernet, "La Géorgie, et au-delà" [Georgia, and Beyond], *Le Monde*, September 10, 2008. My translation.
4. Tara Bahrampour, "Georgians Question Wisdom of War with Russia," *Washington Post*, September 9, 2008: www.washingtonpost.com/wp-dyn/content/article/2008/09/08/AR2008090802449_pf.html.
5. "Vice President's Remarks at the Ambrosetti Forum."

I

Introduction: Rethinking the Cold War in the Middle East

1. Rosemary Hill, "Impervious to Draughts," review of *The English House*, by Hermann Muthesius (London: Frances Lincoln, 2007), *London Review of Books*, May 22, 2008, p. 23.
2. For the full text, see Winston Churchill, "The Sinews of Peace," in Mark A. Kishlansky, ed., *Sources of World History* (New York: Harper Collins, 1995), pp. 298–302. The speech was given in the presence of President Truman. Charles S. Maier, *Among Empires: American Ascendancy and Its Predecessors* (Cambridge, Mass.: Harvard University Press, 2006), p. 326, n. 9, points out that Churchill had already used the phrase "iron curtain" twice in cables to Truman during 1945, well before the Fulton speech.
3. For more on such differences, see Geoffrey Roberts, "Stalin and Soviet Foreign Policy," in *The Origins of the Cold War: An International History*, ed. Melvyn P. Leffler and David S. Painter, pp. 42–57, 2nd ed. (London: Routledge, 2005), and, more generally, Geoffrey Roberts, *Stalin's Wars:*

From World War to Cold War, 1939–1953 (New Haven, Conn.: Yale University Press, 2006). Also, see the discussion of the Novikov telegram in chapter 2 of this book.

4. A. C. Grayling, *Among the Dead Cities: The History and the Moral Legacy of the WWII Bombing of Civilians in Germany and Japan* (New York: Walker, 2006), p. 159, notes Churchill's thinking as early as 1944 about rearming Germany to help in an expected confrontation with the Soviet Union.

5. Churchill was secretary of state for war in 1919–20 and the primary advocate of Allied intervention in Russia, while Stalin was commissar for nationalities and an active figure on many fronts of the civil war. Both had a long-standing previous involvement in the Middle East and the adjacent southern regions of the USSR, where this British-Bolshevik conflict was largely fought out. Stalin was a Georgian native who had been in contact with revolutionary movements throughout the region for much of his life, while Churchill had fought in Sudan under Lord Kitchener in 1898, and was First Lord of the Admiralty in 1911, when the British fleet shifted over to oil, drawn mainly from Iran: See Rashid Khalidi, *Resurrecting Empire: Western Footprints and America's Perilous Path in the Middle East*, rev. ed. (Boston: Beacon Press, 2005), pp. 83–85. In the same capacity, Churchill had also been the great advocate of the Gallipoli landings during World War I, the failure of which led to one of the many eclipses in his career.

6. For a personal view of the impact of the Cold War in several spheres by a perceptive and cosmopolitan observer, see André Schiffrin, *A Political Education: Coming of Age in Paris and New York* (Hoboken, N.J.: Melville House, 2007), pp. 81–152.

7. A good exemplar of the school of historians who are reluctant to abandon analyses that still breathe the frosty air of the Cold War is John Gaddis Smith, whose seminal works on the origins of the Cold War have had a major impact, but whose views have changed little since it ended and Soviet archival materials became available, as is evidenced by his *We Now Know: Rethinking Cold War History* (Oxford: Oxford University Press, 1997).

8. Among the best reflections of a willingness to try to comprehend the actual motivations of both sides in light of new evidence is the work of Melvyn P. Leffler, coeditor with David S. Painter of *The Origins of the Cold War*, which brings much newly discovered material to bear, and is balanced and sober. See also Leffler's *For the Soul of Mankind: The United States, the Soviet Union, and the Cold War* (New York: Hill and Wang, 2007), Tony Judt's excellent *Postwar: A History of Europe since 1945* (New

York: Penguin, 2005), and Odd Arne Westad's Bancroft Prize–winning *The Global Cold War: Third World Interventions and the Making of Our Times* (Cambridge: Cambridge University Press, 2005).

9. Much remains to be discovered in the Soviet archives, which were only partially opened in the 1990s. Access to certain materials has been limited. It is interesting, as Geoffrey Roberts notes in "Stalin and Soviet Foreign Policy" (in *The Origins of the Cold War*, ed. Leffler and Painter, pp. 42–57), that an examination of some formerly inaccessible Soviet material only recently opened to researchers reveals that leading Soviet policymakers' confidential expressions of their views generally appear to track closely with Soviet public statements.

10. The phrase is from Francis Fukuyama's 1989 article, "The End of History?" *National Interest* (summer 1989), and 1992 book, *The End of History and the Last Man* (New York: Free Press, 1992). This apostate neoconservative, after being a charter signatory of the 1997 Statement of Principles of the Project for a New American Century, a neoconservative manifesto for the twenty-first century (about which more later in chapter 1), has since disparaged his erstwhile comrades.

11. A major exception is Westad's *The Global Cold War*.

12. Among the few works published over the past dozen years or so on the Middle East and the Cold War are Yezid Sayigh and Avi Shlaim, eds., *The Cold War and the Middle East* (Oxford: Oxford University Press, 1997), Salim Yaqub, *Containing Arab Nationalism: The Eisenhower Doctrine and the Middle East* (Chapel Hill: University of North Carolina Press, 2004), and Nigel Ashton, ed., *The Cold War in the Middle East: Regional Conflict and the Superpowers, 1967–1973* (London: Routledge, 2007).

13. For a masterful account of some of these examples, see Mahmood Mamdani, *Good Muslim, Bad Muslim: America, the Cold War, and The Roots of Terror* (New York: Pantheon Books, 2004). See also Chalmers Johnson, *Blowback: The Costs and Consequences of American Empire*, 2nd ed. (New York: Holt, 2004).

14. As just one indication of the limits of its global capacities before World War II, it is striking that the United States did not even have an international intelligence arm until the creation in mid-1942 of the Office of Strategic Services (OSS).

15. See Melvyn P. Leffler, "National Security and U.S. Foreign Policy," in *The Origins of the Cold War*, ed. Leffler and Painter, pp. 17ff.

16. Signatories of the initial 1997 PNAC statement included Elliott Abrams, Jeb Bush, Dick Cheney, Francis Fukuyama, Zalmay Khalilzad, I. Lewis Libby, Peter Rodman, Donald Rumsfeld, and Paul Wolfowitz. Its key paragraph is: "As the 20th century draws to a close, the United States

stands as the world's preeminent power. Having led the West to victory in the Cold War, America faces an opportunity and a challenge: Does the United States have the vision to build upon the achievements of past decades? Does the United States have the resolve to shape a new century favorable to American principles and interests?" The statement is available at www.newamericancentury.org/statementofprinciples.htm.

17. I will do this in chapter 2, which discusses the role of oil in the earliest phases of the Cold War.

18. Col. William Eddy, *FDR Meets Ibn Saud* (Washington, D.C.: America-Mideast Educational and Training Services, 1954; repr. Vista, Calif.: Selwa Press, 2005). Eddy had a colorful career. While head of the OSS in North Africa at the time of the American landings there, he went to meet Gen. George Patton and other generals, limping from wounds received as a marine in the Battle of Belleau Wood in World War I. According to one account, he "arrived in uniform, with five rows of ribbons over his left breast pocket, top row left to right, Navy Cross, Distinguished Service Cross, Silver Star with cluster and two Purple Hearts. Patton gazed at the younger officer and exclaimed, 'The son of a bitch's been shot at enough, hasn't he?'" Dick Camp Jr., "And a Few Marines: Colonel William A. Eddy," *Leatherneck*, April 2004, available at www.aramco expats.com/Articles/Community/Annuitants-And-Former-ExPats/1430.aspx.

19. Daniel Yergin, *The Prize: The Epic Quest for Oil, Money, and Power* (New York: Simon & Schuster, 1991), pp. 403–5.

20. Grayling, *Among the Dead Cities,* notes that in the European theater, the U.S. Army Air Force (USAAF) had a devastating effect on the German war effort by bombing exclusively strategic targets, notably oil production facilities, as will be discussed in the next chapter. Britain's RAF Bomber Command followed a different strategy, mainly bombing German cities. In the Pacific theater, the USAAF bombed strategic targets like oil production facilities while also targeting Japanese cities.

21. This company has since been nationalized as Saudi ARAMCO.

22. Eddy, *FDR Meets Ibd Saud,* p. 33.

23. U.S. Department of State, *Foreign Relations of the United States, 1945,* vol. 8 (Washington, D.C.: Government Printing Office, 1969), p. 698.

24. Ibid., p. 755.

25. Eddy, *FDR Meets Ibd Saud,* pp. 34–35. It is not clear whether Eddy was among the four. If not, this is not a first-person account of the meeting.

26. The books of Harry St. John Philby, a former British official and advisor to Ibn Sa'ud who helped influence him to take the American rather than the British bid for an oil contract, are indispensable for understanding

Ibn Saʿud's complex, conflicted relations with the United Kingdom. See, notably, *Arabia of the Wahhabis* (London: Constable, 1928) and *Saudi Arabia* (New York: Praeger, 1958), as well as Elizabeth Monroe, *Philby of Arabia* (London: Faber, 1973).

27. For more about the role of oil in the Cold War in the Middle East, see chapter 2.

28. Libya, a former Italian colony, was another such country, and a U.S. air-field that accommodated over four thousand airmen and a wing of nuclear-armed strategic bombers was set up there. It was vacated a year after Muʿammar Qaddafi came to power in 1969.

29. Until the first truly intercontinental bomber, the B-52, came into service in significant numbers in the late 1950s, and before intercontinental ballistic missiles (ICBMs) and submarine-launched ballistic missiles (SLBMs) were deployed in the 1960s, the American nuclear arsenal was carried by B-29, B-36, and B-47 bombers of the Strategic Air Command (SAC), whose maximum ranges were less than four thousand miles. This necessarily meant that they needed bases all around the periphery of the Soviet Union in order to reach targets in the depth of the Soviet hinterland. As we shall see in subsequent chapters, bases in the Middle East were particularly important in this early period of the Cold War to provide SAC bombers with the ability to reach targets to the east of the Ural Mountains and in central Asia and Transcaucasia, where much of Soviet oil production and industry, especially military industry, were located.

30. For more on these strategic factors in the early phases of the Cold War, see chapters 2 and 3.

31. Saʿud ibn ʿAbd al-ʿAziz succeeded his father, ʿAbd al-ʿAziz ibn Saʿud, on the old king's death in 1953.

32. The text can be found at http://coursesa.matrix.msu.edu/fflhst203/documents/eisen.html.

33. Malcolm H. Kerr, *The Arab Cold War: Gamal 'Abd al-Nasir and His Rivals, 1958–1970*, 3rd ed. (Oxford: Oxford University Press, 1971). To avoid confusion with the larger American-Soviet Cold War, I refer to this conflict hereafter using the term "Arab cold war."

34. Perhaps the best analysis of this process is by Alvin Z. Rubinstein, *Red Star on the Nile: The Soviet-Egyptian Influence Relationship since the June War* (Princeton, N.J.: Princeton University Press, 1977), who started out with the standard American Cold War assumption that the Soviets were manipulating the Egyptians, but found that the data showed the opposite. For another example, see Waldemar J. Gallman, *Iraq under General Nuri: My Recollections of Nuri Al-Said, 1954–1958* (Baltimore: Johns Hopkins University Press, 1964), chaps. 4–5, which shows how Iraqi

prime minister Nuri al-Sa'id constantly stressed the dangers of communism to his American interlocutors in order to extract support from them. Gallman was U.S. ambassador to Iraq for the last four years of the monarchy, 1954–58.

35. For what is still the finest account of these developments, see Hanna Batatu, *The Old Social Classes and the Revolutionary Movements of Iraq: A Study of Iraq's Old Landed and Commercial Classes and of Its Communists, Ba'thists, and Free Officers* (Princeton, N.J.: Princeton University Press, 1978), pp. 764–973.

36. One of the most acute analyses of this American strategy can be found in Mamdani, *Good Muslim, Bad Muslim*.

37. For Iran, see Kermit Roosevelt, *Countercoup: The Struggle for Control of Iran* (New York, McGraw-Hill, 1979), and James Bill, *The Eagle and the Lion: The Tragedy of American-Iranian Relations* (New Haven, Conn.: Yale University Press, 1988). Roosevelt, son of FDR, was in charge of the Iran operations for the CIA. For the Syrian and Lebanon cases, see Wilbur Crane Eveland, *Ropes of Sand: America's Failure in the Middle East* (New York: Norton, 1980). Eveland was involved in U.S. intelligence activity in Syria from an early stage, and personally delivered briefcases of dollars to Chamoun.

38. For this entire period, including the Yemeni civil war and the war in Dhofar, see Fred Halliday, *Arabia without Sultans: A Political Survey of Instability in the Arab World* (London: Penguin, 1974), as well as the indispensable Kerr, *The Arab Cold War*.

39. See reference in n. 25. See also John Snetsinger, *Truman, the Jewish Vote, and Israel* (Stanford, Calif.: Hoover Institution Press, 1974).

40. See Arnold Kramner, *The Forgotten Friendship: Israel and the Soviet Bloc, 1947–53* (Urbana: University of Illinois Press, 1974).

41. The best account of the role played by France in helping Israel to produce nuclear weapons starting in 1956 can be found in Avner Cohen, *Israel and the Bomb* (New York: Columbia University Press, 1998), pp. 49ff.

42. On the Suez War, see Herman Finer, *Dulles over Suez: The Theory and Practice of His Diplomacy* (Chicago: University of Chicago Press, 1964), Diane Kunz, *The Economic Diplomacy of the Suez Crisis* (Chapel Hill: University of North Carolina Press, 1991), and Wm. Roger Louis and Roger Owen, eds., *1956: The Crisis and Its Consequences* (Oxford: Oxford University Press, 1989).

43. For the best account of American policies during this period, see Selim Yaqub, *Containing Arab Nationalism: The Eisenhower Doctrine and the Middle East* (Chapel Hill: University of North Carolina Press, 2004), and Irene Gendzier, *Notes from the Minefield: United States Intervention in*

Lebanon and the Middle East, 1945–1958 (New York: Columbia University Press, 1997).

44. This was notably the case during the 1968–70 Egyptian-Israeli War of Attrition along the Suez Canal, when the United States shipped newly manufactured F-4 Phantoms to Israel although they were sorely needed to make up for losses incurred over North Vietnam, and at the height of the 1973 war, when U.S. stocks of some key weapons systems were depleted in order to replenish the rapidly diminishing Israeli arsenal.

45. On the War of Attrition, see Yaakov Bar-Siman-Tov, *The Israeli-Egyptian War of Attrition, 1969–1970: A Case-Study of Limited Local War* (New York: Columbia University Press, 1980), Edgar O'Ballance, *The Electronic War in the Middle East, 1968–70* (London: Faber, 1974), and Lawrence Whetten, *The Canal War: Four-Power Conflict in the Middle East* (Cambridge, Mass.: MIT Press, 1974).

46. Mohamed Heikal, *The Road to Ramadan* (London: Collins, 1975). For more details here and elsewhere in this section, see chapter 4.

47. Kissinger did not even consult Nixon on this move: Robert Dallek, *Nixon and Kissinger: Partners in Power* (New York: HarperCollins, 2007). On the 1973 war see Heikal, *The Road to Ramadan*; Gen. Saad el-Shazly, *The Crossing of Suez: The October War 1973* (London: Third World Center, 1980); Chaim Herzog, *The War of Atonement* (London: Weidenfeld & Nicolson, 1975); and Zeev Schiff, *October Earthquake: Yom Kippur 1973* (Tel Aviv: University Publishing, 1974).

48. See chapter 2 for details of Stalin's 1945–46 interference in the politics of Kurdistan, Azerbaijan, and other parts of northern Iran.

49. Jonathan C. Randal, *After Such Knowledge, What Forgiveness: My Encounters with Kurdistan* (New York: Farrar, Straus and Giroux, 1997). Kissinger's first book was *A World Restored: Metternich, Castlereagh, and the Problems of Peace, 1812–22* (Boston: Houghton Mifflin, 1957).

50. The indispensable National Security Archive at George Washington University has obtained the government documents chronicling this despicable episode, including a fulsome photo of a smiling Donald Rumsfeld, in his capacity as a special envoy of President Reagan, shaking hands with Saddam Hussein in 1983: www.gwu.edu/fflnsarchiv/NSAEBB/NSAEBB82/press.htm.

51. Several of the key players in this criminal enterprise to subvert the intent of Congress, and in some cases the letter of the law, who were indicted or convicted of various felonies, were later welcomed into the administration of George W. Bush, including Elliott Abrams (pled guilty to two felonies, then was pardoned by President George H. W. Bush); Adm. John Poindexter (convicted of five felony counts, all later reversed on ap-

peal), and John Negroponte (never convicted, though implicated in several of these felonies).

52. Susan Meisalas, with Martin van Bruinessen, *Kurdistan: In the Shadow of History* (New York: Random House, 1997).

53. See "The Sources of Soviet Conduct," *Foreign Affairs,* July 1947, which Kennan published under the pseudonym "X."

54. Perhaps the most thoughtful analysis of the demise of the Soviet Union, Stephen Kotkin, *Armageddon Averted: The Soviet Collapse, 1970–2000* (Oxford: Oxford University Press, 2001), makes this clear.

55. Gar Alperovitz, *Atomic Diplomacy: Hiroshima and Potsdam; the Use of the Atomic Bomb and the American Confrontation with Soviet Power* (New York: Simon & Schuster, 1965).

II
Oil and the Origins of the Cold War

1. Text of President Harry S. Truman's speech before a joint session of Congress, March 12, 1947, Avalon Project at Yale Law School, www.yale.edu/lawweb/avalon/trudoc.htm. A parallel landmark statement that laid out the lineaments of the Cold War as seen from Moscow was Soviet ideologist Andrei Zhdanov's famous "two camps" speech of September 22, 1947, to the Cominform. The text is available at www.cnn.com/SPECIALS/cold.war/episodes/04/documents/cominform.html. Zhdanov's speech is discussed in chapter 5 of this book.

2. Indeed, the southern regions of the Soviet Union became increasingly important strategically as the war wore on, and more and more of the USSR's industrial capacity was moved there to escape the Nazi offensive eastward.

3. In the same year, the entire Middle East produced less than 4 percent of the world's oil, a proportion that was to grow rapidly in the postwar era: see George P. Stevens Jr., "Saudi Arabia's Petroleum Resources," *Economic Geography* 25, no. 3 (July 1949), Table 1, p. 219. See also Peter Odell, "The Significance of Oil," *Journal of Contemporary History* 3, no. 3 (July 1968), 93–110.

4. J. M. Spaight, "The War of Oil," *Military Affairs* 13, no. 3 (autumn 1949): 138–41. By contrast, RAF Bomber Command directed most of its strategic bombing throughout the war against German cities, rather than strictly economic or military targets: see A. C. Grayling, *Among the Dead Cities: The History and Moral Legacy of the WWII Bombing of Civilians in Germany and Japan* (New York: Walker, 2006).

5. Raymond G. Stokes, "The Oil Industry in Nazi Germany," *Business History Review* 59, no. 2 (summer 1985): 272.

6. See Spaight, "The War of Oil."

7. For details, see Rashid Khalidi, *Resurrecting Empire: Western Footprints and America's Perilous Path in the Middle East*, rev. ed. (Boston: Beacon Press, 2005), pp. 83–85.

8. Although initially concerned about the ability of faltering domestic production to meet growing oil needs, by late 1945 Soviet planners decided to return to their traditional autarkic approach of relying entirely on domestic resources. See Fred H. Lawson, "The Iranian Crisis of 1945–1946 and the Spiral Model of International Conflict," *International Journal of Middle East Studies* 21, no. 3 (August 1989), p. 318, citing William Taubman, *Stalin's American Policy: From Entente to Detente to Cold War* (New York: Norton, 1982), p. 121.

9. As we saw in chapter 1, the best account of the meeting is by Col. William Eddy, U.S. minister in Saudi Arabia: *FDR Meets Ibn Saud* (Washington, D.C.: America-Mideast Educational and Training Services, 1954; repr. Vista, Calif.: Selwa Press, 2005).

10. Besides Standard Oil of California (Socal, later Exxon), the partner companies included Texas Oil Company (Texaco), Standard Oil of New Jersey, and the Socony Vacuum Oil (later Mobil). Only Texaco was not part of the former Standard Oil empire, whose successor companies controlled 70 percent of the concession.

11. Stevens, "Saudi Arabia's Petroleum Resources," Table 3, p. 221.

12. Given the continuing Nazi submarine danger to tanker transport from the United States, Middle Eastern oil, refined in the region, was particularly important to the waging of Allied military campaigns in the Middle East, the Mediterranean, and Southeast Asia, and to supplying fleets in these and other regions.

13. Eddy, *FDR Meets Ibn Saud*, p. 28, notes of Roosevelt that "every now and then I would catch him off guard and see his face in repose. It was ashen in color; the lines were deep; the eyes would fade in helpless fatigue. He was living on his nerve. His doctors had told him not to go to Yalta. With Ibn Saud he was at his very best; but he was living on borrowed time, and eight weeks later he was dead."

14. The president had met the preceding day with King Farouk of Egypt and Emperor Haile Selassie of Ethiopia. See chapter 1 for some of Ibn Sa'ud's concerns, specifically those relating to Palestine.

15. According to Eddy, the British were livid about this meeting, which took place in what they considered to be their own Egyptian preserve, and understood perfectly well its import. As soon as they heard about it, they immediately arranged a meeting in Egypt between Churchill and Ibn

Sa'ud, which Eddy claims was less successful than the meeting he had arranged.

16. Woodrow Wilson International Center for Scholars, Cold War International History Project, Collection: Cold War Origins (hereafter CWIHP), "Decree of the USSR State Defense Committee No. 9168 SS Regarding Geological Prospecting Work for Oil in Northern Iran," June 21, 1945.

17. Lawson, "The Iranian Crisis of 1945–1946," pp. 315–18.

18. Ibid, p. 318.

19. CWIHP, Decree of the CC CPSU Central Committee Politburo to Mir Bagirov, CC Secretary of the Communist Party of Azerbaijan, on "Measures to Organize a Separatist Movement in Southern Azerbaijan and Other Provinces of Iran," July 6, 1945. For an account of the role of Bagirov and the Soviet Azeri Communist Party in these events, based on newly accessible documents in the party's archives in Baku, see Fernande Sheide Rainer, "The Iranian Crisis of 1946 and the Origins of the Cold War," in *The Origins of the Cold War: An International History*, ed. Melvyn P. Leffler and David S. Painter, pp. 93–111, 2nd ed. (New York: Routledge, 2005).

20. CWIHP, "Measures to Carry Out Special Assignments throughout Southern Azerbaijan and the Northern Provinces of Iran," July 14, 1945.

21. See George Lenczowski, *Russia and the West in Iran: 1918–1948: A Study in Big Power Rivalry* (Ithaca, N.Y.: Cornell University Press, 1949). See also James A. Bill, *The Eagle and the Lion: The Tragedy of American-Iranian Relations* (New Haven, Conn.: Yale University Press, 1988), and Bruce Kuniholm, *The Origins of the Cold War in the Near East* (Princeton, N.J.: Princeton University Press, 1980).

22. M. Leffler and D. Painter, eds., *The Origins of the Cold War*, pp. 116–19.

23. Lawson, "The Iranian Crisis of 1945–1946," p. 317. For more on these Soviet strategic concerns, see Eduard Mark, "Allied Relations in Iran, 1941–1947: The Origins of a Cold War Crisis," *Wisconsin Magazine of History* 59, no. 3 (autumn 1975).

24. Melvyn Leffler, "Strategy, Diplomacy, and the Cold War: The United States, Turkey, and NATO," *Journal of American History* 71, no. 4 (March 1985), pp. 813–14. A report for Truman by Clark Clifford and another White House aide, cited by Leffler, noted that "the Near East is an area of great strategic interest to the Soviet Union because of the shift of Soviet industry to southeastern Russia, within range of air attack from the Near East."

25. For details, see Thanasis Sfikas, "The Greek Civil War," in *The Origins of the Cold War*, ed. Leffler and Painter, pp. 134–52.

26. Leffler, "Strategy, Diplomacy, and the Cold War," pp. 808–10.

27. The standard work, albeit somewhat dated, on this subject is M. S. An-

derson, *The Eastern Question, 1744–1923: A Study in International Relations* (London: St. Martin's, 1966).

28. Daniel Yergin, *The Prize: The Epic Quest for Oil, Money, and Power* (New York: Simon & Schuster, 1991), pp. 280–302.

29. In his 1796 Farewell Address (http://avalon.law.yale.edu/18th_century/washing.asp), George Washington warned against "permanent, inveterate antipathies against particular nations, and passionate attachments for others," adding: "The great rule of conduct for us in regard to foreign nations is in extending our commercial relations, to have with them as little political connection as possible. So far as we have already formed engagements, let them be fulfilled with perfect good faith. Here let us stop. Europe has a set of primary interests which to us have none; or a very remote relation. Hence she must be engaged in frequent controversies, the causes of which are essentially foreign to our concerns. Hence, therefore, it must be unwise in us to implicate ourselves by artificial ties in the ordinary vicissitudes of her politics, or the ordinary combinations and collisions of her friendships or enmities.... It is our true policy to steer clear of permanent alliances with any portion of the foreign world." Jefferson reprised this theme in his 1801 inaugural address (www.yale.edu/lawweb/avalon/presiden/inaug/jefinau1.htm), calling for "peace, commerce, and honest friendship with all nations, entangling alliances with none."

30. Margaret MacMillan, *Paris, 1919: Six Months That Changed the World* (New York: Random House, 2002), pp. 83–97, points out that Wilson only intended the principle of self-determination to apply to European and a limited range of non-European cases.

31. David S. Painter and Melvyn P. Leffler, introduction to *The Origins of the Cold War*, ed. Leffler and Painter, p. 3.

32. See the June 3, 1921, letter from Georgi Chicherin, the Soviet commissar for foreign affairs, to the Soviet envoy to Afghanistan regarding the respectful line to follow in negotiating with the Afghans, cited in *La politique étrangère soviétique: Textes officielles (1917–1967)* (Moscow: Progress, 1967), pp. 55–57.

33. For the texts of these treaties, see J. C. Hurewitz, *The Middle East and North Africa in World Politics: A Documentary Record* (New Haven, Conn.: Yale University Press, 1979), vol. 2, pp. 240–48, 250–53. The treaty with Turkey was dated March 16, 1921, that with Iran, February 2, 1921, and that with Afghanistan, February 28, 1921. It was by the terms of the former that the Kars and Ardahan districts, previously seized by the Russians, reverted to Turkey.

34. For more on this force, see Floreeda Safiri, "South Persia Rifles," *Encyclopedia Iranica*, www.iranica.com/newsite/index.isc?Article=http://

www.iranica.com/newsite/articles/unicode/ot_grp12/ot_southpersiarif
les_20080407.html.

35. By 1945, the United States had shipped 375,000 trucks to the USSR, providing about two-thirds of the trucks used by the Red Army.

36. The main route for Lend-Lease supplies to Russia, however, was across
the northern Pacific from Alaska to Siberia.

37. John C. Campbell, "The Soviet Union and the Middle East: 'In the General Direction of the Persian Gulf,'" part 1, *Russian Review* 29, no. 2 (April
1970), p. 147.

38. Cited in ibid.

39. Ibid., pp. 150–51.

40. CWIHP, telegram from N. Novikov, Soviet ambassador to the United
States, to the Soviet leadership, September 27, 1946.

41. The full text of the original "Long Telegram," dated February 1946, can
be found at: www.gwu.edu/fflnsarchiv/coldwar/documents/episode-1/
kennan.htm.

42. The "Long Telegram" was published by Kennan under the pseudonym
"X" in modified form in *Foreign Affairs* in July 1947.

43. Silvio Pons, "Stalin and the Italian Commnists," in *The Origins of the
Cold War*, ed. Leffler and Painter, p. 212. Pons notes that according to
Novikov's memoir, this cable reflected mainly Molotov's views, which in
practice meant Stalin's.

44. Novikov ignored the successful post–World War I American efforts to
wrest a 20 percent share of Iraqi oil from British oil interests.

45. CWIHP, telegram from N. Novikov, September 27, 1946.

46. Kennan's "Long Telegram," www.gwu.edu/fflnsarchiv/coldwar/docu
ments/episode-1/kennan.htm. Given what is known about the successes
of Soviet espionage in penetrating the American and British governments at this stage, it cannot be entirely excluded that the text, or at least
the gist, of Kennan's dispatch of February 1946 was known to Novikov
when he drafted his own long missive to Moscow in September 1946, although there appears to be no evidence to this effect in the Soviet diplo-
mat's dispatch.

III

The Middle East and the International System

1. A vestige of these same attitudes is the stated belief of many Europeans,
including leading European politicians, that Turkey cannot be considered for European Union membership, and is not truly "European," because it is not a Christian country.

2. In the case of the Armenians, their state, briefly independent at the end of World War I on a fraction of the national territory they claimed, was incorporated into the USSR as the Armenian Soviet Socialist Republic, and thereby lost its independence until the fall of the Soviet Union. Neither the Kurds nor the Palestinians ever achieved independence, their own efforts and international commitments notwithstanding. On the Kurds and the Palestinians, see David McDowall, *A Modern History of the Kurds* (London: I.B. Tauris, 1996), and Rashid Khalidi, *The Iron Cage: The Story of the Palestinian Struggle for Statehood* (Boston: Beacon Press, 2007).

3. This term is itself Eurocentric, nongeographical, and inherently meaningless: In the middle of what? East of what? For more on the definition of "Middle East" and related topics, see Rashid Khalidi, "The 'Middle East' as a Framework for Analysis: Re-mapping a Region in the Era of Globalization," *Comparative Studies of South Asia, Africa, and the Middle East* 18, no. 2 (1998), pp. 1–8. I and others use this term for want of a better one. Generally, it refers to the area of North Africa and West Asia bounded by the Atlantic, the Caucasus Mountains, Turkmenistan, Afghanistan, and Pakistan. See also Martin W. Lewis and Kären E. Wigan, *The Myth of Continents: A Critique of Metageography* (Berkeley: University of California Press, 1977).

4. C. J. Bartlett, *Castlereagh* (New York: Scribners, 1966), pp. 157–58.

5. Britain's reluctance to abide by such a guarantee prefigured later cases when the United States Congress resisted similar potential restraints on American actions, such as at the end of World War I, when the Senate refused to ratify the Versailles treaty, thereby rejecting U.S. membership in the League of Nations.

6. For details, see Rashid Khalidi, *British Policy in Syria and Palestine, 1906–1914* (Oxford: St. Antony's Middle East Monographs, 1980).

7. The wording is that of the first of Wilson's Fourteen Points of January 8, 1918: wwi.lib.byu.edu/index.php/President_Wilson%27s_Fourteen_Points.

8. "Memorandum on Syria, Palestine, and Mesopotamia: Reflections of Foreign Secretary Arthur James Balfour," August 11, 1919. Text in J. C. Hurewitz, ed., *The Middle East and North Africa in World Politics: A Documentary Record* (New Haven, Conn.: Yale University Press, 1979), vol. 2, p. 188.

9. See in particular Richard Holbrooke's introduction to Margaret MacMillan, *Paris, 1919: Six Months That Changed the World* (New York: Random House, 2002), and pp. 11ff.

10. See Rashid Khalidi, *Palestinian Identity: The Construction of Modern Na-*

tional Consciousness (New York: Columbia University Press, 1997), for more on the constitution of Middle Eastern national identities in this period.

11. Some of the parallels between the Palestinian case and those of the Kurds and Armenians are explored in Khalidi, *The Iron Cage.*

12. For more details, see Erez Manela, *The Wilsonian Moment: Self-Determination and the International Origins of Anti-Colonial Nationalism* (New York: Oxford University Press, 2007).

13. Quoted in MacMillan, *Paris, 1919,* p. viii.

14. "Steps to the Charter: Origins of the United Nations," *UN Chronicle,* April 1985, available at http://findarticles.com/p/articles/mi_m1309/is_ v22/ai_3709366.

15. A total of 81 of 321 Security Council resolutions passed between March 1948 and November 1974 dealt with the Arab-Israeli conflict alone. During the thirteen years of this period that my father, Dr. Ismail Raghib Khalidi, worked in the UN Secretariat's Political and Security Council Division (1955–68) dealing with the Middle East, it was his estimate that nearly half of the Council's meeting time was taken up by Arab-Israeli questions: private communication, I. R. Khalidi, June 1968.

16. The text of the Mandate for Palestine can be found in J. C. Hurewitz, ed., *The Middle East and North Africa in World Politics,* vol. 2, pp. 179–84.

17. For details see the first four chapters of Khalidi, *The Iron Cage.*

18. Susan Pedersen, "Settler Colonialism at the Bar of the League of Nations," in *Settler Colonialism in the 20th Century: Projects, Practices, and Legacies,* ed. Susan Pedersen and Caroline Elkins (New York: Taylor and Francis, 2005).

19. Between 1972 and 2007, the United States used its veto 43 times against Security Council resolutions that were critical of Israel, out of 101 vetoes during that period by all permanent members combined. See Global Policy Forum, "Subjects of UN Security Council Vetoes," www .globalpolicy.org/security/membship/veto/vetosubj.htm.

20. I was in the Security Council visitors' gallery during this session, and witnessed the apparently inexplicable delay, the ulterior motives for which were thereafter explained to me.

21. Yevgeni Primakov, *Missions à Baghdad: Histoire d'une négociation secrète* (Paris: Plon, 1991). Primakov later became Russian foreign minister and prime minister, and was one of the leading candidates opposing Vladimir Putin in the 2000 Russian presidential elections.

22. This was passed on June 8, 2004. Security Council resolution 511 of October 16, 2003, had already rebaptized the American and allied forces as a "Multinational Force" under UN auspices.

23. On the degree to which French Middle East policy a few years after the Iraq invasion had aligned itself on American positions, whether over Iran, Lebanon, or Palestine, see Alain Gresh, "De l'Iran à la Palestine: La voix brouillée de la France," *Le Monde Diplomatique* 627, June 2006, pp. 1, 10–11.

24. "Rapprochement diplomatique libano-syrien sous l'égide de la France," *Le Monde*, July 12, 2008. As Syria had refused to establish diplomatic relations with Lebanon since the 1940s, this was a diplomatic coup for French president Nicolas Sarkozy. France announced at the same time that it would become involved in the Syrian-Israeli negotiations, at the request of both parties.

25. William Widenor, *Henry Cabot Lodge and the Search for an American Foreign Policy* (Berkeley: University of California Press, 1983), pp. 71, 75, cited in Alan Brinkley, "The Idea of an American Century" (paper presented at Columbia University conference, Whose International Community? Universalism and Legacies of Empire, April 29–30, 2005.

26. For details of how the United States frustrated the efforts of the United Nations, see the "End of Mission Report" of May 2007 of Alvaro de Soto, UN special coordinator for the Middle East peace process and envoy to the Quartet, the full text of which was published by the *Guardian*, June 13, 2007: http://www.guardian.co.uk/world/2007/jun/13/usa.israel.

27. See, among others, Michael Hardt and Antonio Negri, *Empire* (Cambridge, Mass.: Harvard University Press, 2000); Charles S. Maier, *Among Empires: American Ascendancy and Its Predecessors* (Cambridge, Mass.: Harvard University Press, 2006); and Craig Calhoun, Frederick Cooper, and Kevin W. Moore, eds., *Lessons of Empire: Imperial Histories and American Power* (New York: New Press, 2006).

28. For reflections on this subject, see Lloyd Gardiner and Marilyn B. Young, eds., *The New American Empire: A 21st Century Teach-In on U.S. Foreign Policy* (New York: Free Press, 2005).

29. For an analysis arguing that the latter is the case in the long term, see Immanuel Wallerstein, *The Decline of American Power: The U.S. in a Chaotic World* (New York: New Press, 2003).

30. This was the burden of the thesis put forward by the framers of the Project for a New American Century, mentioned in chapter 1. For details, see www.newamericancentury.org/statementofprinciples.htm.

31. The American strategy was nowhere more apparent than in the negotiations between the United States and the Iraqi government for a status-of-forces agreement in Iraq. The delicate dance around whether U.S. bases would be permanent, whether this was in fact a treaty that must be submitted to the Senate for ratification, and other crucial matters, like

the ferocious opposition of most political forces in Iraq to the deal the United States was originally trying to force on the government of Nuri al-Maliki, and was later obliged to abandon, went largely unreported in the U.S. press. See Patrick Cockburn, "U.S. Extorts Iraq to Approve Military Deal," *CounterPunch*, June 6, 2008.

32. This quaint term was the Pentagon's original description of some of the many gigantic military installations it has established in Iraq, a term it used until it became clear that these words exposed the Bush team's quiet game of establishing permanent bases in that country.

33. For assorted details on some of these fiascos, in Gaza and Lebanon respectively, see, inter alia, David Rose, "The Gaza Bombshell," *Vanity Fair*, April 2008; Rami G. Khouri, "A New Middle East, but not Condi's," *Daily Star*, May 24, 2008. Regarding what appeared to be covert American efforts directed against the Iranian regime that continued right up to the end of the Bush presidency, see Andrew Cockburn, "Secret Bush 'Finding' Widens Covert War on Iran," *CounterPunch*, May 2, 2008, and Seymour Hersh, "Preparing the Battlefield," *New Yorker*, July 7, 2008.

IV
Superpower Rivalry as a Catalyst for Conflict

1. Johan Huizinga, "The Idea of History," in *The Varieties of History, from Voltaire to the Present*, ed. Fritz Stern (New York: Meridian, 1956), p. 292, cited in Edward Said, *Joseph Conrad and the Fiction of Autobiography*, 2nd ed. (New York: Columbia University Press, 2008), p. 11.

2. In the Bancroft Prize–winning *The Global Cold War: Third World Interventions and the Making of Our Times* (Cambridge: Cambridge University Press, 2005), historian Odd Arne Westad superbly traces this dynamic, perceptively using a broad range of primary sources to analyze the negative impact of the policies of both superpowers on various regions of the third world. However, he does not focus on the Middle East, and mentions (p. 4) that the Arab-Israeli wars are "treated in less depth" than other conflicts in his book.

3. On the latter subject, see Rashid Khalidi, *British Policy in Syria and Palestine, 1906–1914* (Oxford: St. Antony's Middle East Monographs, 1980), pp. 126–29, 183–86, 368–70, and *Resurrecting Empire: Western Footprints and America's Perilous Path in the Middle East*, rev. ed. (Boston: Beacon Press, 2005), pp. 16–24, 79–81, 93–94, 162–64.

4. André Schiffrin, *A Political Education: Coming of Age in Paris and New York* (Hoboken, N.J.: Melville House, 2007), pp. 142–49, gives examples

of CIA-sponsored groups Schiffrin was associated with. See also Frances Stonor Saunders, *Who Paid the Piper? The CIA and the Cultural Cold War* (London: Granta, 1999).

5. Historians now know much more than they did before about the decisions taken in launching this war by the North Korean regime, Stalin, and the new Communist government in China. See Kathryn Weathersby, "Stalin and the Korean War," in *The Origins of the Cold War: An International History,* ed. Melvyn P. Leffler and David S. Painter, pp. 265–82, 2nd ed. (London: Routledge, 2005).

6. Thousands of prisoners seized as a result of the five years of internal strife in South Korea after 1945 were murdered by South Korean security forces in July 1950, just after the outset of the Korean War. See Bruce Cumings, *The Origins of the Korean War,* vol. 2, *The Roaring of the Cataract, 1947–1950* (Princeton, N.J.: Princeton University Press, 1990), and Stewart Lone and Gavan McCormack, *Korea since 1850* (New York: Palgrave Macmillan, 1993), section on "Atrocities," pp. 119–22.

7. Tim Weiner, *Legacy of Ashes: The History of the CIA* (New York: Doubleday, 2007), pp. 258–62. As Weiner shows, pp. 142–54, this was not the only involvement of the CIA in Indonesia: it had earlier attempted an unsuccessful coup against President Sukarno in 1958. See also Westad, *The Global Cold War,* p. 188.

8. This impact in many parts of the third world is brilliantly analyzed by Westad in *The Global Cold War,* although Westad notes that he does not focus on the Indo-Pakistani wars, conflicts that were considerably exacerbated by the superpower rivalry.

9. For details see Soviet ambassador Anatoly Dobrynin's summary of his secret meeting with Robert Kennedy (obtained by the National Security Archive) on October 27, 1962, when the terms of the agreement were fully laid out: www.gwu.edu/fflnsarchiv/nsa/cuba_mis_cri/621027%20Dobrynin%20Cable%20to%20USSR.pdf.

10. M. S. Anderson, *The Eastern Question, 1744–1923: A Study in International Relations* (London: St. Martin's, 1966), and L. Carl Brown, *International Politics and the Middle East: Old Rules, Dangerous Game* (Princeton, N.J.: Princeton University Press, 1984), both explain how this strategic reality became the core of the so-called Eastern Question for well over a century.

11. BP, *Statistical Review of World Energy 2007.*

12. In 2006 the top five international oil companies had profits of over $120 billion: *Le Monde,* January 4, 2008, p. 12.

13. Over thirty years ago, the Israeli scholar Ilana Dimant-Kass noticed the salience of the region for the Soviet military. She pointed out that in the

Soviet Ministry of Defense newspaper, *Kraznaya Zvezda,* the Middle East received "high priority, second only to that given to the United States and NATO, and more than that given to Europe or Southeast Asia," which she ascribes to the region's strategic, political, and economic significance for the West, and by implication for the USSR, and to its proximity to the southern Soviet frontiers: "The Soviet Military and Soviet Policy in the Middle East, 1970–1973," *Soviet Studies* 26, no. 4 (October 1974), p. 506.

14. Brown, *International Politics and the Middle East,* pp. 3–5.

15. For more on the Mandate period, see Rashid Khalidi, *The Iron Cage: The Story of the Palestinian Struggle for Statehood* (Boston: Beacon Press, 2006), chaps. 1–4.

16. For the different motivations of these three powers, see Avi Shlaim, *Collusion across the Jordan: King Abdullah, the Zionist Movement, and the Partition of Palestine* (New York: Columbia University Press, 1988), and Mary Wilson, *King Abdullah, Britain, and the Making of Jordan* (Cambridge: Cambridge University Press, 1987).

17. Abraham Ben-Zvi, *Decade of Transition: Eisenhower, Kennedy, and the Origins of the American-Israeli Alliance* (New York: Columbia University Press, 1998), pp. 97–102, 107–14. See also Warren Bass, *Support Any Friend: Kennedy's Middle East and the Making of the U.S.-Israel Alliance* (New York: Oxford University Press, 2003).

18. Khalidi, *The Iron Cage,* chap. 3.

19. Text in J. C. Hurewitz, *Diplomacy in the Near and Middle East: A Documentary Record, 1914–1956* (Princeton, N.J.: Van Nostrand, 1956), vol. 2, pp. 308–9.

20. Tom Segev, *1967: Israel, the War, and the Year That Transformed the Middle East* (New York: Metropolitan Books, 2007), pp. 265–67. U.S. documents covering the 1967 war are in *Foreign Relations of the United States* (hereafter, FRUS), Johnson Administration, vol. 19, *Arab-Israeli Crisis and War, 1967* available online: www.state.gov/r/pa/ho/frus/johnsonlb/xix/index.htm.

21. In one case, new fighter planes had just been delivered, uncrated, and assembled at a Syrian air base by Soviet personnel when they were destroyed on the ground by Israeli air strikes: personal communication to the author by Soviet official formerly posted in Syria: Beirut, October 12, 1978.

22. Abraham Ben-Zvi, "Influence and Arms: John F. Kennedy, Lyndon B. Johnson, and the Politics of Arms Sales to Israel, 1962–1966," *Israel Affairs* 10, nos. 1–2 (2004), pp. 29–59. The Skyhawks, ordered in 1966, were first delivered after the 1967 war.

23. *Department of State Bulletin* 63 (July 27, 1970), pp. 112–13.

24. On this understudied subject, see Dimant-Kass, "The Soviet Military and Soviet Policy in the Middle East," pp. 502–21.

25. See Vladislav Zubok, *A Failed Empire: The Soviet Union in the Cold War from Stalin to Gorbachev* (Chapel Hill: University of North Carolina Press, 2007), pp. 199–200.

26. The most perceptive student of these matters is Kass, e.g., in "The Soviet Military and Soviet Policy in the Middle East."

27. Rubinstein found specifically that the Egyptians more often got their way than did the Soviets: Alvin Rubinstein, *Red Star on the Nile: The Soviet-Egyptian Influence Relationship since the June War* (Princeton, N.J.: Princeton University Press, 1977). This point is also made by Zubok, *A Failed Empire*. See also Jon Glassman, *Arms for the Arabs: The Soviet Union and War in the Middle East* (Baltimore: Johns Hopkins University Press, 1975), and Mohamed Haikal, *The Sphinx and the Commissar: The Rise and Fall of Soviet Influence in the Middle East* (New York: Harper & Row, 1978).

28. Camille Mansour, *Beyond Alliance: Israel and U.S. Foreign Policy* (New York: Columbia University Press, 1994). See also Noam Chomsky, *The Fateful Triangle: The United States, Israel, and the Palestinians* (Boston: Verso, 1983).

29. The canonical statement of this case is by Steve Walt and John Mearsheimer, *The Israel Lobby and U.S. Foreign Policy* (New York: Farrar, Straus and Giroux, 2007).

30. The War of Attrition is analyzed in Lawrence Whetten, *The Canal War: Four-Power Conflict in the Middle East* (Cambridge, Mass.: MIT Press, 1974); Yaakov Bar-Siman-Tov, *The Israeli-Egyptian War of Attrition, 1969–1970: A Case Study of Limited War* (New York: Columbia University Press, 1980); and Edgar O'Ballance, *The Electronic War in the Middle East, 1968–1970* (London: Faber and Faber, 1974). U.S. documents covering the period from the 1967 war through the end of 1968 are in FRUS, Johnson Administration, vol. 20, *Arab-Israeli Dispute, 1967–68*, available at www.state.gov/r/pa/ho/frus/johnsonlb/xx/index.htm.

31. For details of Egyptian strategy see Mahmud Riyad, *Muthakkirat Mahmud Riyad, 1948–1978: Al-Bahth 'an al-salam wal-sira' fil-sharq al-awsat* [The Memoirs of Mahmud Riyad, 1948–1978: The Search for Peace and the Struggle in the Middle East] (Beirut: al-Mu'assasa al-'Arabiyya lil-Dirasat wal-Nashr, 1981); Abdel Magid Farid, *Nasser: The Final Years* (Reading, England: Ithaca Press, 1994); and Mohamed Heikal, *Secret Channels: The Inside Story of the Arab-Israeli Peace Negotiations* (London: HarperCollins, 1996). Riyad was Egyptian foreign minister, Farid,

secretary general of the Egyptian presidency, and Heikal, a minister and Nasser's closest confidant.

32. Summary of a meeting in Tel-Aviv between Secretary of State William Rogers, Israeli Prime Minister Golda Meir, and other U.S. and Israeli government officials regarding plans for a Middle East peace agreement. Memo, Department of State, May 7, 1971, *Declassified Documents Reference System* (DDRS), doc. CK3100548308 (Farmington Hills, Mich.: Gale Group, 2007). My attention was drawn to these documents by a 2007 unpublished paper by Omer Subhani, to whom I am grateful.

33. "Summary of Henry Kissinger's telephone call to Assistant Secretary of State Joseph Sisco regarding President Richard M. Nixon's request that the State Department soften its dialogue with Israel over that country's decision to violate its cease-fire." Memo, White House, February 28, 1971, DDRS, doc. CK3100573382. Sisco argued to Kissinger that if the United States helped Egypt to negotiate a separate peace with Israel, it would achieve the aim of supplanting the Soviets in Egyptian favor as a by-product, but to no avail.

34. Haikal, *The Sphinx and the Commissar*, provides an Egyptian perspective on this.

35. There is a wealth of Egyptian and Israeli memoir material on the 1973 war: see, e.g., Mohamed Heikal, *The Road to Ramadan* (London: Collins, 1975); Muhammad Fawzi, *Harb Uktubir 'am 1973: dirasah wa-durus* [The October War: Analysis and Lessons] (Cairo: Dar al-Mustaqbal al-'Arabi, 1988); Gen. Saad El-Shazly, *The Crossing of Suez: The October War, 1973* (London: Third World Centre, 1980); Abba Eban, *Abba Eban: An Autobiography* (New York: Random House, 1977); Chaim Herzog, *The War of Atonement, October 1973* (Boston: Little, Brown, 1975); Chaim Herzog, *The Arab-Israeli Wars: War and Peace in the Middle East from the 1948 War of Independence through Lebanon* (London: Greenhill Books, 2004); Avraham Adan, *On the Banks of the Suez: An Israeli General's Personal Account of the Yom Kippur War* (London: Arms & Armour Press, 1980).

36. This is confirmed on the basis of Soviet sources by Zubok, *A Failed Empire*, p. 239. See also Viktor Israelyan, *Inside the Kremlin during the Yom Kippur War* (University Park: Pennsylvania State University Press, 1996).

37. These included some aircraft, like the F-4 Phantom, with limited production runs, for which there was heavy demand from the U.S. military because of equipment losses during the war in Southeast Asia.

38. The only partial exception was the firing by Iraq of several dozen Scud missiles at Israel during the 1991 Gulf War.

39. This was shown, ex post facto, by Syria's acceptance at the end of the 1973 war of UN Security Council resolution 338, which embodied the accept-

ance by Damascus for the first time of resolution 242, and of the principle of a negotiated peaceful settlement of the Arab-Israeli conflict. Egypt, Jordan, and later Israel, had all accepted resolution 242 several years before.

40. The literature on this episode is rich, starting with Henry Kissinger's own memoir *White House Years* (Boston: Little, Brown, 1979), and continuing through works incorporating new archival revelations, notably Robert Dallek, *Nixon and Kissinger: Partners in Power* (New York: HarperCollins, 2007).

41. Dallek, *Nixon and Kissinger*, p. 520.

42. National Security Archive, "The October War and U.S. Policy," ed. William Burr, in particular Document 54: Memcon between Meir and Kissinger, October 22, 1973, 1:35–2:15 p.m: www.gwu.edu/fflnsarchiv/NSAEBB/NSAEBB98/index.htm#docs.

43. Dallek, *Nixon and Kissinger*, pp. 530–31.

44. Richard Holbrooke, review of Michael Dobbs, *One Minute to Midnight: Kennedy, Khrushchev, and Castro on the Brink of Nuclear War* (New York, Knopf, 2008), *New York Times*, June 22, 2008.

45. There had been a Soviet and a UN presence that was purely symbolic at a one-day meeting of a peace conference in Geneva at the end of 1973, which grouped together Egypt, Jordan, and Israel and served only a formal purpose.

46. The text can be found in William Quandt, *The Middle East Ten Years after Camp David* (Washington, D.C.: Brookings Institution Press, 1988), Appendix B, pp. 447–48.

47. As might be imagined, the Soviets looked dimly on this outcome: for a semiofficial reaction, see A. Ustyagov, "The Eygptian-Israeli Deal: A Dangerous Step," *International Affairs* 7 (July 1979), pp. 53–59.

48. An insider perspective on this period can be found in William B. Quandt, *Peace Process: American Diplomacy and the Arab-Israeli Conflict since 1967*, 3rd ed. (Washington, D.C.: Brookings Institution Press, 2005), pp. 177–204.

49. Whether the term used was "terrorism," "banditry," "thuggery," or "lawless elements," colonial powers have traditionally denigrated and tried to delegitimize and diminish the responses to their rule of subject peoples. The lack of historical awareness of this background in American public discourse, while not surprising, is deeply depressing.

50. During the Reagan era, Ross helped to define the misguided "interim" approach to negotiations, which protected Israel from having to make difficult decisions, and played key roles in both subsequent administrations. His book, *The Missing Peace: The Inside Story of the Fight for Mid-*

dle East Peace (New York: Farrar, Straus and Giroux, 2004), is a masterpiece of self-justification. It must be read, if at all, in tandem with Clayton Swisher's more accurate *The Truth about Camp David: The Untold Story about the Collapse of the Middle East Peace Process* (New York: Nation Books, 2004), and with accounts of other participants, including that of the then Israeli foreign minister, Shlomo Ben Ami: *Scars of War, Wounds of Peace: The Arab-Israeli Tragedy* (Oxford: Oxford University Press, 2006).

51. The Oslo Accords have many critics. In *Scars of War,* pp. 201–22, 225–39, Ben Ami, while poorly assessing Palestinian politics, highlights some flaws of Oslo. Idith Zertal and Akiva Eldar, *Lords of the Land: The War over Israel's Settlements in the Occupied Territories, 1967–2007* (New York: Nation Books, 2007), shows how settlements, never slowed by Oslo, torpedoed the prospects of peace. See also Khalidi, *The Iron Cage,* chaps. 5 and 6.

52. See Khalidi, *The Iron Cage,* chap. 6, for details.

53. Brown, *International Politics and the Middle East,* pp. 4–5.

54. For different interpretations of the causes of the 1975–90 war in Lebanon, see Walid Khalidi, *Conflict and Violence in Lebanon: Confrontation in the Middle East* (Cambridge, Mass.: Harvard Center for International Affairs, 1979); Tabitha Petran, *The Struggle over Lebanon* (New York: Monthly Review Press, 1987); Ghassan Tueni, *Une guerre pour les autres* (Paris: Lattes, 1985); Itamar Rabinovich, *The War for Lebanon, 1970–1983* (Ithaca, N.Y.: Cornell University Press, 1984); Rex Brynen, *Sanctuary and Survival: The PLO in Lebanon* (Boulder, Colo.: Westview, 1990); and Naomi Weinberger, *Syrian Intervention in Lebanon: The 1975–76 Civil War* (New York: Oxford University Press, 1986).

55. The massacre took place in a situation of growing sectarian polarization in Lebanon and in the wake of high tension after populist leader Marouf Saad had been shot a few weeks earlier while heading a demonstration of fishermen in the southern port city of Sidon. Saad later died of his wounds.

56. Kissinger's account of the second Sinai disengagement accord and the period that followed, including the war in Lebanon, can be found in *Years of Upheaval* (London: Weidenfeld & Nicolson, 1982).

57. Ilana Dimant-Kass, *The Lebanon Civil War, 1975–76: A Case of Crisis Mismanagement* (Jerusalem, Hebrew University, 1979), pp. 9–17.

58. This discretion did not succeed in hiding all traces of such involvement, as when Iranian-manufactured G-3 automatic rifles and Saudi-manufactured 81 mm mortar ammunition turned up in the hands of the right-wing Lebanese Forces in the 1975–76 phase of the Lebanese war, as

could be attested by the many people in West Beirut in this period who saw expended mortar rounds in the street, or captured G-3 rifles.

59. For one of the better accounts of this complex period, see W. Khalidi, *Conflict and Violence in Lebanon*.

60. There is much material on this episode in *The Kissinger Transcripts: A Verbatim Record of U.S. Diplomacy, 1969–1977*, available online through the National Security Archive via ProQuest. This can be accessed via www.gwu.edu/fflnsarchiv/NSAEBB/NSAEBB193/index.htm.

61. The southern limit of the Syrian deployment in Lebanon was first the Beirut-Damascus road, but later became a line from south of Sidon running eastward. By the spring of 1976, Kissinger was already telling his aides to tell Damascus that "we agree with the Syrian approach": ibid., Memorandum of Conversation, March 26, 1976.

62. For insights into Soviet policy at this point see Rashid Khalidi, "Soviet Policy in the Arab World in 1976: A Year of Setbacks," in *The Yearbook of the Palestine Question: 1976* [Arabic], Camille Mansour, ed. (Beirut: Institute for Palestine Studies, 1979), pp. 397–420.

63. Egypt and Iraq, eager to exploit any situation that would harm their Syrian rivals, both managed to smuggle some weapons and Palestinian Liberation Army cadres based on their territory to the PLO and its allies through the blockade, but their impact was minimal.

64. See Alexander M. Haig Jr., *Inner Circles: How America Changed the World; A Memoir* (New York: Warner Books, 1992); Rashid Khalidi, *Under Siege: P.L.O. Decisionmaking During the 1982 War* (New York: Columbia University Press, 1986); and Ze'ev Schiff and Ehud Yaari, *Israel's Lebanon War* (New York: Simon & Schuster, 1984).

65. Primakov, then a member of the Central Committee of the Soviet Communist Party (he later became foreign minister and prime minister of the Russian Federation), spoke to PLO leaders and thereafter to Palestinian researchers at the Institute for Palestine Studies in Beirut: personal information of the author.

66. This was the case even though Ronald Reagan was finally moved to try to put some restraints on America's client by the outcry provoked by the magnitude of the casualties and damage inflicted by Israel's indiscriminate air and artillery bombardments of Beirut from June 5 until August 12, 1982. Over nineteen thousand people, the great majority of them Lebanese and Palestinian civilians, died in the 1982 war according to Lebanese police figures quoted in the *Washington Post*, December 2, 1982, and cited in R. Khalidi, *Under Siege*, p. 200, n. 5.

67. Everyone in West Beirut saw these flares, and many, myself included, wondered why they were being fired when the fighting was over and the

city had been occupied by Israeli troops, with very little resistance. It was only in the following days that the awful truth became known. Journalist Jonathan Randal was in West Beirut at the time, and his contemporary reports in the *Washington Post,* and those of his colleague Loren Jenkins, who won a Pulitzer for his coverage of the massacres, can be consulted with great benefit for details, as can Randal's book, *Going All the Way: Christian Warlords, Israeli Adventurers, and the War in Lebanon* (New York: Viking, 1984).

68. In an interview with the Israeli newspaper *Yediot Aharanot on* May 2, 2008. Barak later became defense minister and prime minister.

69. R. Khalidi, *Under Siege,* pp. 168–71, details the unfulfilled pledges made via the Lebanese government and other third parties by the American envoy, Ambassador Philip Habib, to protect the Palestinian civilian population in the refugee camps around Beirut after the withdrawal of the PLO.

70. The best work on the Iraqi Communist Party remains Hanna Batatu, *The Old Social Classes and the Revolutionary Movements of Iraq: A Study of Iraq's Old Landed and Commercial Classes and of its Communists, Ba'thists, and Free Officers* (Princeton, N.J.: Princeton University Press, 1978).

71. Weiner, *Legacy of Ashes,* pp. 140–41; 576–77. See also Marion Farouk-Sluglett and Peter Sluglett, *Iraq since 1958: From Revolution to Dictatorship* (London: I.B. Tauris, 2003).

72. After Saddam Hussein's regime smashed the Kurdish revolt, it "resettled" many Kurds far from Iraqi Kurdistan. A University of Chicago archaeological team working at Nippur before the Iran-Iraq War found that local workers who had formerly labored on the site had been drafted, and consequently hired relocated Kurds, only to find that none of them spoke Arabic. The problem was resolved when some Kurds turned out to speak Hebrew as a result of their having been trained by Israeli operatives. Since some of the archaeologists could speak Hebrew, communication became possible and the work proceeded: personal communication to the author, Chicago, January 12, 1994.

73. Jonathan C. Randal, *After Such Knowledge, What Forgiveness: My Encounters with Kurdistan* (New York: Farrar, Straus and Giroux, 1997), p. 176.

74. Among such justificatory works, see Yevgeni Primakov, *Anatomy of the Middle East Conflict* (Moscow: Progress, 1979), R. A Ulyanovsky, *The Revolutionary Process in the East: Past and Present* (Moscow: Progress, 1985), and K. H. Brutents, *National Liberation Revolutions Today,* part 2 (Moscow: Progress, 1977). See also Ilana Kass, *Soviet Involvement in the*

Middle East: Policy Formulation, 1966–1973 (Boulder, Colo.: Westview, 1978), chap. 5.

75. For the Iraqi Communist Party, see Batatu, *The Old Social Classes,* pp. 574–1112; and Oles Smolansky and Bettie Smolansky, *The USSR and Iraq: The Soviet Quest for Influence* (Durham, N.C.: Duke University Press, 1991); for the Egyptian Communist Party, see Tareq Ismael and Rifa'at El-Said, *The Communist Movement in Egypt, 1920–1988* (Syracuse, N.Y.: Syracus University Press, 1990); and Selma Botman, *The Rise of Egyptian Communism, 1939–1970* (Syracuse, N.Y.: Syracuse University Press, 1988).

76. The Iranian government accused both superpowers, the Soviets through the medium of the Tudeh Party and other leftist formations, and the United States through other covert actions, of trying to undermine, destabilize, and overthrow the Islamic regime. Classified U.S. documents seized in the American Embassy in Tehran in 1979 and published in seventy-seven volumes in 1979–95 under the title *Documents from the U.S. Espionage Den,* cover the period up to the seizure of the embassy, and shed little light on any such effort; nor does Tim Weiner in *Legacy of Ashes.*

77. See Henner Furtig, *Iran's Rivalry with Saudi Arabia between the Gulf Wars* (Reading, England: Ithaca Press, 2002), and Thomas Naff, *Gulf Security and the Iran-Iraq War* (Washington, D.C.: National Defense University Press, 1985).

78. "Shaking Hands with Saddam Hussein: The U.S. Tilts Towards Iraq, 1980–1984," Joyce Battle, ed.: www.gwu.edu/fflnsarchiv/NSAEBB/NSAEBB82/index.htm.

79. Weiner, *Legacy of Ashes,* p. 404.

80. During the Iran-Iraq War, Iraq ran up $12.9 billion in debts to the USSR for weapons, most of which the Russian government wrote off in early 2008: "Moscow Cancels $US 12 Billion Iraqi Debt," *Russia Today,* February 12, 2008, www.russiatoday.ru/news/news/20765.

81. This category, generally held to encompass nuclear and biological weapons and poison gas, tends to blur important distinctions. Poison gas, which was internationally banned after its hideous effects were revealed during World War I, is still weaponized mainly for battlefield use, making it only questionable whether it is primarily a "weapon of mass destruction." Biological weapons have never been used in modern warfare (or by terrorists) and would seem to be intended mainly for use against civilian populations, while nuclear weapons have so far only been used against civilian populations, in 1945 at Hiroshima and Nagasaki, and would still appear to be primarily directed at civilian targets.

The latter two are therefore in a certain sense more truly "weapons of mass destruction."

82. There is a prolific literature on the Iran-Contra affair. For primary sources on this topic, see Peter Kornbluh and Malcolm Byrne, *The Iran-Contra Scandal: The Declassified History* (New York, New Press, 1993).

83. Weiner, *Legacy of Ashes*, p. 404.

84. Stephen R. Shalom, "The United States and the Iran-Iraq War," *Z Magazine*, February 1990.

V
The Cold War and the Undermining of Democracy

1. The main two exceptions are Turkey, where military rule has alternated with democracy for nearly fifty years, and where what Turks call the "deep state," including elements of the military, the judiciary, the police, and much of the bureaucracy, still retain a powerful hold over many areas of political life; and Israel, which is a democracy for its citizens (with non-Arabs having far more rights than the 20 percent of its citizens who are Arab) but which for over forty-one years—more than two-thirds of its existence—has imposed military rule over 3.5 million Palestinians who are denied self-determination in the occupied West Bank, Gaza Strip, and East Jerusalem. In Lebanon, Kuwait, Jordan, Morocco, Egypt, and Iran, limited forms of democracy exist, but there are crippling constraints on the free exercise of democratic rights by the citizenry, ranging from overt and covert foreign intervention in Lebanon, to the autocracy of the ruling elites in the four other Arab states (monarchical in the first three cases), to a dictatorial theocracy in the case of Iran.

2. See Rashid Khalidi, *Resurrecting Empire: Western Footprints and America's Perilous Path in the Middle East*, rev. ed. (Boston: Beacon Press, 2005), chap. 2, for a brief history of the trials and tribulations of the democratic experiments in the Middle East and the role of external intervention in undermining it.

3. L. Carl Brown, *International Politics and the Middle East: Old Rules, Dangerous Game* (Princeton, N.J.: Princeton University Press, 1984), pp. 3–5

4. James Madison to Thomas Jefferson, "Political Observations," April 20, 1795, in *Letters and Other Writings of James Madison* (Philadelphia: J. B Lippincott, 1867), vol. 4, p. 491.

5. Odd Arne Westad, *The Global Cold War: Third World Interventions and the Making of Our Times* (Cambridge: Cambridge University Press, 2005), chaps. 1 and 2, pp. 9–72.

6. Westad, *The Global Cold War*, p. 30.

7. J. C. Hurewitz, ed., *The Middle East and North Africa in World Politics: A Documentary Record* (New Haven, Conn.: Yale University Press, 1979), vol. 2, p. 179.

8. For an examination of this and other options explored by the Soviets in Arab countries, see John R. Swanso, "The Soviet Union and the Arab World: Revolutionary Progress through Dependence on Local Elites," *Western Political Quarterly* 27, no. 4 (1974), pp. 637–56.

9. For details, see Alexandre Bennigsen and S. Enders Wimbush, *Muslim National Communism in the Soviet Union: A Revolutionary Strategy for the Third World* (Chicago: University of Chicago Press, 1979), and Helene Carrere d'Encausse and Stuart Schram, *Marxism and Asia: An Introduction with Readings* (London: Allen Lane, 1969).

10. See Elizabeth Valkenier, *The Soviet Union and the Third World: An Economic Bind* (New York: Praeger, 1983); Roger E. Kanet, ed., *The Soviet Union and the Developing Nations* (Baltimore: Johns Hopkins University Press, 1974); Alvin Rubinstein, *Moscow's Third World Strategy* (Princeton, N.J.: Princeton University Press, 1990); and Bruce Porter, *The USSR in Third World Conflicts: Soviet Arms and Diplomacy in Local Wars 1945–1980* (Cambridge: Cambridge University Press, 1984). Regarding the Middle East, see Walter Laqueur, *The Soviet Union and the Middle East* (New York: Praeger, 1959), and Jaan Pennar, *The USSR and the Arabs: The Ideological Dimension* (New York: Crane, Russak, 1973).

11. Mostafa Elm, *Oil, Power, and Principle: Iran's Oil Nationalization and Its Aftermath* (Syracuse, N.Y.: Syracuse University Press, 1992), pp. 1–22, gives this background.

12. The Conservatives, again led by an increasingly aged but still vigorously imperialist Winston Churchill, had returned to power in October 1951, and although they did not privatize the nationalized British industries, they took an even dimmer view of Iran's action than had the previous Labour government of Clement Attlee.

13. Indeed, in the words of Daniel Yergin, in *The Prize: The Epic Quest for Oil, Money, and Power* (New York: Simon & Schuster, 1991), p. 472, during the Truman administration, "antitrust lawyers in the Justice Department were very suspicious of any cooperation among the major oil companies," and pressed for a criminal antitrust prosecution of these companies that was only finally rejected by Truman a few days before he left office.

14. Tim Weiner, *Legacy of Ashes: The History of the CIA* (New York: Doubleday, 2007), pp. 93–105.

15. Interestingly, it was Amir Faisal, effectively his father's foreign minister, whom King Ibn Sa'ud sent to Moscow to launch diplomatic ties with the

Soviets. This was further evidence of Ibn Sa'ud's constant efforts to diminish the hitherto predominant influence of Great Britain.

16. See Arnold Kramner, *The Forgotten Friendship: Israel and the Soviet Bloc, 1947–53* (Urbana: University of Illinois Press, 1974).

17. For a brilliantly rendered evocation of how the residents of Saudi Arabia first perceived the American oilmen and other foreigners when they started arriving in the kingdom in the 1930s, and the initial impact of oil revenues, see Abdel Rahman Munif's *Cities of Salt*, trans. Peter Theroux (New York: Vintage, 1989).

18. As was noted in chapter 2, "The Sources of Soviet Conduct" was published in *Foreign Affairs* in July 1947 under the pseudonym "X."

19. For a good overview, see John Campbell, *Defense of the Middle East: Problems of American Policy* (New York: Harpers, for the Council on Foreign Relations, 1960).

20. Malcolm H. Kerr, *The Arab Cold War: Gamal 'Abd al-Nasir and His Rivals, 1958–1970*, 3rd ed. (London: Oxford University Press, 1971).

21. Zhdanov stated in a September 1947 speech to the Cominform: "The fundamental changes caused by the war on the international scene and in the position of individual countries has entirely changed the political landscape of the world. A new alignment of political forces has arisen. The more the war recedes into the past, the more distinct become two major trends in postwar international policy, corresponding to the division of the political forces operating on the international arena into two major camps: the imperialist and anti-democratic camp, on the one hand, and the anti-imperialist and democratic camp, on the other": www.cnn.com/SPECIALS/cold.war/episodes/04/documents/cominform.html.

22. For internal Soviet ideological debates, see Werner Hahn, *Postwar Soviet Politics: The Fall of Zhdanov and the Defeat of Moderation, 1946–53* (Ithaca, N.Y.: Cornell University Press, 1982), and Vladislav Zubok and Constantine Pieshakov, *Inside the Kremlin's Cold War: From Stalin to Khrushchev* (Cambridge, Mass.: Harvard University Press, 1996).

23. See Miles Copeland, *The Game of Nations: The Amorality of Power Politics* (New York: Simon & Schuster, 1970), for a fascinating account by a former CIA operative of the frustrations of dealing with dogmatic policymakers in Washington at this time. See also Salim Yaqub's excellent *Containing Arab Nationalism: The Eisenhower Doctrine and the Middle East* (Chapel Hill: University of North Carolina Press, 2004).

24. For detailed analysis of these events, see Rashid Khalidi, "The Revolutionary Year of 1958 in the Arab World," in *A Revolutionary Year: The Middle East in 1958*, ed. Wm. Roger Louis and Roger Owen (Washington,

D. C.: Woodrow Wilson Center Press; London: I.B. Tauris, 2002), pp. 181–208, on which this section draws.

25. Readers seeking more detail about how this happened can refer to Khalidi, *Resurrecting Empire*, chap. 2.

26. The French role is analyzed in Gerard Khoury, *La France et l'Orient arabe: Naissance du Liban moderne 1914–1920* (Paris : Armand Colin, 1993).

27. For details see Rania Maktabi, "The Lebanese Census of 1932 Revisited: Who Are the Lebanese?" *British Journal of Middle East Studies* 26, no. 2 (1999), pp. 219–41.

28. See Albert Hourani, *Syria and Lebanon: A Political Essay* (London: Oxford University Press, 1946), pp. 163–85.

29. Until 1946, when it became the Hashemite Kingdom of Jordan, the territory was known as the Emirate of Transjordan. I will refer to it as Jordan throughout.

30. See Eugene Rogan, *Frontiers of the State in the Late Ottoman Empire: Transjordan, 1850–1921* (New York: Cambridge University Press, 1999), and Beshara Doumani, *Rediscovering Palestine: Merchants and Peasants in Jabal Nablus, 1700–1900* (Berkeley: University of California Press, 1955), for details of these pre–World War I relationships.

31. For an account of the conference, see Aaron S. Klieman, *Foundations of British Policy in the Arab World: The Cairo Conference of 1921* (Baltimore: Johns Hopkins University Press, 1970).

32. Winston Churchill is supposed to have claimed he created Jordan "in an afternoon": John Kifner, "The Ruling Class: Building Modernity on Desert Mirages," *New York Times*, February 7, 1999.

33. For the earliest origins of the band of British-controlled territory running from the Mediterranean to the Gulf, in the pre–World War I "railway partitions" between the great powers, see Rashid Khalidi, *British Policy in Syria and Palestine, 1906–1914* (Oxford: St. Antony's Middle East Monographs, 1980), chap. 3.

34. The force raised in the Hijaz during the great Arab Revolt of 1916 onward went under the name of al-Jaysh al-'Arabi (literally "the Arab Army"), became part of Gen. Allenby's forces fighting the Ottomans, helped to liberate Damascus in 1918, and became the backbone of the army of Faisal's Syrian state. The forces Amir Abdullah rode northward with into Jordan from the Hijaz in 1921 included remnants of this force, but in 1923 after the British takeover it was purged of nationalist officers, placed under a British commander, Capt. Frederick Peake, and rebaptized the Arab Legion.

35. Hussein was sixteen when his grandfather was killed by his side in Jerusalem, and assumed the throne a year later.

36. These events are best treated in Louis and Owen, ed., *A Revolutionary Year*. See Patrick Seale's indispensable *The Struggle for Syria: A Study of Postwar Arab Politics, 1945–1958*, rev. ed. (London: I.B. Tauris, 1986) for events leading up to 1958, and Malcolm H. Kerr's excellent *The Arab Cold War* for subsequent developments. See also Irene Gendzier, *Notes from the Minefield: United States Intervention in Lebanon and the Middle East, 1945–1958* (New York: Columbia University Press, 1997).

37. That these fears were widely shared in the West can be seen from a *Le Monde* editorial dated July 15, 1958, describing the Iraqi revolution as part of a larger concerted effort: "Tout indique sinon l'existence d'un plan concerté, du moins celle de mouvements 'parallèles' s'inspirant des mêmes mots d'ordre, utilisant la meme tactique et recevant probablement les mêmes encouragements." [Everything indicates the existence, if not of a concerted plan, at least that of "parallel" movements, inspired by the same instructions, using the same tactics, and probably receiving the same support.]

38. For a sensitive account of the changes in Jordan during this period from a perceptive observer who grew up there, see Abdel Rahman Munif, *Story of a City: A Childhood in Amman* (London: Quartet, 1998).

39. British Foreign Office correspondence, FO 371/127880, Johnston to Lloyd, no. 26, May 8, 1957. I am grateful to Professor Roger Louis for providing me with copies of this and other documents used in this chapter.

40. British Foreign Office correspondence, FO 371/127882, Johnston to Lloyd, no. 64, November 6, 1957. The prime minister during the brief interregnum between democracy and authoritarianism in Jordan was my uncle, Dr. Hussein Fakhri al-Khalidi.

41. Ibid.

42. For repeated exaggerated and often lurid estimations by Western diplomats of the role of the Soviet Union in the Jordan case, see Khalidi, "The Revolutionary Year of 1958," pp. 181–208.

43. Wilbur Crane Eveland, *Ropes of Sand: America's Failure in the Middle East* (New York: Norton, 1980), p. 252. Eveland notes: "Throughout the elections I traveled regularly to the presidential palace with a briefcase full of Lebanese pounds, then returned late at night to the embassy with an empty twin case I'd carried away for Harvey Armada's CIA finance-office people to replenish."

44. Malik did seem to share the lurid fears regarding communism of his American interlocutors, as was apparent when I heard him in New York in 1958 speaking heatedly and with passionate conviction on the subject at a private gathering.

45. One of the best reflections of this belief is Amin Maalouf's novel, *The Rock of Tanios*, trans. Dorothy S. Blair (New York: G. Braziller, 1994).

46. In the first of two parliamentary elections in 1954, only 16 nationalist or leftist deputies were returned out of a total of 135, but this large number displeased the U.S. ambassador and the British. The problem was resolved after pro-Western strongman Nuri al-Said returned as prime minister and saw to it that almost none of these deputies were returned in the second, even more thoroughly rigged, election. See Waldemar J. Gallman, *Iraq under General Nuri: My Recollections of Nuri Al-Said, 1954–1958* (Baltimore: Johns Hopkins Press, 1964), and Peter Sluglett, "The Pan-Arab Movement and the Influence of Cairo and Moscow," in *A Revolutionary Year*, ed. Louis and Owen, pp. 209–20.

47. For details, see Elizabeth Bishop, "Talking Shop: Egyptian Engineers and Soviet Specialists at the Aswan High Dam" (PhD diss., University of Chicago, Department of History, 1999).

48. This was Graham Fuller, who had the distinction of being the only person to be removed from his post for the Iran-Contra fiasco, perhaps—this being Washington—because he had vigorously opposed this illegal, foolish initiative when it was proposed by those in the Reagan White House who devised it. For this disaster, sadly, few of those actually responsible were ever punished. Some individuals who were convicted of felonies, like Elliott Abrams, were pardoned by George H. W. Bush, and returned to serve in equally illustrious fashion (albeit so far escaping indictment) in the administration of his son.

VI
Victory in the Cold War, and the Global War on Terror

1. Martin W. Lewis and Kären E. Wigan, in *The Myth of Continents: A Critique of Metageography* (Berkeley: University of California Press, 1997), acutely point out that the "continents" of Africa, Asia, and Europe are in fact a single landmass. While Europe, although just one of many protuberances from this huge landmass, is dignified with the title of a "continent" in conventional geographic terminology, South Asia, another larger extension from the same landmass, is commonly referred to as a mere "subcontinent."

2. The cliffs at Nahr al-Kalb, north of Beirut, at a point where the coastal plain narrows greatly, are marked with inscriptions, steles, and other evidence carved in the stone that attests to the passage of armies, from those of the pharaohs and the Assyrians to the Roman and, much later, the British empires.

3. Recent research on the Phoenicians dates their rise to the middle of the

second millennium BCE rather than the beginning of the first, as had been thought previously: see Glenn E. Markoe, *Phoenicians* (Berkeley: University of California Press, 2000), p. 11.

4. These conflicts are brilliantly analyzed in Alfred Thayer Mahan, *The Influence of Sea Power upon History, 1660–1783*, rev. ed. (Boston: Little, Brown, 1902), a book that has had great influence on British and American strategic thinking.

5. See Rashid Khalidi, "Lebanon in the Context of Regional Politics: Palestinian and Syrian Involvement in the Lebanese Crisis," *Third World Quarterly* 7, no. 3 (July 1985), pp. 495–514; Naomi Weinberger, *Syrian Intervention in Lebanon: The 1975–76 Civil War* (New York: Oxford University Press, 1986); Rex Brynen, *Sanctuary and Survival: The PLO in Lebanon* (Boulder, Colo.: Westview, 1990); and Itamar Rabinovich, *The War for Lebanon, 1970–1983* (Ithaca, N.Y.: Cornell University Press, 1984).

6. For details, see Rashid Khalidi, *Under Siege: PLO Decision-Making during the 1982 War* (New York: Columbia University Press, 1986). Also important in limiting this conflict was the fact stated bluntly by Soviet envoy Yevgeni Primakov to his Palestinian interlocutors in Beirut on the eve of the June 1982 Israeli invasion of Lebanon, that the USSR did not have the capability to confront Israel and its American backer in Lebanon, and could only guarantee protection of the territory of its Syrian protégé: personal information of the author. For further details, see chap. 4, n. 65.

7. Malcolm H. Kerr, *The Arab Cold War: Gamal 'Abd al-Nasir and His Rivals, 1958–1970*, 3rd ed. (London: Oxford University Press, 1971).

8. Kerr, *The Arab Cold War*, and David Hirst, *The Gun and the Olive Branch: The Roots of Violence in the Middle East*, 2nd ed. (London: Faber and Faber, 1984), show how the rivalry with Saudi Arabia affected Egyptian decision-making.

9. Lawrence Whetten, *The Canal War: Four-Power Conflict in the Middle East* (Cambridge, Mass.: MIT Press, 1974), correctly describes the fighting along the Suez Canal of 1968–70 as a four-power conflict, showing how deeply the superpowers were engaged, and also how the Egyptian military managed to push their antiaircraft missile batteries forward to the banks of the Suez Canal in spite of intense Israeli bombardment, later making possible the 1973 crossing. See also Yaakov Bar-Siman-Tov, *The Israeli-Egyptian War of Attrition, 1969–1970: A Case-Study of Limited Local War* (New York: Columbia University Press, 1980).

10. See Yezid Sayigh and Avi Shlaim, eds., *The Cold War and the Middle East* (Oxford: Oxford University Press, 1997), and Nigel Ashton, ed., *The Cold War in the Middle East: Regional Conflict and the Superpowers, 1967–1973*

(London: Routledge, 2007), for interpretations based partly on newly released archival materials. Another book based on such materials, Isabella Ginor and Gideon Remez, *Foxbats over Dimona: The Soviets' Nuclear Gamble in the Six-Day War* (New Haven, Conn.: Yale University Press, 2007), appears to come to a number of unfounded conclusions.

11. Some of the key leaders of this neo-Ba'th regime had been volunteers with the National Liberation Front (FLN) in the Algerian war of liberation and came away with a belief in the effectiveness of a "long-term people's war of liberation," to use the Maoist catchphrase of the era, and this was the basis of their support for Palestinians who espoused similar ideas.

12. See Robert Pranger, *American Policy for Peace in the Middle East, 1969–1971: Problems of Principle, Maneuver, and Time* (Washington, D.C.: American Enterprise Institute, 1974), and Hirst, *The Gun and the Olive Branch*.

13. A work that reflects well this transitory moment in Arab politics is Walid Kazziha, *Revolutionary Change in the Arab World: Habash and His Comrades from Arab Nationalism to Marxism* (London: Hurst, 1975).

14. For a recent book that deals with this war, see Nubar Hovsepian, ed., *The War on Lebanon: A Reader* (New York: Olive Branch Press, 2007).

15. According to UN figures, the number of Palestinians killed by various forms of conflict in the Gaza Strip went up from 75 in the first five months of 2006 (13 of them children) to 462 in the subsequent seven months, of whom 109 were children. A total of 25 Israelis were killed in Israel and inside the occupied territories in 2006 as a direct or indirect result of the conflict, 2 of them children: www.ochaopt.org/documents/PoC_tables_June_08.pdf.

16. Lebanon was little involved in the first three Arab-Israeli wars of 1948, 1956, and 1967, except as the recipient of large numbers of Palestinians driven in 1948 from their homes in Galilee, Haifa, and Jaffa by Israeli forces.

17. To mention only one precedent, the revolutionary movements in the Arab world and other parts of the Middle East in the 1960s, mentioned earlier in this chapter, were also connected, in some cases very closely, to one another, as well as to states and groups outside the Middle East: see, inter alia, Kazziha, *Revolutionary Change in the Arab World*. There were similar, shadowy connections between Arab revolutionaries and military officers in several Arab countries and Turkey in the immediate wake of the collapse of the Ottoman Empire in 1918.

18. *Yediot Aharanot*, May 2, 2008. He also said that "twenty years ago we supported the establishment of the Hamas."

19. Robert Scheer, "Obama on the Brink," July 22, 2008, www.truthdig.com/ report/item/20080722_obama_on_the_brink.

20. On the underlying basis of this ideological drive, see Jane Mayer, *The Dark Side: The Inside Story of How the War on Terror Turned into a War on American Ideals* (New York: Doubleday, 2008).

21. I owe this formulation to my friend Jim Chandler of the University of Chicago.

22. The Baker-Hamilton Report issued by the Iraq Study Group in December 2006 did not describe how poorly the Iraq War had been waged by the United States at the outset, but was critical of the war generally and said "U.S. efforts in Afghanistan have been complicated by the overriding focus of U.S. attention and resources on Iraq": www.usip.org/isg/ iraq_study_group_report/report/1206/iraq_study_group_report.pdf.

   Among many others, see also Richard Clarke, *Against All Enemies: Inside America's War on Terror* (New York: Free Press, 2004), and Paul R. Pillar, "Intelligence, Policy, and the War in Iraq," *Foreign Affairs,* March/ April 2006: www.foreignaffairs.org/20060301faessay85202/paul-r-pillar/ intelligence-policy-and-the-war-in-iraq.html.

23. This was the October 2, 2002, "Joint Resolution to Authorize the Use of United States Armed Forces against Iraq": www.whitehouse.gov/news/ releases/2002/10/20021002–2.html.

24. There is a growing body of new work that makes the link between the dramatic extension of American presidential power, the growing infringements on citizens' rights and liberties, and interventions abroad justified under the banner of the global war on terror. Besides Mayer, *The Dark Side,* among the best are Frederick Schwarz Jr. and Aziz Huq, *Unchecked and Unbalanced: Presidential Power in a Time of Terror* (New York: New Press, 2007); Matthew Crenson and Benjamin Ginsberg, *Presidential Power: Unchecked and Unbalanced* (New York: Norton, 2007); and Stephen Holmes, *The Matador's Cape: America's Reckless Response to Terror* (Cambridge: Cambridge University Press, 2007).

25. Perhaps the most dramatic of these announcements was that by Attorney General John Ashcroft while on a visit to Moscow of the arrest of José Padilla on charges of planning a terrorist attack involving nuclear materials, charges that were quietly dropped long before Padilla was charged and convicted on more mundane grounds.

26. For a brilliant legal analysis of these infringements on liberty, see Michael Tigar, "A System of Wholesale Denial of Rights," *Monthly Review* 59, no. 4 (2007), pp. 11–24.

27. Geoffrey Stone, *Perilous Times: Free Speech in Wartime from the Sedition Act of 1798 to the War on Terrorism* (New York: Norton, 2004).

28. Figures in constant 2005 dollars. Information from the Stockholm International Peace Research Institute (SIPRI) Military Expenditure Database: www.sipri.org/contents/milap/milex/mex_database1.html. Essentially the same core constellation of neoconservatives and muscular nationalists that has called for and waged the global war on terror in the George W. Bush era was responsible during the Reagan administration for artificially inflating the Soviet threat. They used, among other methods, the fantastic exaggerations of the Soviet defense budget concocted in 1976 by the "Team B" group (inspired by University of Chicago right-wing academic Albert Wohlstetter, himself a disciple of Leo Strauss, and supported by Donald Rumsfeld and Dick Cheney), including Richard Perle and Paul Wolfowitz, as well as Richard Pipes and Paul Nitze, to claim that what we now know to have been the already inflated estimations of the CIA and the rest of the intelligence community of Soviet military spending were too low. See: "November 1976: Team B Browbeats CIA Analysts," www.historycommons.org/context.jsp?item=a1176 teambversusteama.

29. In the materials produced by the Project for a New American Century and other far-right-wing groupings out of which emerged most of the key foreign policy decision-makers of the new administration, China was prominently featured as the great danger to be feared: newamericancentury.org/RebuildingAmericasDefenses.pdf.

30. Official American military casualty figures are as of July 2008: www.defenselink.mil/news/casualty.pdf. The World Health Organization in January 2008 released the results of a survey of 9,345 households to ascertain Iraqi civilian casualties. On the basis of this survey, it estimated the number of Iraqis killed violently between the invasion of March 19, 2003, and the end of February 2008 as about 220,000, with deaths "linked to the conflict" totaling 600,000: *Le Monde,* March 19, 2008.

31. The supplemental appropriation request for fiscal year 2007 was estimated at $100–$128 billion. That for 2006 was $66 billion; for 2005, $82 billion; for 2004, $72 billion, and for 2003, $74 billion, all on top of the regular defense budget: Ivan Eland, "Hidden Costs," *American Conservative,* January 15, 2007, pp. 16–17.

32. The ineffable Richard Perle has written (with David Frum, in *An End to Evil*): "For us, terrorism remains the great evil of our time, and the war against this evil, our generation's great cause. . . . There is no middle way for Americans: It is victory or holocaust," cited in Jim Lobe, "From Holocaust to Hyperpower," Inter Press Service, January 26, 2005. He has also said: "For those of us who are involved in foreign and defense policy today, my generation, the defining moment of our history was certainly the Holocaust. It was the destruction, the genocide of a whole

people, and it was the failure to respond in a timely fashion to a threat that was clearly gathering. We don't want that to happen again; when we have the ability to stop totalitarian regimes we should do so, because when we fail to do so, the results are catastrophic," cited in Jim Lobe, "'Moral Clarity' or Moral Abdication?" TomPaine.com, May 11, 2005: www.tompaine.com/articles/2005/05/11/moral_clarity_or_moral_abdi cation.php.

33. Pillar, "Intelligence, Policy, and the War in Iraq." This account is corroborated by that of Richard Clarke, the senior counterterrorism official at the outset of the George W. Bush administration in his book *Against All Enemies.* The run-up to the Iraq War witnessed a reprise of the identical tactic utilized by the Team B group in 1976 of stampeding public opinion with distortions, exaggerations, and concoctions about Soviet military prowess in order to justify massive American arms budgets (which finally could be adopted during the Reagan administration). Having been taken in by these neocon con men once, the American public sadly failed to see through the same shameless charade when it was performed a quarter-century later.

34. Jeff Stein, "Can You Tell a Sunni from a Shiite?" *New York Times,* October 17, 2006.

35. For an analysis of the underlying rationale behind the extremist conservative takeover of the Republican Party in recent years, and the role played by the right-wing think tanks, see Tom Frank, "The Wrecking Crew: How a Gang of Right-Wing Con Men Destroyed Washington and Made a Killing," *Harper's,* August 2008, pp. 35–45.

36. A good example in the think-tank world would be Danielle Pletka, the highly visible vice president for strategy of the American Enterprise Institute, whose sole credentials for her repeated fatuous but quotable pronouncements on the Middle East would appear to be a brief stint in Israel, work on a right-wing newspaper, and service as a junior aide to Senator Jesse Helms. The administration of George W. Bush pullulated with officials dealing with the Middle East in a range of departments and agencies, some in senior positions, with equally slim résumés as far as any real in-depth Middle East expertise goes.

37. For details on the Ottoman background, and the role of former Ottoman officers, see Muhammad Tarbush, *The Role of the Military in Politics: A Case Study of Iraq to 1941* (London: I.B. Tauris, 1982); Peter Sluglett, *Britain in Iraq: Contriving King and Country* (New York: Columbia University Press, 2007); and Toby Dodge, *Inventing Iraq: The Failure of Nation-Building and a History Denied* (New York: Columbia University Press, 2005).

38. Andrew Cockburn, in *CounterPunch,* and Seymour Hersh, in the *New*

Yorker, have reported on a "presidential finding" authorizing the waging of a covert campaign against the Iranian regime and its influence both inside Iran and from Lebanon to Afghanistan, and the appropriation of $300–$400 million for this purpose: Andrew Cockburn, "Secret Bush 'Finding' Widens War on Iran," *CounterPunch,* May 2, 2008; Seymour Hersh, "Preparing the Battlefield," *New Yorker,* July 7, 2008.

39. See Rashid Khalidi, *The Iron Cage: The Story of the Palestinian Struggle for Statehood* (Boston: Beacon Press, 2006), chaps. 5 and 6, for details.

40. See Christine Spolar, "14 'Enduring Bases' Set in Iraq: Long-Term Military Presence Planned," *Chicago Tribune,* March 23, 2004.

41. For details, see the Defense Department's website for the new command: www.defenselink.mil/africom/.

42. In an op-ed titled "It's Time to Begin a Troop Pullout," *New York Times,* July 14, 2008.

43. According to a March 2008 poll done for the BBC, ABC, ARD, and NHK, 72 percent of Iraqis opposed the presence of "coalition forces," 61 percent felt that the presence of U.S. forces made the security situation worse, and 1 percent wanted American forces to stay permanently: www .globalpolicy.org/security/issues/iraq/poll/2008/0308opinion.pdf.

44. According to Andrew Kohut and Richard Wike, "All the World's a Stage," *National Interest,* May 6, 2008, in several years of polling done by the Pew Global Attitudes Project: "Between 2002 and 2007, the number of people with a favorable view of the United States fell in twenty-six countries out of the thirty-three where trend data are available. Ratings of the United States are disturbingly low among many of our longtime European allies, and they have dipped in Latin America and other parts of the world as well. The findings are especially dismal in Muslim nations." www.nationalinterest.org/Article.aspx?id=17502.

45. In fourteen CNN polls from May 2007 until June 2008, disapproval ranged from 63–68 percent: www.pollingreport.com/iraq.htm. The president's approval rating was equally dismal: 28 percent of respondents approved of his performance in a poll in April 2008, and 81 percent were dissatisfied with the country's direction: www.nytimes.com/2008/04/04/us/04poll.html.

46. One only has to read accounts of the inner workings of the Nixon administration, reputed for its expertise in foreign and strategic matters, to see how much of an illusion this may have been: see, e.g., the revelations about Nixon's distraction from matters of foreign policy during the 1973 Middle East war, leading up to the dangerous nuclear confrontation with the USSR, in Robert Dallek, *Nixon and Kissinger: Partners in Power* (New York: HarperCollins, 2007),pp. 520–33.

47. The populations of these six states are: Libya: 6 million; UAE: 4.6 million; Oman: 3.3 million; Kuwait: 2.7 milllion; Qatar: 900,000; Bahrain 700,000. Very large proportions of these 14 million people are non-citizens, a majority in some states. Their respective 2007 GDPs (today much inflated by the rise in the price of oil) are $74 billion; $167 billion; $61 billion; $130 billion; $57 billion; and $24 billion. Central Intelligence Agency, 2008 World Factbook, https://www.cia.gov/library/publications/the-world-factbook/index.html.

48. One can contrast the $105.8 million that the U.S. Congress appropriated in FY 2007 as its entire budget for international education, including the Fulbright-Hays programs, National Resource Centers, and Foreign Language and Area Studies Fellowships, with the currently estimated $275 million unit cost of one new FA-22 Raptor (which recently entered service with the U.S. Air Force), originally "conceived as the air superiority aircraft to . . . give the U.S. the ability to conduct Offensive Counter Air Operations deep inside Russia during the Cold War" (Col. Everest Riccioni, USAF ret., "Description of our Failing Defense Acquisition System as Exemplified by the History, Nature and Analysis of the USAF F-22 Raptor Program": www.pogo.org/m/dp/dp-fa22-Riccioni-03082005.pdf).

49. For one of many efforts by Bush administration spokespersons to blur the lines between war abroad and the threat of terrorism at home, see the statements by Fran Townsend, the president's advisor for homeland security, on July 17, 2007, in which she unveils a new report on the terrorist threat to the United States and links this directly to the war in Iraq: "Townsend: al-Qaida Plots New Attack," *New York Times,* July 18, 2007.

50. Speaking on January 17, 1961, Eisenhower also stated: "We have been compelled to create a permanent armaments industry of vast proportions. Added to this, three and a half million men and women are directly engaged in the defense establishment. We annually spend on military security alone more than the net income of all United States corporations. Now this conjunction of an immense military establishment and a large arms industry is new in the American experience. The total influence—economic, political, even spiritual—is felt in every city, every Statehouse, every office of the Federal government. We recognize the imperative need for this development. Yet, we must not fail to comprehend its grave implications. Our toil, resources, and livelihood are all involved. So is the very structure of our society." The text of Eisenhower's Farewell Address is available at www.americanrhetoric.com/speeches/dwightdeisenhowerfarewell.html.

51. Washington's Farewell Address is available at www.yale.edu/lawweb/avalon/washing.htm.

52. It is worth noting as factors that seem to have mitigated this war's impact that, unlike both the French and American wars in Indochina, a conscript army is not involved in the Iraq War, and the size of the forces committed and the casualties have both been considerably smaller there than they were in either Indochina war.

53. Daniel Yergin, *Shattered Peace: The Origins of the Cold War and the National Security State* (Boston: Houghton Mifflin, 1977).

54. James Madison to Thomas Jefferson, "Political Observations," April 20, 1795, in *Letters and Other Writings of James Madison* (Philadelphia: J. B. Lippincott, 1867), vol. 4, p. 491.

BIBLIOGRAPHY

For a bibliography of Sowing Crisis, please go to www.beacon.org/SowingCrisis.

INDEX